JOURNAL FOR THE STUDY OF THE NEW TESTAMENT SUPPLEMENT SERIES
129

Executive Editor
Stanley E. Porter

Editorial Board
Richard Bauckham, David Catchpole, R. Alan Culpepper,
Margaret Davies, James D.G. Dunn, Craig A. Evans, Stephen Fowl,
Robert Fowler, Robert Jewett, Elizabeth Struthers Malbon

Sheffield Academic Press

The Name and Way
of the Lord

Old Testament Themes,
New Testament Christology

Carl Judson Davis

Journal for the Study of the New Testament
Supplement Series 129

To Lynn

Proverbs 31.10-31

Copyright © 1996 Sheffield Academic Press

Published by Sheffield Academic Press Ltd
Mansion House
19 Kingfield Road
Sheffield S11 9AS
England

Printed on acid-free paper in Great Britain
by Bookcraft Ltd
Midsomer Norton, Bath

British Library Cataloguing in Publication Data

A catalogue record for this book is available
from the British Library

ISBN 1-85075-604-X

CONTENTS

PREFACE

In Fall of 1986, Dr Murray J. Harris left his position as Warden of Tyndale House, Cambridge to become Professor of New Testament Exegesis and Theology at Trinity Evangelical Divinity School. As his first class, he conducted a seminar on Jesus as θεός in the New Testament, the subject of his then forthcoming book.[1] My contribution to that class was an investigation of Heb. 1.8-9 which applies Ps. 45.7-8 to the Son and is one of the few New Testament passages which probably calls the Son θεός. The context of that ascription in Hebrews is one where the author in the next verses applies Ps. 102.25-27[26-28] to the Son and implies that the Son as Lord created the world.[2] My exegesis of those verses led to a great interest in similar passages. I continued to study such passages in my MA thesis on Paul's use of the definite article with κύριος.[3] There, I studied the definite article as the determinative factor in the reference of κύριος to Jesus or God. I also studied passages which take the title κύριος, use it as a surrogate for the word Yahweh, and apply it to Jesus. That work, for all its disguise as a grammatical work, was really my own initiation to the problems of monotheism and New Testament Christology. While at work on my Master's thesis, I read Dunn's *Christology in the Making* and was surprised at how little he discussed the phenomenon of Old Testament passages about God applied to Christ.[4] When he did discuss it, he seemed to think such application was of little christological import. A little later, I read Maurice

1. M.J. Harris, *Jesus as God: The New Testament Use of* Theos *in Reference to Jesus* (Grand Rapids: Baker, 1992).

2. See O. Cullmann, *Christ and Time: The Primitive Conception of Time and History* (trans. F.V. Filson; London: SCM Press, 1962), pp. 25-26 (rev. edn with an new introductory chapter), and *The Christology of the New Testament* (trans. S.C. Guthrie and C.A.M. Hall; Philadelphia: Westminster Press, rev. edn, 1959), p. 311.

3. C.J. Davis, 'The Articular and Anarthrous κύριος in Paul' (MA thesis, Trinity Evangelical Divinity School, 1989).

4. J.D.G. Dunn, *Christology in the Making: A New Testament Inquiry into the Origins of the Doctrine of the Incarnation* (London: SCM Press, 2nd edn, 1989).

Casey's suggestion that such application had parallels in regard to
intermediaries in pre-Christian Judaism and that therefore such application was no evidence that the early Church believed in the divinity of
Jesus.[5] In my mind, such suggestions differed radically from what I saw
as the implications of the texts. Their suggestions, therefore, sparked my
interest which has resulted in this book.

This book is a slightly altered version of my 1993 PhD thesis at the
University of Sheffield. Special thanks goes to Ralph P. Martin who
supervised this work and who, at the beginning of my study, suggested I
use Salvation History as a perspective with which to examine the New
Testament data. I have come to see the great wisdom in his suggestion. I
would, also, like to thank my parents, Carl and Ermine Davis, who
sacrificially paid my tuition bills. Lastly, I thank my wife Lynn, to whom
this book is dedicated. Without her, it would have never seen the light of
day.

5.   M. Casey, 'Chronology and the Development of Pauline Christology', in
Paul and Paulinism: Essays in Honour of C.K. Barrett (ed. M.D. Hooker and
S.G. Wilson; London: SPCK, 1982), pp. 124-34.

ABBREVIATIONS*

AB	Anchor Bible
ABD	*The Anchor Bible Dictionary* (6 vols.; ed. D.N. Freedman; New York: Doubleday, 1992).
ACNT	Augsburg Commentary on the New Testament
ANCL	Ante-Nicene Christian Library
ANET	J.B. Pritchard (ed.), *Ancient Near Eastern Texts*
ANRW	*Aufstieg und Niedergang der römischen Welt*
APOT	R.H. Charles (ed.), *The Apocrypha and Pseudepigrapha of the Old Testament in English*
ASNU	Acta Seminarii Neotestamentici Uppsaliensis
ArB	The Aramaic Bible
ATR	*Anglican Theological Review*
BAGD	W. Bauer, W.F. Arndt, F.W. Gingrich and F.W. Danker, *Greek–English Lexicon of the New Testament*
BBB	Bonner biblische Beiträge
BDB	F. Brown, S.R. Driver and C.A. Briggs, *Hebrew and English Lexicon of the Old Testament*
BGBE	Beiträge zur Geschichte der biblischen Exegese
BHS	*Biblia Hebraica Stuttgartensia*
BHT	Beiträge zur historischen Theologie
BIOSCS	*Bulletin of the International Organization for Septuagint and Cognate Studies*
BIRS	Bibliographies and Indexes in Religious Studies
BKAT	Biblischer Kommentar Altes Testament
BJRL	*Bulletin of the John Rylands Library*
BL	Bampton Lectures
BMI	The Bible and its Modern Interpreters

---

* All translations of the Old Testament, Apocrypha and New Testament are those of the NRSV unless otherwise stated. All works in the Pseudepigrapha are those of J.H. Charlesworth, *Old Testament Peusepigrapha* (2 vols.; Garden City, NY: Doubleday, 1983–85). Translations of Philo are those of F.H. Colson, G.H. Whitaker and R. Marcus, *Philo* (12 vols.; LCL; Cambridge, MA: Harvard University Press, 1929–53). Those of Josephus belong to H.StJ. Thackeray, R. Marcus, A. Wikgren and L.H. Feldman, *Josephus* (10 vols.; LCL; Cambridge, MA: Harvard University Press, 1926–65). Translations of the Dead Sea Scrolls are those of G. Vermes, *The Dead Sea Scrolls in English* (London: Penguin Books, 3rd edn, 1987).

BNTC	Black's New Testament Commentaries
CBQ	*Catholic Biblical Quarterly*
CHJ	W.D. Davies and Louis Finkelstein, *The Cambridge History of Judaism* (2 vols.; Cambridge: Cambridge University Press, 1984–89).
CNT	Commentaire du Nouveau Testament
CRINT	Compendia rerum iudaicarum ad Novum Testamentum
CCWJCW	Cambridge Commentaries on Writings of the Jewish & Christian World 200 BC to AD 200
DBI	R.J. Coggins and J.L. Houlden, *A Dictionary of Biblical Interpretation* (London: SCM Press, 1990; Philadelphia: Trinity Press International, 1990).
DJD	Discoveries in the Judaean Desert
EB	Etudes Bibliques
EcB	Die neue Echter Bibel
EDT	W.A. Elwell (ed.), *Evangelical Dictionary of Theology* (Grand Rapids: Eerdmans, 1984).
EGG	Exegetical Guide to the Greek New Testament
EKK	Evangelisch-Katholischer Kommentar zum Neuen Testament
EvQ	*Evangelical Quarterly*
ETL	*Ephemerides theologicae louvanienses*
ExpTim	*Expository Times*
GHAT	Göttinger Handkommentar zum Alten Testament
GNB	Good News Bible
HNTC	Harper's New Testament Commentary
HSM	Harvard Semitic Museum
HT	Helps for Translators
HTKNT	Herders theologischer Kommentar zum Neuen Testament
ICC	International Critical Commentary
ICT	Issues in Contemporary Theology
Int	*Interpretation*
ISBE	G.W. Bromiley (ed.), *International Standard Bible Encyclopedia*, rev. edn
ITQ	*Irish Theological Quarterly*
JB	Jerusalem Bible
JBL	*Journal of Biblical Literature*
JJS	*Journal of Jewish Studies*
JSNT	*Journal for the Study of the New Testament*
JSNTSup	*Journal for the Study of the New Testament*, Supplement Series
JSOTSup	*Journal for the Study of the Old Testament*, Supplement Series
JWSTP	M.E. Stone (ed.), *Jewish Writings of the Second Temple Period. Apocrypha, Pseudepigrapha, Qumran Sectarian Writings, Philo, Josephus* (CRINT 2.2; Assen: Van Gorcum, 1984).
KEK	Kritisch-exegetischer Kommentar über das Neue Testament

KJV	King James Version
Lamsa	*Holy Bible from the Ancient Eastern Test (Peshitta)*, trans. George M. Lamsa (San Francisco: Harper and Row, 1968).
LCC	Library of Christian Classics
LCL	Loeb Classical Library
LEC	Library of Early Christianity
LL	Lutterworth Library
LSJ	Liddell–Scott–Jones, *Greek–English Lexicon*
NASB	New American Standard Bible
NDCT	A. Richardson and J. Bowden (eds.), *New Dictionary of Christian Theology* (London: SCM Press, 1983).
NEB	New English Bible
NCB	New Century Bible
NICNT	New International Commentary on the New Testament
NICOT	New International Commentary on the Old Testament
NIGTC	New International Greek Testament Commentary
NIDNTT	C. Brown (ed.), *New International Dictionary of New Testament Theology*
NIV	New International Version
NJB	New Jerusalem Bible
NRSV	New Revised Standard Version
NovTSup	*Novum Testamentum*, Supplements
NPNF	Nicene and Post-Nicene Fathers
NTD	Das Neue Testament Deutsch
NTS	*New Testament Studies*
OS	*Oudtestamentische Studiën*
OTA	*Old Testament Abstracts*
OTP	J.H. Charlesworth (ed.), *Old Testament Pseudepigrapha*
PG	J. Migne (ed.), *Patrologia graeca*
PTR	*Princeton Theological Review*
REB	Revised English Bible
RevQ	*Revue de Qumran*
SBLMS	Society of Biblical Literature Monograph Series
SBLRBS	Society of Biblical Literature Resources for Biblical Study
SBLSBS	Society of Biblical Literature Sources for Biblical Study
SBT	Studies in Biblical Theology
SEÅ	*Svensk exegetisk årsbok*
SECT	Sources of Early Christian Thought
SJLA	Studies in Judaism in Late Antiquity
SJT	*Scottish Journal of Theology*
SNTSMS	Society for New Testament Studies Monograph Series
SVT	Septuaginta Vetus Testamentum Graecum Auctoritate Academiae Litterarum Gottingensis
SNT	Studien zum Neuen Testament

Tanakh	*Tanakh. A New Translation of the Holy Scriptures according to the Traditional Hebrew Text* (Jerusalem: Jewish Publication Society, 1985).
TDNT	G. Kittel and G. Friedrich (eds.), *Theological Dictionary of the New Testament*
THAT	E. Jenni and C. Westermann (eds.), *Theologisches Handwörterbuch zum Alten Testament* (2 vols.; Munich: Kaiser, 1971–76).
TNTC	Tyndale New Testament Commentaries
TS	*Theological Studies*
TSAJ	Texte und Studien zum Antiken Judentum
TSK	*Theologische Studien und Kritiken*
TU	Texte und Untersuchungen
TynBul	*Tyndale Bulletin*
VTSup	*Vetus Testamentum*, Supplements
WBC	Word Biblical Commentary
WUNT	Wissenschaftliche Untersuchungen zum Neuen Testament
ZAW	*Zeitschrift für die Alttestamentliche Wissenschaft*
ZNW	*Zeitschrift für die Neutestamentliche Wissenschaft*
ZRGG	*Zeitschrift für Religions- und Geistesgeschichte*

Chapter 1

INTRODUCTION*

Primary Questions and Summary of Recent Proposals

The New Testament is replete with Old Testament citations and allusions about the divine which the New Testament writers apply to Christ.[1] Recent discussion of this phenomenon centres upon two questions: What was its source and chronology, and what was its significance to first-century Christians? On the first score, some hold that such application stems from Jesus himself[2] and/or the early Palestinian church.[3] Some

---

* In this section I am only summarizing views. My critique shall be throughout the remainder of this book. Some works on the Old Testament in the New do not deal in any substantial way with application of Old Testament passages about God applied to Christ. These include, B. Lindars, *New Testament Apologetic. The Doctrinal Significance of the Old Testament Quotations* (London: SCM Press, 1961); R.B. Hays, *Echoes of Scripture in the Letters of Paul* (New Haven: Yale University Press, 1989); and D.A. Carson and H.G.M. Williamson, *It is Written: Scripture Citing Scripture. Essays in Honour of Barnabas Lindars, SSF* (Cambridge: Cambridge University Press, 1988).

1. See Appendix.

2. R.T. France, *Jesus and the Old Testament. His Application of Old Testament Passages to himself and his Mission* (London: Tyndale Press, 1971), pp. 150-59; and D.B. Capes, 'Paul's Use of Old Testament Yahweh-Texts and its Implication for his Christology' (PhD dissertation, Southwestern Baptist Theological Seminary, 1990), pp. 299-303 (now *Old Testament Yahweh Texts in Paul's Christology* [WUNT, 2.47; Tübingen: Mohr (Siebeck), 1992]). Others see Jesus as the source of Christology in general: C.F.D. Moule, *The Origin of New Testament Christology* (Cambridge: Cambridge University Press, 1977), p. 4; E.E. Ellis, 'Biblical Interpretation in the New Testament Church,' in *Miqra. Text, Translation and Interpretation of the Hebrew Bible in Ancient Judaism and Early Christianity* (ed. M.J. Mulder; CRINT 2.1; Philadelphia: Fortress Press; Assen: Van Gorcum, 1989), p. 718 n. 149; R.N. Longenecker, *The Christology of Early Jewish Christianity* (London: SCM Press, 1970), pp. 155 and 138 n. 48; F.F. Bruce, 'Jesus is Lord', in *Soli Deo Gloria. New Testament Studies in Honor of William Childs Robinson* (ed. J. McDowell Richards; Richmond: John Knox, 1968), p. 35; M. Hengel, 'Christology and New Testament

suggest it is the result of Jewish exegetical work.[4] Others take it as a
non-Jewish or Hellenistic Jewish development.[5] On the second, some
take this application as implicit evidence that the early church held to
an embryonic Trinitarian theology,[6] that they blurred the boundaries

Chronology. A Problem in the History of Earliest Christianity', in *Between Jesus and
Paul: Studies in the Earliest History of Christianity* (trans. J. Bowden; London: SCM
Press; Philadelphia: Fortress Press, 1983), p. 44. See too E. Käsemann, 'Blind Alleys
in the "Jesus of History" Controversy', in *New Testament Questions of Today*
(London: SCM Press, 1969), pp. 42-43; and L.W. Hurtado, 'New Testament
Christology: A Critique of Bousset's Influence', *TS* 40 (1979), p. 317.

3.   L. Cerfaux, *Christ in the Theology of St Paul* (trans. G. Webb and A. Walker;
New York: Herder & Herder, 1959), p. 346; E. Schweizer, 'Discipleship and Belief in
Jesus as Lord from Jesus to the Hellenistic Church' (trans. H. F. Peacock, *NTS* 2
(1956), p. 93; Joseph A. Fitzmyer, *Pauline Theology. A Brief Sketch* (Englewood
Cliffs, NJ: Prentice-Hall, 1967), p. 36; Joseph A. Fitzmyer, 'The Semitic Background
of the New Testament κύριος-Title', in *A Wandering Aramean. Collected Aramaic
Essays* (SBLMS, 25; Missoula: Scholars Press, 1979), pp. 128, 130. See too
Ethelbert Stauffer, *New Testament Theology* (trans. J. Marsh; London: SCM Press,
1955), p. 115; D. Guthrie, *New Testament Theology* (Leicester: Inter-Varsity Press,
1981), p. 292; W.G. Kümmel, *The Theology of the New Testament According to its
Major Witnesses, Jesus-Paul-John* (trans. J.E. Steely; Nashville: Abingdon Press,
1973), p. 114.

4.   A.T. Hanson, *The Prophetic Gospel: A Study of John and the Old Testament*
(Edinburgh: T. & T. Clark, 1991), p. 67. T. Nagata, 'Philippians 2.5-11: A Case
Study in Contextual Shaping of Early Christian Christology' (PhD dissertation,
Princeton University, 1981), p. 283; Capes, 'Paul's Use', p. 283; W.L. Schutter,
Hermeneutic and Composition in 1 Peter (WUNT, 2.30; Tübingen: Mohr [Siebeck],
1989), pp. 130, 147-50.

5.   W. Bousset, *Kyrios Christos. A History of the Belief in Christ from the
Beginnings of Christianity to Irenaeus* (trans. J.E. Steely; Nashville: Abingdon Press,
1970), p. 130 (pre-Pauline Hellenistic Church); R. Bultmann, *Theology of the New
Testament* (trans. K. Grobel; New York: Scribner's, 1951), I, p. 128 (Hellenistic
development before Paul).

6.   B.B. Warfield, *The Lord of Glory. A Study of the Designations of our Lord in
the New Testament with Especial Reference to his Deity* (London: Evangelical Press,
1907), pp. 231-32; W.C. Robinson, 'Jesus Christ is Jehovah', *EvQ* 5 (1933),
pp. 144-55, 271-90; C.E.B. Cranfield, 'Some Comments on Professor J.D.G. Dunn's
Christology in the Making with Special Reference to the Evidence of the Epistle to the
Romans', in *The Glory of Christ in the New Testament. Studies in Christology in
Memory of George Bradford Caird* (ed. L.D. Hurst and N.T. Wright; Oxford:
Clarendon Press, 1987), p. 274; C.E.B. Cranfield, *A Critical and Exegetical
Commentary on the Epistle to the Romans* (Edinburgh: T. & T. Clark, 1975–79), II,
p. 839.

between the one God and Christ,[7] that they held to the deity of Christ,[8] that 'God was in Christ',[9] that Jesus was 'one with Jehovah',[10] that Jesus was on a par with Yahweh,[11] that Jesus shared the functions and divine nature of God,[12] and/or that Jesus in some undefined sense was God.[13] Some suggest that these or similar views of God stem from the idea of God as a corporate personality,[14] from hints of such a view in the Old Testament,[15] from parallel developments regarding similar messianic figures,[16] from speculation about God's Wisdom, Word, Name

7. Bousset, *Kyrios Christos*, p. 149; F. Hahn, *The Titles of Jesus in Christology: Their History in Early Christianity* (trans. H. Knight and G. Ogg; London: Lutterworth, 1969), p. 108.

8. H.P. Liddon, *The Divinity of Our Lord and Saviour Jesus Christ. Eight Lectures Preached before the University of Oxford* (BL [1866]; London: Rivingtons, 1875), p. 328; See too Bruce, 'Lord', pp. 35-36; F.F. Bruce, *This is That. The New Testament Development of Some Old Testament Themes* (Exeter: Paternoster Press, 1968), p. 36; W. Elwell, 'The Deity of Christ in the Writings of Paul', in *Current Issues in Biblical and Patristic Interpretation. Studies in Honor of Merrill C. Tenney Presented by his Former Students* (ed. G.F. Hawthorne; Grand Rapids: Eerdmans, 1975), p. 299; Ellis, 'Biblical Interpretation', p. 720; Capes, 'Paul's Use', p. 278; L. Goppelt, *Theology of the New Testament* (trans. J.E. Alsup; ed. J. Roloff; Grand Rapids: Eerdmans, 1981–82), II, pp. 83-85; Guthrie, *Theology*, p. 299; and L.J. Kreitzer, *Jesus and God in Paul's Eschatology* (JSNTSup, 19; Sheffield: JSOT Press, 1987), p. 25.

9. D.E.H. Whiteley, *The Theology of St Paul* (Philadelphia: Fortress Press, 1964), p. 101; see too p. 106.

10. F. Prat, *The Theology of Saint Paul* (trans. J.L. Stoddard; London: Burns, Oates and Washbourne, 1957), II, p. 119.

11. Fitzmyer, *Pauline*, p. 37; and Fitzmyer, 'Semitic Background', pp. 130-31.

12. I.H. Marshall, 'Jesus is Lord', in *The Origins of New Testament Christology* (ICT; Leicester: Inter-Varsity Press, 1976), p. 106; and *idem*, 'Jesus as Lord: The Development of the Concept', in *Jesus the Saviour: Studies in New Testament Theology* (London: SPCK, 1990), p. 208.

13. G.E. Ladd, *A Theology of the New Testament* (Grand Rapids: Eerdmans, 1974), pp. 416-17, 577; and O. Cullmann, *The Christology of the New Testament*, (trans. S.C. Guthrie and C.A.M. Hall; London: SCM Press; Philadelphia: Westminster Press, rev. edn, 1959), p. 311.

14. Ellis, 'Biblical Interpretation', p. 718 n. 149; Capes, 'Paul's Use', p. 293 n. 401. Cf. S.E. Porter, 'Two Myths: Corporate Personality and Language/Mentality Determinism', *SJT* 43 (1990), pp. 289-307, and the literature cited there.

15. Liddon, *Divinity*, pp. 44-96; G. van Groningen, *Messianic Revelation in the Old Testament* (Grand Rapids: Baker, 1990), pp. 931-36.

16. Kreitzer, *Jesus*, p. 190 n. 37.

or Angel,[17] from reflection over Jesus' absolute life,[18] from Paul's Damascus road experience,[19] and/or from the concept of divine agency together with the religious experience of the early Christians.[20] Still others question such implications and ideas. Most notably, Maurice Casey postulates that such application in its pre-Johannine stage has pre-Christian parallels in application of God-texts to intermediaries.[21] By 'intermediary', Casey means human agents of high status (e.g. the Davidic king, Moses), aspects of deity (e.g. Wisdom, Word), or supernatural beings (e.g. angels).[22] The second group in Casey's analysis are divine, but these aspects of deity never attain deity in terms of being distinct from God and at the same time thought of in terms similar to God.[23] In his view, Jewish belief in intermediaries offers static and dynamic parallels to New Testament christological development. Static parallels are those in which one function of God becomes the function of an intermediary. Dynamic parallels are those which show a trend to an ever increasing status of intermediaries based on the needs of a subgroup within Judaism.[24] According to Casey, Paul and the Synoptics regard Jesus as not fully divine in his second usage of divine.[25] For Casey, belief in the deity of Jesus came when the Gentile Christians abandoned strict numeric monotheism, elevated Jesus to divine status, and then unsuccessfully reinterpreted strict numeric monotheism so as to accommodate a plurality of

---

17. Longenecker, *Christology*, pp. 41-46; D. Juel, *Messianic Exegesis. Christological Interpretation of the Old Testament in Early Christianity* (Philadelphia: Fortress Press, 1988), p. 148. See too Moule, *Origin*, pp. 43-44; A.F. Segal, *Two Powers in Heaven. Early Rabbinic Reports about Christianity and Gnosticism* (SJLA, 25; Leiden: Brill, 1977), pp. 205-19; and D. Steenburg, 'The Worship of Adam and Christ as the Image of God', *JSNT* 39 (1990), pp. 95-109.

18. Moule, *Origin*, pp. 43-44.

19. S. Kim, *The Origin of Paul's Gospel* (Grand Rapids: Eerdmans, 1982).

20. L.W. Hurtado, *One God, One Lord. Early Christian Devotion and Ancient Jewish Monotheism* (Philadelphia: Fortress Press, 1988), pp. 126-28.

21. M. Casey, 'Chronology and the Development of Pauline Christology', in *Paul and Paulinism. Essays in Honour of C.K. Barrett* (ed. M.D. Hooker and S.G. Wilson; London: SPCK, 1982), pp. 124-34; idem, *From Jewish Prophet to Gentile God. The Origins and Development of New Testament Christology* (Cambridge: James Clarke, 1991), pp. 79-85, 147, 159.

22. Casey, *Prophet*, p. 78.

23. Casey, *Prophet*, p. 90. For a further discussion of 'divine' in Casey's argument, see Chapter 6 below.

24. Casey, *Prophet*, pp. 79-85.

25. Casey, *Prophet*, pp. 98 and 135.

figures under the rubric of the one God.[26]

Casey's thesis is similar to the earlier one of Wilhelm Bousset who suggests that during the period between Paul and establishment of the early Jewish-Christian community, christological mutation took place.[27] Within this time, the Hellenistic Christian community saw the surrounding pagans revere deities subordinate to the higher gods or incarnations of the supreme deities.[28] Simultaneously, the community took these categories and applied them to Jesus.[29] As a result, Jesus was κύριος, and the worshipping community transferred the Old Testament name of God to Jesus before Paul's ministry.[30] In this Hellenistic community, the shift meant deification on a second range, subordinate to the supreme deity.[31] During this process, the Hellenistic church loosened monotheism.[32] Originally, the Palestinian Church did not understand Jesus as Lord in a religious sense, but at a later date, the Hellenistic Jewish tradition influenced the Palestinian tradition.[33] At that point, Paul found the κύριος Jesus in the Old Testament although Paul did not lead the way in this understanding of the Old Testament.[34] Thus, application of Old Testament passages about the LORD to Jesus occurred very early in the Hellenistic community and meant that Paul and these Christians understood Jesus as a second range of divine being along side the one supreme God. This view leads 'in the direction of beginning gradually to obliterate all boundary lines between the Old Testament God and the Christ.'[35]

Others work with a nuanced version of Bousset's theory because of a pervasive criticism of one point of his thesis.[36] Hahn, for example, sees

26. Casey, *Prophet*, pp. 163-81, and 175 in particular.

27. Bousset, *Kyrios Christos*, pp. 119-20.

28. Bousset, *Kyrios Christos*, pp. 131, 139, 146-47.

29. Bousset, *Kyrios Christos*, p.136.

30. Bousset, *Kyrios Christos*, p. 130. Similarly see Bultmann, *Theology*, I, pp. 51-52, 124-26.

31. Bousset, *Kyrios Christos*, p. 147 n. 103.

32. Bousset, *Kyrios Christos*, p. 147.

33. Bousset, *Kyrios Christos*, pp. 126, 128, 149.

34. Bousset, *Kyrios Christos*, pp. 149-50.

35. Bousset, *Kyrios Christos*, p. 149.

36. Many questioned the idea of κύριος coming exclusively from the Hellenistic community (Bousset, *Kyrios Christos*, p. 128). See in particular J.A. Fitzmyer, 'New Testament *Kyrios* and *Maranatha* and their Aramaic Background', in *To Advance the Gospel. New Testament Studies* (New York: Crossroad, 1981), pp. 218-35; Fitzmyer, 'Semitic Background', pp. 115-42. S. Schulz, 'Maranatha und Kyrios Jesus', *ZNW*

κύριος as applied to Christ developing along two lines.[37] The Palestinian early church used κύριος as a secular mode of address and as an appellation of the soon returning Christ.[38] Hellenistic Jewish Christianity, on the basis of Ps. 110.1, linked the exaltation of the messiah with the title Lord which at first was adoptionistic and functional.[39] The impetus for applying Old Testament LORD-texts to him came when members of the Hellenistic church took the idea of the returning Lord and then applied day-of-the-LORD passages to him.[40] The Hellenistic church then blurred the boundaries between Jesus and God.[41] By the time of the New Testament documents, this Hellenistic part of the early church had irreversibly injected κύριος with a meaning it did not hold for the Palestinian community. Such application suggested the divinity or near divinity of Christ.[42]

Similarly Dulière suggests κύριος as applied to Jesus was at first a title of respect.[43] The church then recognized two Lords, Lord-Adonai of the Old Testament and the new Lord Jesus.[44] The ambiguity in the term led in part to the deification of Jesus since one could not distinguish if the referent of κύριος were Lord-Adonai, the Lord Jesus or both at

---

53 (1962), pp. 125-44, suggests that *maranatha* does not give a divine ascription to Jesus but rather hails him as the Son of Man coming as judge (see the summary of H. Boers, 'Where Christology is Real. A Survey of Recent Research on New Testament Christology', *Int* 26 [1972], pp. 315-17). I have not read Schulz's article first-hand. Bousset offers two views concerning 1 Cor. 16.22. Maranatha may have been 'a formula of confirmation and oath-taking with reference to God' (Bousset, *Kyrios Christos*, p. 129 n. 36), or maranatha developed on the 'bilingual region of the Hellenistic communities of Antioch, Damascus, and even Tarsus' (Bousset, *Kyrios Christos*, p. 129). Cf. A.E.J. Rawlinson, *The New Testament Doctrine of the Christ* (BL 1926; London: Longmans, Green & Co., 1926), pp. 231-37; G. Vos, 'The Continuity of the Kyrios-Title in the New Testament', *PTR* 13 (1915), pp. 161-89; Bruce, 'Lord', pp. 23-36; Cullmann, *Christology*, pp. 195-237.

    37. Hahn, *Titles*, pp. 68-128. See p. 68.
    38. Hahn, *Titles*, pp. 88-89, 102-103.
    39. Hahn, *Titles*, p. 113.
    40. Hahn, *Titles*, pp. 107-108.
    41. Hahn, *Titles*, p. 108.
    42. Hahn, *Titles*, pp. 113-14.
    43. W. Dulière, 'Theos Dieu et Adonai-Kurios, Conséquences de l'addition d'un Jésus-Kurios à l'Adonai-Kurios dans la terminologie chrétienne', *ZRGG* 21 (1969), p. 193.
    44. Dulière, 'Theos', p. 193.

the same time.[45] This practice led to the diffusion of divinity of Lord-Adonai to the Lord Jesus.[46] After that period, a sorting out of terminology occurred: θεός referred to God while κύριος referred to the new Lord.[47] It was Christian desire to honour Jesus which led to this application.[48] One could associate this view with the development of a view of the divine wherein one assigned different divine names to different aspects of his character. The wrathful aspect (κύριος in Philo, אלהים in the Rabbis) and the gracious aspect (θεός in Philo, יהוה in the Rabbis) bore different names.[49]

Kramer, like Bousset and Bultmann, holds that application of such passages to Christ stems from the pre-Pauline period.[50] For him, too, such application could occur only on Hellenistic soil and was not part of the original Palestinian community's belief about Jesus.[51] Either the κύριος title for Jesus arose, and with it application of Old Testament texts about the LORD to Jesus, in connection with the κύριος acclamation of Hellenistic cult deities, or it arose as a mutation of the confession 'Jesus is the messiah' when that confession passed on to Hellenistic soil.[52] Kramer sees either the Jewish Greek-speaking Christians or the Hellenistic Gentiles as responsible for the first application of the LORD passages to Jesus.[53] He also believes that κύριος as applied to Jesus denotes his absolute status, his function as God in relation to the world.[54] Kramer, furthermore, draws a distinction between proper quotations about God applied to Jesus and mere allusions or imprecise quotations applied to him.[55] Kramer implies that the latter are of lesser theological significance than the former.

A different line of argument comes from George Howard who suggests in New Testament times, the writers wrote the Tetragram, יהוה,

---

45. Dulière, 'Theos', pp. 193-94.
46. Dulière, 'Theos', p. 194.
47. Dulière, 'Theos', p. 195.
48. Dulière, 'Theos', p. 195.
49. See Segal, *Two Powers*, pp. 43-50.
50. W. Kramer, *Christ, Lord, Son of God*, SBT 50 (trans. B. Hardy; London: SCM Press, 1966), p. 157.
51. Kramer, *Christ*, p. 158.
52. Kramer, *Christ*, pp. 72-73, by implication.
53. Kramer, *Christ*, p. 84.
54. Kramer, *Christ*, pp. 82-83.
55. Kramer, *Christ*, pp. 156-57.

rather than using the surrogate κύριος.[56] Toward the end of the first century, scribes substituted κύριος and less frequently θεός for the יהוה which stood in the New Testament documents.[57] When this change took place, the New Testament documents lost the original significance of the Old Testament quotations and allusions.[58] Mk 1.3; 1 Cor. 1.31; Rom. 10.16-17; 14.10-11; 1 Cor. 2.16; 1 Pet. 3.14-15; 1 Cor. 10.9 and Jude 5 are cases where later scribes changed the first-century New Testament text into a christological statement.[59] Howard further suggests that when this second-century change took place, second- and third-century scribes changed many other texts to reconcile the original Christologies with the later ones.[60]

Some scholars suggest the application of such passages is insignificant theologically. For Dunn, the application of passages about God to Jesus stems from God's desire to share his dominion with man (Isa. 45.23 in particular).[61] Dunn makes no comment on when this application first took place although his view allows for such application from an early date.[62] Dunn, furthermore, suggests between John and Jesus the early church held to an undefined divinity of Christ which he defines in terms of God's immanent presence.[63]

Similarly, to Adam Christology one could argue that the New

---

56. G. Howard, 'The Tetragram and the New Testament', *JBL* 96 (1977), p. 63.

57. Howard, 'Tetragram', pp. 76-77.

58. Howard, 'Tetragram', p. 77.

59. Howard, 'Tetragram', pp. 78-82.

60. Howard, 'Tetragram', p. 83, by implication.

61. J.D.G. Dunn, 'Was Christianity a Monotheistic Faith from the Beginning?' *SJT* 35 (1982), pp. 327-28; *idem*, *Christology in the Making. A New Testament Inquiry into the Origins of the Doctrine of the Incarnation* (London: SCM Press, 2nd edn, 1989), pp. 157-58. Cf. J.D.G. Dunn, 'Christology', *ABD*, I, p. 984.

62. Dunn, 'Monotheistic', p. 321.

63. Dunn, 'Monotheistic', p. 330. R.H. Fuller, 'Lower and Higher Christology in the Fourth Gospel', in *The Conversation Continues. Studies in Paul & John in Honor of J. Louis Martyn* (ed. R.T. Fortna and B.R. Gaventa; Nashville: Abingdon, 1990), p. 363, describes Dunn's view as the anhypostatic Logos and Wisdom becoming hypostatic in Jesus (see Dunn, 'Monotheistic', pp. 330-31). Fuller points out that this view was that of J.A.T. Robinson. This position seems close to Beryllus who believed that the Son did not pre-exist his human birth and that his divinity was only that of the Father (see E. Burton, *Testimonies of the Ante-Nicene Fathers to the Doctrine of the Trinity and the Divinity of the Holy Ghost* [Oxford: Oxford University Press, 1831], p. 92; see too Eusebius, *History* 6.33 and the positions of Noetus and Praxeas outlined in Liddon, *Divinity*, p. 16).

Testament applied such passages to Jesus because Jesus is God's agent.[64] A.E. Harvey submits that the concept שליח/ἀπόστολος allows one to treat the representative as if he were the person himself.[65] Accordingly, there would be no limits to the transactions which the agent might undertake on God's behalf, even standing for him as the object of worship.[66] Such a view, one could suggest, explains why Christians applied such passages to Jesus who was the fully authorized representative of God.

Several authors suggest continuity between the early church's κύριος Christology and its later developments. This continuity may exist in one of two ways. Fuller connects the historical Jesus and the later christological kerygma of the church[67] and sees Christianity interacting with three successive environments: Palestinian Judaism, Hellenistic Judaism and the Graeco-Roman World.[68] For Fuller, the Palestinian church did not call Jesus אדני.[69] However, when κύριος became a title for Jesus in Hellenistic Judaism (translating מר of Palestinian Jewish Christianity) the way stood open for the transfer of Old Testament passages about Yahweh to Jesus, and such transfer pointed to the functional identity of Jesus and God.[70] Fuller also suggests pre-Christian Jews saw a distinction within the being of God on the basis of Wisdom.[71] They could thus identify the Son with one such distinction. Furthermore, Jesus' words

64. The New Testament allows for the idea of agency (Mt. 10.40-42; 26.40, 45; Lk. 10.16; Jn 13.20; Gal. 4.14). See too Ignatius, *Ephesians* 6.1; *Didache* 11.2, 4; Justin Martyr, *Apology* 1.16.10; 1.63.5; Eusebius, *History of the Church* 6.12.3; and *Letter to Diognetus* 7-10 (J.F. Bethune-Baker, *An Introduction to the Early History of Christian Doctrine to the Time of the Council of Chalcedon* [London: Methuen, 1903], p. 123).

65. A.E. Harvey, 'Christ as Agent', in *The Glory of Christ in the New Testament. Studies in Christology in Memory of George Bradford Caird* (ed. L.D. Hurst and N.T. Wright; Oxford: Clarendon Press, 1987), p. 247.

66. Harvey, 'Agent', pp. 247-48; cf. Hurtado, *One God*, p. 97.

67. R.H. Fuller, *The Foundations of the New Testament Christology* (LL; London: Lutterworth, 1965), p. 11.

68. Fuller, *Foundations*, p. 16.

69. Fuller, *Foundations*, pp. 50, 185-86.

70. Fuller, *Foundations*, p. 50.

71. Fuller, *Foundations*, p. 255, writes, 'God-in-Action is ontically distinguishable from God-in-himself, but not separable. For God-in-his-own-being is essentially a God who is ever ready to go out in action and communication, while God-going-out-of-himself-in-action is always God-in-his-own-being. All this is meant in the statement that the pre-existent One was in the μορφή (form) of God and equal to God, that he was θεός, God, and yet πρὸς τὸν θεόν, in relation to God.'

and deeds point to an implicit Christology in which Jesus understands himself as 'an immediate confrontation with "God's presence and his self"'.[72] Thus, by the time of Phil. 2.6-11, Paul possessed a certain identity between Jesus and God.[73] Therefore, Fuller submits the terminological shift of κύριος is true to the Christology of the early church and of Jesus.[74]

Representative of the second view is Marshall, who holds that at an early stage Christians extended the meaning of κύριος by applying texts about the LORD to Jesus.[75] For Marshall such application connotes an early Christian belief that Jesus shared in the functions and divine nature of God.[76] Marshall further posits that Jesus pointed to a coming Master in his parables. Thus when the early church identified Jesus as the coming Son of Man they identified Jesus as the coming Master, the Lord.[77] Furthermore, Jesus identified the messiah as not merely David's son but also his Lord.[78] To these ideas, the resurrection added an understanding of Jesus as the one exalted to Heaven.[79] Marshall sees then a connection with Jesus as Lord at his resurrection, then postulates a belief in Jesus as Lord in the past and future.[80] Thus, a process which began in the early church and stood complete by the earliest books of Paul, meant that New Testament writers did what was tantamount to classing Jesus as divine.[81]

Similarly, Fitzmyer sees the κύριος title first applied to Jesus in regard to the parousia and then to different stages of his existence.[82] Fitzmyer understands the word as having a Palestinian Jewish Religious background and demonstrates that 'the Lord' was a possible title for God in Jewish usage.[83] Furthermore, Fitzmyer understands its background as a

---

72. Fuller, *Foundations*, p. 106

73. Fuller, *Foundations*, p. 214.

74. Fuller, *Foundations*, p. 254. See similarly P. Pokorny, *The Genesis of Christology. Foundations for a Theology of the New Testament* (Edinburgh: T. & T. Clark, 1987), pp. 75-96.

75. Marshall, *Jesus*, p. 208.

76. Marshall, *Origins*, p. 106.

77. Marshall, *Jesus*, p. 204.

78. Marshall, *Jesus*, pp. 204-206.

79. Marshall, *Jesus*, p. 206.

80. Marshall, *Jesus*, pp. 207-208.

81. Marshall, *Jesus*, pp. 208-209.

82. Fitzmyer, 'Semitic Background', p. 129.

83. Fitzmyer, 'Semitic Background', pp. 123-27.

rendering of the absolute title of God. Part of the significance which the early church recognized from the word when applied to Jesus was just such an absolute title.[84] Such application meant Jesus shared in the transcendence of God 'in an egalitarian sense, not in an identifying sense'.[85]

One may group these theories as follows: concerning the chronological question, some posit the passages come from a shift in cultures away from the Palestinian church (e.g. Bousset, Hahn, Kramer, Fuller). This option allows for either incongruity between the Jerusalem church and the later formulations (Casey, Bousset, Hahn) or the development of what was implicit in the Palestinian church's Christology at an early date (Fuller, Pokorny). Others suggest connection between the early church's Christology and the later ones (Marshall, see too n. 3). Concerning the significance of such application, some suggest such application reflects the deity, divinity or divine equality of Christ (see nn. 9-14). Others deny that such application is theologically very significant (Casey, Dunn).

Goals

In spite of the difference of opinion regarding such application, little detailed historical and exegetical work has been done on individual passages in regard to their theological import.[86] Recently this situation has begun to change: L.J. Kreitzer has studied the theological import of Paul's eschatological expectations in particularly the day-of-the-LORD passages applied to Christ.[87] Also, David Capes has examined all LORD-texts in Paul to determine which ones apply to Jesus and which apply to the Father.[88] Capes has dealt with the significance which such passages have when applied to Christ. What remains is to trace the theological associations of particular Old Testament passages in pre-Christian and first-century Judaism to compare with the New Testament usage of those same passages to Jesus. I propose to offer such work on two passages (Isa. 40.3 and Joel 2.32[3.5]a). This work shall survey the application of

---

84. Fitzmyer, 'Semitic Background', p. 126.

85. Fitzmyer, 'Semitic Background', p. 130.

86. See Hurtado, 'New Testament', pp. 316-17; and Kreitzer, *Jesus*, p. 18. Capes, 'Paul's Use', examines individual passages, but much of his work is a grammatical inquiry into whether certain passages have Jesus or God as their referents even though the scope of his work covers the same theological question as this one.

87. Kreitzer, *Jesus*, pp. 165-83.

88. Capes, 'Paul's'.

ideas contained in Isa. 40.3 and Joel 2.32 [3.5] in a representative sample
of pre-Christian and first-century CE Jewish literature to find pre-
Christian Jewish parallels for applying the respective passages to a second
figure.[89] I also shall collect some of the major pre- and post-Christian
Jewish parallels for applying any passage about the divine to a second
figure, and then I shall compare these parallels to New Testament application of such passages to Jesus. I shall ask the question: do such parallels
explain the New Testament phenomenon, or does the New Testament
have a different hermeneutical axiom in applying such passages to Jesus?
Or do the New Testament and pre-Christian Jewish literature provide
enough data to decide the question at all?

My choice of these two texts depends on two factors. They appear in
more than one tradition: Paul and Luke use Joel 2.32[3.5] while
Matthew, Mark, Luke and John use Isa. 40.3; moreover, both Isa. 40.3
and Joel 2.32[3.5] are important christologically since Paul implies that
'calling on the name of the Lord Jesus' was something widespread even
fundamental within Christianity before 53–57 CE (see Rom. 10.13 and
1 Cor. 1.2) and determinative in whether or not one is a Christian (Rom.
10.12-13), and since Luke implies 'calling on the name of the Lord
Jesus' characterized the first Christian converts (Acts 2.21 and 38 by
implication) and figured in the conversion of Paul (Acts 9.14, 21; and
22.16). In addition, Isa. 40.3 prefaces Jesus' ministry in all four of the
Gospels and in Mark forms the very beginning of the Gospel. The application of these two texts in more than one tradition and their implied
Christological importance make them an excellent prospect from which
to mine information about the early church's application of Yahweh-
texts to Jesus.

Methodology

The question then of this book is, 'To what extent may one know what
Christians between 50 and 90 CE probably understood by the New

---

89. K. Snodgrass, 'Streams of Tradition Emerging from Isaiah 40.1-5 and their
Adaptation in the New Testament', *JSNT* 8 (1980), pp. 24-45, makes an excellent start
on this task. His study is, however, preliminary since he does not deal in any substantial way with the christological application of the text. D.L. Phelps, 'Implications
of Lucan-Peter's Pentecost Homily for Christian Preaching of the Old Testament'
(PhD dissertation, Southwestern Baptist Theological Seminary, 1990), pp. 53-57,
collects the Rabbinic usage of Joel 2.28-32[3.1-5].

Testament application of Isa. 40.3 and Joel 2.32 [3.5]a to Jesus?'[90] My research includes first a search for pre-Christian parallels for applying a text about the divine to a second figure. The only way of finding inter- textual application of an Old Testament passage about God is to read the Old Testament closely, and then read carefully the pre-Christian Jewish literature in hope of identifying intertextual application.[91] This work shall identify some of these major intertextual examples and compare and contrast such application to the New Testament application of Isa. 40.3 and Joel 2.32 [3.5]. Some pre- and post-Christian documents have scrip- ture indexes, such as Philo, Josephus, Qumran and the Rabbinic material. However, neither indexes nor computerized searches can replace reading. Much of my contribution, therefore, is the collection and analy- sis of these parallels. I shall include some investigation of the Nag Hammadi, Mishnah, Midrash and Talmud, but the late date of these documents and the magnitude and complexity of their areas of study mean that other scholars must provide their careful analyses. I shall limit my historical research to a reconstruction of a probable historical meaning of the text in regard to the author/final redactor and his first readers.[92] For the Old Testament, such limitation has ample justification since I am striving for the New Testament writers' and readers' prob- able understanding of the text. For the New Testament, such a limitation has less clear justification since some scholars suggest that one is able to find a hermeneutical principle buried in the substratum of a text which differs from that of the whole.[93] However, such limitation has justifica- tion in the New Testament since many recent writers on Christology

90. In this regard, I am combining a literary critical question and a historical one; see L. Chouinard, 'Gospel Christology: A Study of Methodology', *JSNT* 30 (1987), pp. 26-27.

91. Similarly see J.H. Charlesworth, 'The Concept of the Messiah in the Pseudepigrapha', in *ANRW*, II,19.1, p. 197.

92. My method agrees with that of N.T. Wright, *The Climax of the Covenant. Christ and the Law in Pauline Theology* (Edinburgh: T. & T. Clark, 1991), p. 57. On the question of authorial intent, see W.K. Wimsatt, Jr and M.C. Beardsley, 'The Intentionality Fallacy', in *The Verbal Icon. Studies in the Meaning of Poetry* (Lexington: University of Kentucky Press, 1954); cf. Hays, *Echoes*, p. 201 n. 90; A.J. Hultgren, *New Testament Christology. A Critical and Annotated Bibliography* (BIRS; New York: Greenwood, 1988), p. 3; Dunn, *Christology*, p. xiv; Wright, *Climax*, p. xiii.

93. See for example Lindars, *Apologetic*.

have called for such work.[94] Moreover, New Testament scholars have produced much useful work on the exegesis of sources behind the Gospels and other books, but in this minute work, the messages of documents as a whole have sometimes been lost or neglected.[95] Furthermore, exegesis of the whole documents allows for firm historical data: one may be able to conclude that by such and such a date, early Christians held such and such a view of Jesus when they applied certain Old Testament texts to him. It is only with such a historical reconstruction in hand that scholars will be able to ask questions over the likely sources of christological development in the period 30–50 CE and then confirm or question other historical work.

Several recent scholars have raised important issues regarding New Testament christological research. Dunn has stressed the necessity of reading texts as they probably would have been read by their first audiences. He urges New Testament interpreters to read texts not in the light of the later formulations of fully developed ideas but as readers might understand those same ideas as they were semi-developed.[96] Larry Chouinard emphasizes the need to read documents as whole documents and with the realization that a narrator may 'want the reader to see a title [or idea] on more than one level'.[97] The result is that a statement or idea in the Gospels may take on new meaning when read in light of the whole.[98] Similarly, Leander Keck reminds readers that particular titles or ideas are but partial strands in the writer's Christology.[99] Thus, while my method is grammatico-historical, I shall take into account the methodological emphases of Dunn, Chouinard and Keck.

---

94. See Marshall, *Origins*, p. 127; B. Witherington, III, *The Christology of Jesus* (Minneapolis: Fortress Press, 1990), p. 27; L.E. Keck, 'Toward the Renewal of New Testament Christology', *NTS* 32 (1986), p. 372; P.A. Rainbow, 'Monotheism and Christology in I Corinthians 8.4-6' (DPhil thesis, Oxford University, 1987), pp. 18-19; Chouinard, 'Gospel', p. 23. On a similar subject, see Marinus de Jonge, 'John the Baptist and Elijah in the Fourth Gospel', in Fortna and Gaventa, *Conversation*, p. 302.

95. See the criticism of Cranfield, 'Comments', p. 269.

96. J.D.G. Dunn, 'In Defence of a Methodology', *ExpTim* 95 (1984), p. 298. See too G.H. Boobyer, 'Jesus as "Theos" in the New Testament', *BJRL* 50 (1967), pp. 254-55.

97. Chouinard, 'Gospel', p. 30.

98. Chouinard, 'Gospel', p. 30.

99. Keck, 'Christology', p. 371.

Conclusions

Recent work on the application of Old Testament passages about God to Jesus centres upon two questions: What were the theological implications of such application for the writer and his first readers, and in what time frame did such application come about? The question I seek to answer is particularly the first one. Between 50 and 90 CE, what did Christians understand by applying Old Testament passages about God to Jesus? Did all or some of these Christians include the Father and Jesus under the rubric of the one God, or were other hermeneutical axioms in play? The second question is more difficult since the data are less clear. In this regard, I shall only offer some tentative suggestions.

Chapter 2

SOME PRE- AND POST-CHRISTIAN PARALLELS:
AN ASSESSMENT OF THEIR SIGNIFICANCE

Important Parallels

What parallels existed in pre-Christian Judaism for application of passages about God to a second figure? What was their significance? Was such application widespread? And what evidence exists for such application to the or a messiah? In this chapter, I identify a 'parallel' as any text which reinterprets an earlier text about God so as to apply it to a second figure. I am dealing here with the final forms of the Old Testament and not the sources of tradition. Thus, 'earlier' may be earlier only in appearance.[1] Since I am dealing with the first-century perspective on the texts, the precise dating of the Old Testament texts is unimportant so long as they had appeared in their basic final form by New Testament times. This point is important since I am striving to find parallels which New Testament writers and readers might have used in interpreting Old Testament passages about the divine applied to Jesus. By 'second figure' I mean any reality which a text presents in personal terms and at the same time in any way distinct from God.[2] This 'distinction' need not be

---

1.   For examples of the difficulty involved in determining what text or tradition a later Old Testament text is quoting, see the Old Testament essays in D.A. Carson and H.G.M. Williamson, *It is Written: Scripture Citing Scripture. Essays in Honour of Barnabas Lindars, SSF* (Cambridge: Cambridge University Press, 1988).

2.   My usage of 'second figure' is close to the idea of 'hypostasis' as defined by P.A. Rainbow, 'Monotheism and Christology in I Corinthians 8.4-6' (DPhil thesis, Oxford University, 1987), p. 86, who gives 'hypostasis' a phenomenological definition dealing only with the linguistic level of the text. I have avoided the term 'hypostasis' since it has a technical meaning from the fourth century CE christological debates (see L.W. Hurtado, *One God, One Lord. Early Christian Devotion and Ancient Jewish Monotheism* [Philadelphia: Fortress Press, 1988], p. 37). Some scholars use 'hypostasis' to denote a 'quasi-personification of certain attributes proper to God' ... which 'occupy an intermediate position between personalities and

absolute, and I shall show that many of the second figures are ways to describe God's immanence or his immanent activity. Also, I take a broad interpretation of 'application' meaning citation or allusion.

The Angel of the LORD in the Old Testament and Elsewhere

Some uses of 'the angel of the LORD' provide a reverse parallel to the phenomenon under investigation in that the Old Testament reinterprets a number of texts about the angel of the LORD as about the LORD or God.[3] For instance, in Gen. 16.7-14 Hagar identifies the angel of the LORD as 'the LORD who spoke to her' and as 'God' (v. 13).[4] Gen. 32.9[10] identifies the angel of 31.31 as the LORD. In Exod. 3.2, the angel of the LORD appears (מלאך־יהוה וירא), yet the dialogue continues between Moses and the LORD. Moreover, while in 3.2 the angel is in the bush (מתוך־הסנה), v. 4 locates God there (מתוך־הסנה, see too Deut. 33.1).[5] Furthermore, in 3.16 God orders Moses to tell the elders, 'The LORD, the God of your ancestors...has appeared to me', yet in v. 16 the verb 'appeared' (נראה) is the same as 3.3 referring to the angel (וירא) and in this stem occurs nowhere else in the passage. In Num. 22.35, the angel of the LORD says to Balaam, '...speak only what I tell you to speak', yet in v. 38, Balaam says, 'The word God puts in my mouth, that is what I must say'. Here again the text interprets the angel's actions as those of God (see too 23.12 and 16). In Josh. 5.13-14, the captain of the army of the LORD orders Joshua to remove his sandals

abstract beings' (W.O.E. Osterley and G.H. Box, *Religion and Worship of the Synagogue. An Introduction to the Study of Judaism from the New Testament Period* [London: Isaac Pitman & Sons, 2nd edn, 1911], p. 195). Similarly see H. Ringgren, *Word and Wisdom. Studies in the Hypostatization of Divine Qualities and Functions in the Ancient Near East* (Lund: Ohlsson, 1947), p. 8.

3.   To be sure, the angel of the LORD is not always the same figure in the Old Testament (see Mal. 2.7; Hag. 1.13). Sometimes the angel of the LORD is an ambiguous figure (see 2 Kgs 1.3; 19.35; 2 Chron. 32.8, 21; cf. too Ps. 135.8; Exod. 11.4; 12.12, 23 and 29).

4.   Even a cursory glance over the first chapters of Genesis shows that a characteristic of God is to make promises (Gen. 2.18; 3.15-19; 6.18; 7.4; 8.21; 9.5; 9.9, 11, 15, 16; 12.2, 3, 7; 14.15, 17; 15.18). In 16.10, the angel is speaking like God. To be sure, prophets also speak in the first person for God (e.g. 1 Kgs 21.20-22; 2 Kgs 19.6-7).

5.   Early Church Fathers connect this figure with Christ (e.g. Justin, *Apology* 1.62).

for the place was holy. This command is an echo of Exod. 3.4-5. Like Exodus 3, the text allows Yahweh to speak directly to Joshua (Josh. 6.2). Further information comes from 23.3 where the text identifies 'the LORD your God' as the one who fought for Israel. This reference is perhaps an allusion to the figure in 5.13-14 (see too 23.9-10). In Judg. 2.1, the angel of the LORD claims to have brought Israel out of Egypt and to have promised never to break his covenant (cf. v. 15).[6] These words sound strangely like those of God elsewhere (Exod. 20.2; Judg. 6.8; Gen. 17.8; Lev. 26.42-44; Deut. 7.9). In Judg. 6.11-22, the angel of the LORD comes to Gideon (vv. 11-12), yet the LORD turns to Gideon and continues the discourse (v. 14). Furthermore, the LORD promises to wait for Gideon (v. 18), yet when Gideon returns, the angel of the LORD is the one awaiting him (v. 20). Gideon assumes that he will die because he has seen the angel of the LORD face to face (v. 22), yet in the context of the first books of the Old Testament, it is a face to face encounter with God which is death-dealing (see Gen. 32.30 and Exod. 33.20). Judg. 13.3-25 makes a similar equation between seeing God and seeing the angel.[7]

Hosea provides a possible positive parallel to the phenomenon under investigation. In Hos. 12.3-5, the prophet probably uses the word שׂרה to describe Jacob's struggle against God and the angel.[8] This verb occurs only in Hos. 12.4-5 and Gen. 32.29 where Jacob struggles with God (שׂרית עם־אלהים) and with men, and overcomes (ותוכל). 'Overcomes' occurs in the Gen. 32.28, yet the prophet uses it of Jacob's victory over the angel (Hos. 12.5).[9] To be sure, the reference 'with men' may have allowed for insertion of reference to the angel, but it is equally possible

---

6. The angel of the LORD in Exod. 14.19 moves in conjunction with the pillar of cloud which is the locus of God's particularised earthly presence. It may be this angel is the angel in whom God's name dwells (Exod. 23.21). Cf. *Num. R.* § 16.1 which applies Judg. 2.1 to Phineas the son of Eleazar.

7. Josephus, *Ant.* 5.284, takes vision of this angel as a vision of God. Similarly Josephus, *Ant.* 9.20 rereads 2 Kgs 1.3 and the angel of the LORD as simply God, and in *Ant.* 5.277-84, he rereads Judges 13 as about a 'spectre' (277) which is a vision of God (284), yet it is the angel (281).

8. So A. Even-Shoshan, *A New Concordance of the Bible. Thesaurus of the Language of the Bible* (Jerusalem: Kiryat Sepher, 1985), p. 1208. BDB, p. 975, treat the second word as if it were from an otherwise non-existent שׂור though they prefer וַיָּשַׂר an apocopated form of וַיִּשְׂרֶה.

9. See H. Gunkel, *Genesis. Übersetzt und erklärt* (GHAT; Göttingen: Vandenhoeck & Ruprecht, 1917), p. 187.

that the parallelism between 'God' and 'the angel' is an explanation of 'God' in Gen. 32.29. Other texts compare God and the LORD to the angel of the LORD (see Zech. 12.8; Ps. 34.7-8; and 35.1-8).[10]

An important question concerns the angel's distinction from God. Pre-Christian Jews could have read several angel-of-the-LORD passages as supporting a plurality of figures bearing the name Yahweh. In Gen. 18.2, three men appear to Abraham, one of whom is Yahweh (see vv. 1 and 10). According to 19.1, the two remaining men are two angels. However, in 18.33 the LORD leaves Abraham and then overthrows (ויהפך) Sodom and Gomorrah (19.25). The difficulty lies in v. 21 where one of the angels says to Lot, 'I...will not overthrow (לבלתי הפכי) the city of which you have spoken.' Verse 21 suggests that it is the angel who will destroy the cities while v. 25 attributes this action to the LORD. It is possible to see one of the two angels of 19.1 as the LORD of v. 24. Philo, for example, sees the two angels as the two potencies of God. One of these two is 'the Lord' distinct in some undefined way from the central figure who converses with Abraham (*Abr.* 114-46).[11] *T. Abr.* B 2.10 identifies the three figures of Gen. 18.1-8 as angels, one of whom is Michael (see A. 6.1-8; and B 6.4).[12] The problematic nature of these verses continued into the second and third centuries CE.[13] Moreover, 19.24 attributes the destruction to the LORD who rains down fire 'from the LORD out of heaven'.[14] One could argue, as did later Jewish heretics, that 'from the LORD' suggests that two figures bear the name Yahweh; that is, one rains down the destruction from the other in

10. Cf. 2 Sam. 14.17 and 19.27 which compare David to the angel of God.

11. See too Philo, *Quaest. in Gen.* 4.2. Cf. Josephus, *Ant.* 1.196-204. See too the fuller discussion of Philo beginning on p. 46 below.

12. E.P. Sanders, 'Testament of Abraham', in *OTP*, I, p. 875, dates the work between 75 and 125 CE. The event in B 3.1-10 is not the three men theophany at Mamre, but the washing of Michael's feet parallels Gen. 18.4. Cf. B 4.4 where Michael worships God.

13. See too A.F. Segal, *Two Powers in Heaven. Early Rabbinic Reports about Christianity and Gnosticism* (SJLA, 25; Leiden: Brill, 1977), p. 131; and later Augustine, *Trinity* 2.12.

14. J. Skinner, *A Critical and Exegetical Commentary on Genesis* (ICC; Edinburgh: T. & T. Clark, 1910), p. 309, sees this distinction as improbable. He posits that originally the subject was the three men or that מאת יהוה is a doublet to מן השמים or that the latter is a gloss. G.J. Spurrell, *Notes on the Text of the Book of Genesis* (Oxford: Clarendon, 1896), p. 191, takes one phrase explaining the other.

heaven.[15] Moreover, the second generation amora, Abba Hilfi b. Samkai identified the 'LORD who rained down fire from the LORD out of heaven' (Gen. 19.24) as the named angel Gabriel.[16] Furthermore, at the beginning of the story, Abraham first addresses one figure (18.3), and then all three (vv. 4-5); in v. 5, all three figures grant Abraham's request.[17] These bits of data from the MT suggest the possibility that some Jews could have read this text as supporting application of God's name to more than one figure.[18] Philo makes such an interpretation possible in the first century CE. The LXX could support a similar reading (see 18.1, 2, 3, 5, 16, 17, 33; 19.1, particularly vv. 18-24).

In Zech. 3.1, Joshua, the high priest, and Satan stand before the angel of the LORD. The LORD then says, 'The LORD rebuke you, O Satan! The LORD who has chosen Jerusalem rebuke you!'[19] In v. 4, the angel then says, 'See, I have taken your guilt away from you' while in v. 9, he speaks for the LORD who says, 'I will remove the guilt of this land in a single day.' In this passage the angel speaks sometimes in his own voice and sometimes for the LORD. Enigmatically, the LORD speaks as

15. See Justin Martyr, *Dialogue with Trypho* 56.

16. See *Gen. R.* 51.2 and J. Fossum, 'Kyrios Jesus as the Angel of the Lord in Jude 5-7', *NTS* 33 (1987), p. 229.

17. On the Jewish interpretation of Gen. 18, see A.T. Hanson, *The Prophetic Gospel: A Study of John and the Old Testament* (Edinburgh: T. & T. Clark, 1991), p. 128.

18. So G. von Rad, *Genesis. A Commentary* (trans. J.H. Marks; London: SCM Press, 1961), p. 199. Cf. S.R. Driver, *The Book of Genesis with Introduction and Notes* (London: Methuen, 3rd edn, 1904), p. 196. Some Christian commentators used these data to identify the Son as one of the three figures (see Gregory of Nyssa, *Theological Orations* 3.17). Cf. Augustine, *Trinity* 2.12-34 (see H.P. Liddon, *The Divinity of Our Lord and Saviour Jesus Christ. Eight Lectures Preached before the University of Oxford* [BL (1866); London: Rivingtons, 1875], pp. 56-58).

19. Zech. 3.2 has a slight textual problem. The Syriac of SA and SW reflects the Hebrew *Vorlage* יהוה מלאך. Other witnesses to the Hebrew text read יהוה including the LXX and the Targum (see K.J. Cathcart and R.P. Gordon, *The Targum of the Minor Prophets. Translated with a Critical Introduction, Apparatus and Notes* [ArB, 14; Edinburgh: T. & T. Clark, 1989], p. 190). The Syriac eliminates the difficulty of the MT text as it stands and therefore could be a correction or interpretation of יהוה. If מלאך יהוה were the original reading, I see little reason for the change to יהוה. I thus read the shorter and more difficult text, יהוה (so NRSV, NIV, NASB, and NEB) against מלאך יהוה (so JB and NJB; REB reads 'the Angel').

though another will rebuke Satan (v. 2; cf. 1.12). Thus, one could read the LORD in 3.2 as the angel of the LORD, yet the same angel speaks of another who is the LORD (v. 9; 1.12). The LXX and Targum could support a similar reading.

In 1 Chron. 21.15-30, God sends the angel of the LORD who appears at the threshing floor of Ornan. When David sees this angel, he prays to God (vv. 16-17). As a result of David's prayer, the angel sends David word to build an altar. One could thus understand that the angel was the object of his prayer. At this threshing floor, David falls down before the angel and offers sacrifices to the LORD (vv. 21, 26). Again the relationship between the angel and the LORD is unclear. David then calls upon the LORD who answers him from heaven (v. 26; see too 21.15). The text suggests that the angel is on earth in the immediate presence of David while the LORD is in heaven. However, in 2 Chron. 3.1-2, the narrator states, 'Solomon began to build the house of the LORD in Jerusalem on Mount Moriah, where the LORD had appeared to his father David…on the threshing floor of Ornan'. Yet the only one appearing there is the angel of the LORD. The LXX presents similar data. Thus, one could see two figures bearing the name Yahweh, or Yahweh partially manifesting himself through this angel.

Some MSS of the LXX of Dan. 7.13 translate 'And he came to the Ancient One' (ועד־עתיק יומיא מטה) as 'he was present as the ancient of days' (ὡς παλαιὸς ἡμερῶν παρῆν).[20] If they connected this son of man figure with Michael in Daniel 10, readers may have interpreted this figure as the angel of the LORD who in an unspecified sense comes as the Ancient of Days.

Some non-canonical texts furnish information about the angel of the LORD. Demetrius the Chronographer, fragment one, states, 'But when he was about to sacrifice him, he was prevented by an angel, who provided him with a ram for the offering.'[21] In the biblical text, it is Yahweh

20. Manuscript 88 and the Syrohexaplar (followed by Rahlfs, *Septuaginta*, II, p. 914) read ὡς παλαιός ἡμερῶν παρῆν. This reading also appears in ms 967 (second century CE). For dating and assessment of these data see J. Lust, 'Daniel 7.13 and the Septuagint', *ETL* 54 (1978): 62-63. Theodotion reads ἕως τοῦ παλαιοῦ τῶν ἡμερῶν ἔφθασεν. See too the discussion of Dan. 7.13 in C. Rowland, 'The Vision of the Risen Christ in Rev. i.13ff: The Debt of an Early Christology to an Aspect of Jewish Angelology', *JTS* 31 (1980), pp. 2-3.

21. See J. Hanson, 'Demetrius the Chronographer', in *OTP*, II, p. 848. Hanson dates the text to the third century BCE. Demetrius's work appears in the first century BCE text of Alexander Polyhistor which in turn Eusebius preserves in *Pr. Ev.* 9.19.4.

who provides (Gen. 22.14), although the close proximity of the angel of the LORD in this account may mean that the change of Demetrius was not a conscious one. Sir. 48.21 puts the LORD and the angel in parallelism.[22] Wis. 18.15-19 reinterprets the destroyer in the exodus narrative as the Word leaping from the throne of God (cf. 18.25). This passage may be a tradition which connects the Word as the angel of the LORD. *Jub.* 1.29 associates the angel of the presence as the one who went before the camp of Israel.[23] The angel is distinct in some way from the LORD (see v. 27). This distinction also appears in *Jub.* 48.13, which introduces a figure who stood between Egypt and the Israelites during the Red Sea incident (see Exod. 14.19). The text continues, 'We delivered Israel'.[24] It is very unusual that a second figure jointly shares credit for this deliverance.[25] This text shows that some Jewish inter- preters could give this angel real distinction from the LORD. *Ezek. Trag.* 159 identifies 'God' who will pass over Israel (Exod. 12.13) as the 'fearsome angel.'[26] *Ezek. Trag.* 99 attributes the 'divine word' as shining forth from the burning bush.[27] The *Apocalypse of Abraham* perhaps identifies the angel of the LORD as Iaoel who bears and medi- ates the name of God.[28] It is this angel who commands Abraham to cut the animals of sacrifice in two (*Apoc. Abr.* 12.8; cf. Gen. 15.9). In *Apoc. Abr.* 17.1, Abraham and the angel worship the Eternal One. One could

22. On the difficulties of dating Sirach see M. Gilbert, 'Wisdom Literature', in *JWSTP*, pp. 290-92.

23. G.W.E. Nickelsburg, 'The Bible Rewritten and Expanded', in *JWSTP*, p. 103, dates the book to around 168 BCE.

24. P. Hayman, 'Monotheism—A Misused Word in Jewish Studies?', *JJS* 42 (1991), pp. 8-9, points out this text and the similarity of it to Dan. 8-12 and 1QM 15.13-14.

25. Cf. Josephus, *Ant.* 3.298, where Moses says, 'God... and I, though vilified by you, will never cease our efforts on your behalf'.

26. In l. 187, it is Death which will 'pass over.' See R.G. Robertson, 'Ezekiel the Tragedian', in *OTP*, II, p. 815 n. 2. Robertson (p. 804) dates the text to the first part of the second century BCE.

27. See Robertson, 'Ezekiel', II, p. 813 n. g2. The biblical context of v. 99 is the theophany/angelophany of Exodus 3.

28. See C. Rowland, 'A Man Clothed in Linen: Dan. 10.6ff. and Jewish Angelology', *JSNT* 24 (1985), p. 106, who suggests on the basis of *Joseph and Asenath*, *Apocalypse of Abraham* and Revelation, that there was an established tradi- tion which combines description of the being in Daniel 10 with features of the theophany in Dan. 7.9. R. Rubinkiewicz, 'Apocalypse of Abraham', in *OTP*, I, p. 683, dates the text between 70 and the second century CE.

see this action as an indication that the angel is not God or the immanent presence of God.[29] The text, however, is ambiguous since if the angel were the immanence of the Eternal One (a possible interpretation of 'the mediation of my ineffable name' [10.3]), the angel could be subordinate to the Eternal One in his transcendence. *2 Esdras* contains a complex tradition concerning the angel of the LORD, and in this document it is unclear who the angel is.[30] In *Bel and the Dragon* 34, the angel of the LORD appears to Habakkuk and transports the prophet to Babylon (v. 36).[31] In v. 37, he announces to Daniel that God has sent him food which according to v. 34 the angel sent. In 2 Macc. 3.30, one finds, 'And the temple, which a little while before was full of fear and disturbance, was filled with joy and gladness, now that the Almighty LORD had appeared.'[32] But in v. 26, it is two young men who appear (cf. 11.6, 13). *Life of Adam and Eve* 25.1-3 [Vita] identifies Michael as the messenger of God whom the text associates with the divine chariot. This chariot is separate from the LORD who is sitting in heaven.[33] *Pseudo-Philo* 42.8

29. Cf. D.B. Capes, 'Paul's Use of Old Testament Yahweh-Texts and Its Implications for His Christology' (PhD dissertation, Southwestern Baptist Theological Seminary, 1990), p. 290, who sees 17.13 as an indication that Abraham also worships Iaoel, but Iaoel may be the Eternal One's name as opposed to Iaoel the Angel.

30. M.E. Stone, 'Apocalyptic Literature', in *JWSTP*, p. 412, dates the work around 95–100 CE. *2 Esdras* 5.31-40 records Ezra's visitation by Uriel whom Ezra calls the 'sovereign Lord' (v. 38; see too 6.11; 7.17, 45, 58; cf. 13.51) and who is the one who judges, who makes promises and to whom belong the people of Israel (5.40) (see 'my salvation' [6.25; 9.8]; 'my judgment' [6.20]; 'my borders' [9.8]). Uriel is distinct from the Lord who sends him (v. 31 by implication; 6.32) and from the presence of the Lord (vv. 22-31). This angel (see 6.12, 30) speaks as the creator (5.43; 7.11), as the one through whom the end of the world shall come (6.6), and as one who shall visit the earth (v. 18) (cf. 9.2 where the Most High is about the visit the world he has made and 'Then I will come and talk to you' [9.25]). Ezra prays in the presence of the Lord (6.35-59), and the angel returns and says, 'I made the world for their sake' (7.11). He has a son, the messiah (7.28). Elsewhere this angel speaks of the Most High in the third person (7.98; 8.1, 56, 59; 10:50, 52, 54, 57, 59; cf. 7.102, 132-40; 8.6-36). Thus, in *2 Esdras*, the author/final redactor's understanding of this angel is enigmatic. 9.28-29 speaks of the Most High who showed himself in the exodus (see too 14.1-3).

31. The date of Bel and the Dragon is uncertain. See G.W.E. Nickelsburg, 'Stories of Biblical and Early Post-Bibilcal Times', in *JWSTP*, p. 40.

32. The date of 2 Maccabees is between 125–63 BCE. See H.W. Attridge, 'Historiography', in *JWSTP*, p. 177.

33. Nickelsburg, 'Bible Rewritten', p. 117, is uncertain of the date. He cites a

has Manoah of Judges 13 separate the angel from God (cf. v. 10).[34] *T. Jac.* 2.14-15 says, 'Blessed are you also, O Jacob, for you have seen God face to face. You saw the angel of God—may he be exalted!— ...Then you beheld the LORD sitting at [the ladder's] top with a power which no one could describe.'[35] 'God' and the angel are in parallelism; the LORD is distinct from the angel. *Apoc. Zeph.* 6.11-13 allows an equation between 'a great angel' and the LORD of Hosts, but in 6.15 the angel Eremiel denies this identification.[36]

Several later post-Christian texts add to one's understanding of the angel of the LORD. *3 En.* 12.5 interprets Metatron as 'the lesser Yahweh' and as the angel of Exod. 23.21.[37] *3 En.* 16.1 identifies Metatron as the glory of the highest heaven. In 16.1-5, Metatron receives punishment for allowing himself to be identified as one of the two powers in heaven. *B. Sanh.* 38b offers a similar interpretation of Metatron and the angel of the LORD who speaks in Exod. 24.1.[38] In a different way, *Judg. R.* 16.1 applies Judg. 2.1 (an angel-of-the-LORD passage) to Phineas Son of Eleazar.

Several positions in regard to the angel of the LORD are possible.[39]

---

number of scholars who date the work in the first or second century CE.

34. D.J. Harrington, 'Pseudo-Philo', in *OTP*, II, p. 299, supports a date around the time of Christ.

35. W.F. Stinespring, 'Testament of Jacob', in *OTP*, I, p. 913, tentatively dates the text between the second and third centuries CE.

36. On the relationship of Eremiel to the figure in Dan. 10:5-14 see O.S. Wintermute, 'Apocalypse of Zephaniah', in *OTP*, I, pp. 504-505. He dates the text between 100 BCE–175 CE, perhaps earlier than 70 CE (pp. 500-501).

37. P. Alexander, '3 (Hebrew Apocalypse of) Enoch', in *OTP*, I, p. 229, dates the text between the fifth and sixth centuries CE. Metatron, according to S.F. Noll, 'Angelology in the Qumran Texts' (PhD dissertation, University of Manchester, 1979), p. 65, was probably the esoteric name of Michael. See too G.G. Scholem, *Jewish Gnosticism, Merkabah Mysticism and Talmudic Tradition* (New York: Jewish Theological Seminary, 1965), pp. 43-51; and Alexander, 'Shekhinah', pp. 162-63.

38. See Segal, *Two Powers*, p. 68, and his discussion of *b. Sanh.* 38b.

39. One could argue that the angel exists only as the message of God (see C. Westermann, *Genesis 12–36* [trans. J.J. Scullion; Minneapolis: Augsburg, 1985], pp. 242, 244). Some scholars believe the 'angel of the LORD' is a device to lessen the idea of theophany (see G. von Rad, 'ἄγγελος', in *TDNT*, I, p. 78; see too Gunkel, *Genesis.*, p. 187). One could argue that the angel is merely the representative of the LORD (see R. Ficker, 'מַלְאָךְ', in *THAT*, I, p. 907). Others suggest that the angel is the immanence of God or his immanent activity (see J.D.G. Dunn, *Christology in the Making. A New Testament Inquiry into the Origins of the Doctrine of the Incarnation*

The question concerning readers is, What was the pre-Christian Jewish perspective on this angel? It seems likely that several different views existed within Judaism. Philo, on the one hand, takes the angel as manifestation of one attribute of God. His distinction from God is minimal. Philo also mentions God's ability to take angelomorphic form (*Som.* 1.232).[40] *Jubilees*, on the other hand, suggests that the angel had real existence apart from God though it is unclear whether the angel there was divine. Other texts present unclear evidence. The New Testament data of Christ as the angel of the LORD are subject to dispute.[41] One could suggest that Hebrews 1 is a clarification of a misunderstood angel-of-the-LORD Christology. Perhaps Jude 5 understands Jesus as the angel of the LORD.[42] Some suggest a connection between Jesus and the angel of the LORD in Revelation.[43] In Acts 7.30-34, Stephen mentions the theophany/angelophany of Exodus 3, perhaps to connect this figure with Christ.[44] The unfortunate thing is there is still much that is ambiguous. I do know that Jesus as the angel of the LORD was a standard interpreta-

(Hurtado, *One God*, pp. 85-90). Still others see the two as identified yet distinct in some unexplained way (see T.E. McComiskey, 'Angel of the Lord', in *EDT*, p. 48). Still others connect the angel with God's glory, presence and name (W. Eichrodt, *Theology of the Old Testament* [trans. J.A. Baker; Philadelphia: Westminster Press, 1967], II, pp. 23-45; and Noll, 'Angelology', p. 18 n. 27).

40. From F.G. Downing, 'Ontological Asymmetry in Philo and Christological Realism in Paul, Hebrews and John', *JTS* 41 (1990), p. 432. See too Philo, *Abr.* 118.

41. Compare Dunn, *Christology*, pp. 149-51; Rowland, 'Vision', pp. 1-11; C. Rowland, 'The Visions of God in Apocalyptic Literature', *JSJ* 10 (1979), pp. 137-54; Rowland, 'A Man', pp. 99-110; and Fossum, 'Kyrios', pp. 226-43. W.G. MacDonald, 'Christology and "The Angel of the Lord"', in *Current Issues in Biblical and Patristic Interpretation. Studies in Honor of Merrill C. Tenney Presented by his Former Students* (ed. G.F. Hawthorne; Grand Rapids: Eerdmans, 1975), pp. 324-35, argues that an interpretation of Christ as the angel of the LORD denies the traditional understanding of Jesus' true *humanity*. He implies too that one may not think of the angel as God in the Old Testament. Cf. A. Grillmeier, *Christ in Christian Tradition. From the Apostolic Age to Chalcedon (451)* (trans. J. Bowden; London: Mowbrays, 1965], pp. 52-55.

42. See Fossum, 'Kyrios', pp. 226-43.

43. See G.K. Beale, 'Revelation', in Carson and Williamson, *It is Written*, p. 321 and his comments on Rev. 10.1-6. Cf. L.A. Brighton, 'The Angel of Revelation: An Angel of God and an Icon of Jesus Christ' (PhD dissertation, St Louis University, 1991).

44. See F.F. Bruce, *This is That. The New Testament Development of Some Old Testament Themes* (Exeter: Paternoster, 1968), pp. 35-36. Cf. Acts 7.2 and 12.11-17.

tion from the second to fourth centuries CE and that this category was a support for Christ's deity.[45] It is unclear if such an interpretation occurred in New Testament times. In regard to the meaning of the application of Old Testament passages about God to the angel of the LORD, the reader has conflicting evidence. Some Jews applied Old Testament passages about God to this second figure because in an unexplained way they included this figure in their understanding of God. Other data are unclear.[46] So in spite of the clear parallel between the New Testament application of passages about God to Jesus with the Old Testament application of passages about God to the angel of the LORD, these data leave one hardly better off in postulating the early Christian hermeneutic in applying such passages to Jesus.

Melchizedek in 11Q Melchizedek

11Q Melchizedek, discovered in 1956, consists of fourteen fragments which comprise part of three columns. The twenty five lines of column 2 provide the bulk of the document.[47] The primary edition of this document first appeared in 1965, and 11Q Melchizedek has subsequently been the subject of extensive work.[48] 11Q Melchizedek dates on palaeo-

45. See Dunn, *Christology*, p. 132; and MacDonald, 'Christology', pp. 325-28, for examples. MacDonald continues the list up to modern times. See too J.W. Trigg, 'The Angel of Great Counsel: Christ and the Angelic Hierarchy in Origen', *TS* 42 (1991), pp. 35-51. Augustine, *Trinity* 2.18.35, denies the idea that the Son was seen as opposed to the Father (see too Liddon, *Divinity*, pp. 56-58).

46. J. Fossum, 'The New Religionsgeschichtliche Schule: The Quest for Jewish Christology', in *SBL 1991 Seminar Papers* (ed. E.H. Lovering, Jr; Atlanta: Scholars Press, 1991), pp. 644-46. See too D.R. de Lacey, 'Jesus as Mediator', *JSNT* 29 (1987), pp. 106-107.

47. See P.J. Kobelski, *Melchizedek and Melchiresa* (CBQMS, 10; Washington, DC: Catholic Biblical Association of America, 1981), p. 3.

48. A.S. van der Woude, 'Melchisedek als himmlische Erlösergestalt in den neugefundenen eschatologischen Midraschim aus Qumran Höhle XI', *OS* 14 (1965), pp. 354-73; and M. de Jonge and A.S. van der Woude, '11Q Melchizedek and the New Testament', *NTS* 12 (1965–66), pp. 301-26. For bibliography up to 1981 see Kobelski, *Melchizedek*, pp. 142-54. Some of the major studies since that time include, Gareth Lee Cockerill, 'Melchizedek or "King of Righteousness"', *EvQ* 63 (1991), pp. 305-12; P. Sacchi, 'Esquisse du Développement du Messianisme Juif à la Lumière du Texte Qumranien 11QMelch', *ZAW* 100 supplement (1988), pp. 202-14; and E. Puech, 'Notes sur le manuscrit de 11QMelkîsédeq', *RevQ* 12 (1987), pp. 483-513.

graphic grounds to 50–25 BCE.[49] There is some question over the relationship of the document to the other documents at Qumran.[50] This document applies a number of texts about the divine to Melchizedek. The name/title appears in the Old Testament at Gen. 14.18-24 and Ps. 110.4, yet it is unclear whether the figures are one and the same.[51] 11QMelch 2.16 quotes Isa. 52.7 as follows:

Isa. 52.7	מה־ נאוו	על	ההרים
11QMelch 2.15	[מה] נאו	על	הרים
NRSV	How beautiful upon the mountains		
Kobelski	How] beautiful on (the) mountains		

Isa. 52.7	רגלי	מבשׂר
11QMelch 2.16	רגלי	מבש[ר
NRSV	are the feet of the messenger	
Kobelski	are the feet of the heral[d	

Isa. 52.7	משמיע	שלום
11QMelch 2.16	מ[שמיע	שלום
NRSV	who brings good news,	
Kobelski	who pro]claims peace,	

Isa. 52.7	מבשׂר	טוב	משמיע	ישעה
11QMelch 2.16	מב[שׂר	טוב	משמיע	ישוע]ה
NRSV	who		announces salvation,	
Kobelski	the her[ald of good who proclaims salvati]on,			

Isa. 52.7	אמר	לציון	מלך	אלהיך
11QMelch 2.16	אומר	לציון	מל[ך	אלהיך
NRSV	who says to Zion, 'Your God reigns.'			
Kobelski	saying to Zion, 'Your God [is king.']			

49. See Kobelski, *Melchizedek*, p. 3. For a later date, see F.L. Horton, Jr, *The Melchizedek Tradition. A Critical Examination of the Sources to the Fifth Century A.D. and in the Epistle to the Hebrews* (SNTSMS, 30; Cambridge: Cambridge University Press, 1976), p. 82.

50. Horton, *Melchizedek*, p. 72, writes, 'The language of the document is not that of the majority of the scrolls, but shows, rather, dialectic features which are limited to a smaller number of Qumran documents. These features are (a) the heavier suffixes מה- and המה-, (b) the pronoun forms הואה and היאה, and (c) an example of the so-called 'pseudo-pausal', ות]שפוטו in line 11. None of these features can be due simply to a different orthography, and they point to a dialect of Hebrew different from that of the majority of scrolls.'

51. See Horton, *Melchizedek*, pp. 79-80; Noll, 'Angelology', p. 66; and Cockerill, 'Melchizedek', pp. 305-12.

11QMelch 2.17-25 is an interpretation of the different elements of Isa. 52.7.[52] For instance, 11QMelch 2.23-24 seems to interpret 'Your God' of Isa. 52.7 as Melchizedek. That is, in 2.24, the author's need to interpret 'Your God' makes its usual reference to God unlikely. Thus, the reconstruction of most scholars 'Your God is [Melchizedek...]' is probably correct.[53] A second text is Ps. 82.1 which reads,

Ps. 82.1	אלהים	נצב בעדת אל
11QMelch 2.10	אלהים	[נ]צב בעדת [אל]
NRSV	God has taken his place	in the divine council;
Kobelski	Elohim [st]ands	in the assembly [of El,]

Ps. 82.1	בקרב אלהים ישפט	
11QMelch 2.10	בקורב אלהים ישפות	
NRSV	in the midst of the gods	he holds judgment.
Kobelski	in the midst of Elohim	he judges.

The question here is Does this text imply that 'Elohim' is Melchizedek? The decisive issue is how to translate ועליו at the beginning and end of 2.10. The options are 'concerning him' or 'concerning it.' The two possible antecedents of עליו are מלכי צדק and משפת of 2.9. If Melchizedek is correct, this text applies Ps. 82.1 to him.[54] If Justice is the antecedent, Elohim may simply be a reference to God.[55] Since 11QMelch 2.24 probably applies Elohim to Melchizedek, the first option

52. In 2.18, the document identifies the herald as 'the anointed of the spirit who is a prince' alluding to Dan. 9.25. He or a second herald will comfort the mourners of Zion and instruct them according to 2.19-20 alluding to Isa. 61.2-3.

53. So J.T. Milik, 'Milkî-sedeq et Milkî-resa dans les anciens êcrits juifs et chrétiens', *JJS* 23 (1972), p. 125; Horton, *Melchizedek*, p. 75; Noll, 'Angelology', pp. 62-3; W.R.G. Loader, *Sohn und Hoherpriester. Eine traditionsgeschichtliche Untersuchung zur Christologie des Hebäerbriefes* (WMANT, 53; Neukirchen–Vluyn: Neukirchener Verlag, 1981), p. 219; Kobelski, *Melchizedek*, pp. 54, 60; and Puech, 'Notes', p. 511. J. Carmignac, 'Le document de Qumrân sur Melkisédeq', *RevQ* 7 (1969-71): pp. 365-66, denies this application.

54. So Horton, *Melchizedek*, p. 74-75; G. Vermes, *The Dead Sea Scrolls in English* (London: Penguin, 3rd edn, 1987), p. 301; and Kobelski, *Melchizedek*, pp. 59-60.

55. So Carmignac, 'Melchisédeq', pp. 353, 365-67. See too J.A. Fitzmyer, 'Further Light on Melchizedek from Qumran Cave 11', in *Essays on the Semitic Background of the New Testament*, SBLSBS 5 (Missoula, MT: Scholars Press, 1974), p. 36.

is almost irresistible.[56] A last text is Ps. 7.8-9 in 11QMelch 2.10-11 which reads,

Ps. 7.8-9	עליה למרום שובה	
11 Q Melch 2.10	עליה למרום שובה	
NRSV	over it	take your seat on high.
Kobelski	Above it,	to the heights, return!

Ps. 7.8-9	ידין עמים	יהוה
11 Q Melch 2.11	ידין עמים	אל
NRSV	The LORD judges the peoples.	
Kobelski	El judges the nations.	

Again the question is Does this text imply that Melchizedek is 'El'? Is Melchizedek the one who returns to preside over the assembly in 2.10-11?[57] In the biblical narrative, ועליה למרום שובה is the psalmist's imperative to Yahweh.[58] Yahweh is the one who presides over the assembly and who judges the peoples. Does 11Q Melchizedek simply rename Yahweh as 'El'? And is he the one who will שובה?[59] I believe that Melchizedek is in fact the El here for the following reasons: (1) Ps. 82.8 reads, 'Rise up, O God, judge the earth' (קומה אלהים שפטה הארץ). Since Elohim probably refers to Melchizedek in 11QMelch 2.10 quoting Ps. 82.1, I suggest the writer of 11Q Melchizedek probably saw Melchizedek as the figure mentioned in Ps. 82.8. Melchizedek is the figure 'Elohim' who stands in the assembly (Ps. 82.1; 11Q Melch 2.10) and the figure 'Elohim' who will rise up and judge the earth (Ps. 82.8). If the writer combined the similar texts of Ps. 82.1 and 82.8, he probably saw Melchizedek as El of Ps. 7.8-9 since Ps. 82.1 and 8 are similar to Ps. 7.8-9. in both cases the chief figure, אל / אלהים is the one who judges (ידין in

56. Interestingly, rabbinic usage of Ps. 82.1 included the idea of God's Shekinah in the midst of those who study the Torah (see J. Sievers, '"Where Two or Three…": The Rabbinic Concept of the Shekhinah and Matthew 18.20', in *The Jewish Roots of Christian Liturgy* (ed. E.J. Fisher; New York: Paulist Press, 1989), p. 49.

57. It is important to notice that the NRSV corrects the Hebrew text so as to read 'take your seat' rather than 'return'.

58. So NIV, NASB, JB, NEB, REB, NRSV, LXX and BDB, p. 997. The MT reads שׁוּבָה (the Q masc. sing. imper.). The editors of BHS suggest reading שֵׁבָה. Cf. Horton, *Melchizedek*, p. 77.

59. Kobelski, *Melchizedek*, p. 17, takes the only option to be application to the captives. Cf. S.R. Garrett, 'Exodus from Bondage: Luke 9.31 and Acts 12.1-24', *CBQ* 52 (1990), p. 668 n. 4. On a similar subject, see Martin Hengel, *Judaism and Hellenism. Studies in their Encounter in Palestine during the Early Hellenistic Period* (trans. J. Bowden; London: SCM Press, 1974), I, p. 154.

11QMelch 2.11[Ps. 7.9] and ישפות י in 2.10[Ps.82.1]).[60] Both passages
have their chief figure in some kind of assembly (עדת לאמים in Ps. 7.8
and עדת־אל in Ps. 82.1).[61] There are structural similarities קומה אלהים
(Ps. 82.8), קומה יהוה (Ps. 7.7), and שובה (Ps. 7.8 [11QMelch 2.11]).
(2) 11QMelch 2.10 implies that Melchizedek is 'standing in the midst of
the gods.' This position may be the result of the exaltation/enthronement
possibly alluded to in 2.10-11 and its use of Ps. 7.8-9.[62] 1QM 17.5-6
may envision a similar exaltation.[63] (3) שובה implies that the subject will
move from one place to another. If Yahweh is the subject, this movement would be a clear reason to ascribe the text to a second figure.

אל in 11QMelch 2.11 replaces יהוה of Ps. 7.8. The net result is the
possibility that the author of 11Q Melchizedek interprets אל = אלוהים
(יהוה of MT) = מלכי צדק.[64] However, it is possible that El is a reference
to God as opposed to Melchizedek. I do not take this position because of
the reasons listed above and because of the writer's usage of the
'vengeance of El' and the 'inheritance of El' where El = YHWH =
Melchizedek (see below).

11Q Melchizedek applies to Melchizedek a number of phrases associated with God. In 11QMelch 2.9, the text speaks of 'the year of grace
for Melchizedek' (לשנת הרצון למלכי צדק). In the Old Testament a similar
phrase occurs in Isa. 61.2 'to proclaim the year of the LORD's favour'
(לקרא שנת־רצון ליהוה).[65] Thus, 2.9 suggests that the author of 11Q
Melchizedek replaced ליהוה with למלכי [צדק] perhaps within the context

60. Noll, 'Angelology', p. 61, also notices this parallelism.
61. Interestingly, 4Q400 2 speaks of 'your glory' and 'your kingship' amid 'all
the camps of the "gods"'. 4Q400 locates God in 'the congregation of all the gods.'
Cf. God's glory in 4Q400 2. Sir. 24.2 has Wisdom open her mouth in 'the assembly
of the gods.'
62. Garrett, 'Exodus', p. 668 n. 4. The Akkadian Creation Epic 1.150 and 2.29-
40 associates exaltation of a consort in the council of the gods.
63. See C. Rowland, *The Open Heaven. A Study of Apocalyptic Judaism and
Early Christianity* (London: SPCK, 1982), p. 89.
64. See Vermes, *Scrolls*, pp. 300, 301. Noll, 'Angelology', p. 61, suggests on the
basis of the parallelism of the preceding line that El refers to Melchizedek.
65. So M.P. Miller, 'The Function of Isa 61 1-2 in 11Q Melchizedek', *JBL* 88
(1969), p. 468; Milik, 'Milkî-sedeq', p. 125; Fitzmyer, 'Further Light', p. 252;
Loader, *Sohn*, p. 219; Noll, 'Angelology', p. 63; Kobelski, *Melchizedek*, p. 60; and
Puech, 'Notes', p. 510. The word רצון occurs with several designations for time in the
Old Testament. One finds עת רצון in Isa. 49.8 and Ps. 69.13 [14], יום רצון in Isa.
58.5. All of the uses of רצון and time refer to something pleasing to Yahweh.

of a biblical allusion. A further possible allusion in 11Q Melchizedek is the ויום נקם לאלהינו of Isa. 61.2[b]. The רצון מלכי צדק possibly goes back to Isa. 61.2[a].[66] If this suggestion is correct, the 'day of the vengeance of our God' may lie behind 2.13, 'And Melchizedek will avenge the vengeance of the judgments of God.'[67] A similar Old Testament phrase applied to Melchizedek is 'from the inheritance of Melchizedek' (מנחלת מלכי צדק, 2.5).[68] 'The inheritance of Melchizedek' is similar to גורל 'lot' in 2.8. Both 'inheritance and 'lot' point to this special group. The significant feature is that גורל usually refers to the גורל of God in the other Qumran documents when speaking of a group opposed to the 'lot' of Belial.[69] This use of גורל elsewhere, the replacement of Melchizedek for Yahweh in 2.9, and the use of גורל־מלכי צדק suggest that the document takes נחלת־מלכי צדק from an Old Testament idea which referred to נחלת־יהוה/ אלהים.

On the basis of the above exegesis, one must ask if any of the uses of אלוהים/אל in 11Q Melchizedek refer to someone other than Melchizedek. Here the data are unclear. 11Q Melch 2.3-4 mentions God's release שמטה לאל. This release is a reference to the שמטה ליהוה of Deut. 15.2. In 2.6, it is Melchizedek who proclaims liberty to the captives of 2.4-6, so it is possible that the text presupposes שמטה לאל as the release belonging to Melchizedek. This understanding is possible given the author's use of יהוה/אל for Melchizedek in 2.11 although in the final analysis this אל is unclear. If אל does not refer to Melchizedek, one might argue that 11QMelch 2.10 draws the distinction between Elohim = Melchizedek, Elohim = the wicked angels or good angels, and El = God.[70] In that case, the application of אלוהים to him may signify only his heavenly status.[71]

66. So Miller, 'Isa 61', p. 468. See Lk. 4.19. J. Jeremias, *Jesus' Promise to the Nations. The Franz Delitzsch Lectures for 1953* (trans. S.H. Hooke; SBT, 24; London: SCM Press, 1958), pp. 45-46, suggests Jesus' removal of the promised vengeance was the source of the crowds astonishment (Lk. 4.22). Cf. 11Q Melch 2.9; 2.4.

67. So Miller, 'Isa 61', p. 468.

68. So Milik, 'Milkî-sedeq', p. 125; and Puech, 'Notes', p. 510. See for example 1 Sam. 26.19; 2 Sam. 14.16; 20.19; 21.3; Ps. 127.3 and *Jub.* 1.12.

69. See 1QM 1.5; 13.5; 1QS 2.2, 5; and Horton, *Melchizedek*, p. 78.

70. Similarly Kobelski, *Melchizedek*, p. 74; cf. 2 Kgs 18.12; and 19.4.

71. See Exod. 4.16; 7.1; 1 Kgs 18.24; 1 Sam. 28.13; Horton, *Melchizedek*, pp. 75-77; Kobelski, *Melchizedek*, n. 35, p. 60; see C.A. Newsome, *Songs of the Sabbath Sacrifice. A Critical Edition* (HSM, 27; Atlanta: Scholars Press, 1985), p. 24, for evidence of angels called אלוהים at Qumran.

The problem with this explanation is Isaiah 61 which presupposes Melchizedek's replacement of Yhwh not Elohim.

The majority opinion is that Melchizedek is another name for Michael.[72] The question remains open how this angel relates to the angel of the LORD, and whether this angel is a 'hypostasis' of God.[73] Some evidence connects Melchizedek with God. One argument against this connection is the document would have a dualistic outlook as if God and Belial were on a similar plane.[74] However, elsewhere in Qumran God is in fact opposed to Belial.[75] Moreover, if Melchizedek is the angel of the LORD, the distinction between God and his angel could allow for a way to guard against the absolute equality of Good and Evil in dualism. Another objection is that the angelology of Qumran has passed beyond that stage.[76] Yet, the firm evidence for that angelology is lacking. I see no major reason for rejecting Melchizedek = Michael = the angel of the LORD, even though there is little further evidence that this possibility is in fact a probability. It is possible that the group which produced 11Q Melchizedek had an esoteric angelology.[77]

The further question remains whether Melchizedek is a heavenly high priest.[78] Melchizedek could be the figure who offers expiation for the sons of light at the end of the tenth Jubilee.[79] While Melchizedek/Michael

---

72.   See 4Q'Amram[b] 2.3 and 4QTeharot[d] 2.2 which identify the chief evil angel as having three names one of which is Melkiresha'. Since Michael is the opponent of this angel elsewhere in Qumran (1QS 3.20-21; 1QM 13.5-6, 10-16), and since he too has three names (4Q'Amram), a fair guess is that one of these names is Melchizedek. Furthermore Melchizedek executes judgment against Belial which is a function of Michael in 1QM 13.10-12 and 17.5-8. Those who identify Melchizedek with Michael are Noll, 'Angelology', p. 68; Newsome, *Songs*, p. 37; Dunn, *Christology*, p. 152; and Vermes, *Scrolls*, p. 300. Horton, *Melchizedek*, pp. 81-82, notes some similarities and some differences between the two.

73.   Noll, 'Angelology', p. 66, sees Michael identified as the angel bearing the name of God. See too Kobelski, *Melchizedek*, p. 73 n. 70.

74.   So Puech, 'Notes', p. 512, although in n. 48 he concedes the possibility of Melchizedek as a divine hypostasis.

75.   See 4Q280-82; 1QM 18. Similarly Barnabas 18.1-2 contrasts the ways of light and darkness while implicitly contrasting the Lord and Satan.

76.   Kobelski, *Melchizedek*, p. 74, though he gives no support for this statement.

77.   Moreover, one should also keep in mind that Josephus attributes an esoteric angelology to the Essenes (*War* 2.142, from Noll, 'Angelology', p. 9).

78.   See Cockerill, 'Melchizedek', p. 307 n. 4; Kobelski, *Melchizedek*, pp. 64-67; Noll, 'Angelology', pp. 66-67; Puech, 'Notes', p. 512; and Newsome, *Songs*, p. 37.

79.   So Puech, 'Notes', p. 512; cf. Kobelski, *Melchizedek*, pp. 64-65. See too

may be high priest, 2.9 is odd in that the writer applies רצון to him which the biblical narrative associates with God's favour. At least one Qumran scholar suggests that expiation is made not by Melchizedek but to him since it is his favour which the sons of light must gain.[80] Furthermore, if Melchizedek is the one who offers expiation, it does not necessarily follow that he is excluded from the writer's concept of God.[81]

It is possible to see Melchizedek as the personified righteousness of God. In 1QM 17.6-8, one reads,

> He [God] will raise up the kingdom of Michael in the midst of the gods,
> and the realm of Israel in the midst of all flesh. Righteousness shall rejoice
> on high, and all the children of His truth shall jubilate in eternal knowledge.

Righteousness and Michael are parallel as are the children of his truth and the realm of Israel.[82] These data make possible the connection of Melchizedek/Michael and the personified Righteousness of God. It is also possible that 1QM 10–19 associates Michael with the hand of God though the exact significance of this association is unclear.[83] This connection would be natural if the Qumran writers connected the eschatological

Cockerill, 'Melchizedek', p. 307 n. 4; and Newsome, *Songs*, p. 37.

80. During the 1991 British New Testament Conference's study group, 'Apocrypha, Pseudepigrapha, Qumran', G.J. Brooke made the suggestion that sacrifice would be offered to Melchizedek according to 11Q Melchizedek. I take his suggestion as stemming from רצון in that in the Old Testament 'acceptable' frequently has cultic association connected with sacrifice. Here what is 'acceptable' refers to what is acceptable to Melchizedek.

81. The Logos is priest in Philo (see Philo, *Rer. Div. Her.* 206; *Migr. Abr.* 102; *Som.* 1.215; *Cher.* 17; *Gig.* 52; and *Fug.* 106-12; and R. Williamson, *Jews in the Hellenistic World: Philo* [CCWJCW, 1.2; Cambridge: Cambridge University Press, 1989], p. 120). In the later material, *2 En.* 71.34 speaks of a last archpriest who is 'the Word and Power of God.'

82. See J.M. Baumgarten, 'The Heavenly Tribunal and the Personification of Ṣedeq in Jewish Apocalyptic', in *ANRW*, II.19.1 p. 224. It is possible that this document has a chronology similar to Dan. 9.24 and that of 11Q Melchizedek (p. 222) and that some could read Ps. 110 as an address of God to Melchizedek the embodiment of Sedeq (see Baumgarten, 'Heavenly', p. 229; Puech, 'Notes', p. 512 n. 48; and D. Flusser, 'Jesus in the Context of History', in *The Crucible of Christianity. Judaism, Hellenism and the Historical Background to the Christian Faith* [ed. A. Toynbee; London: Thames and Hudson, 1969], p. 229).

83. J. Duhaime, 'Dualistic Reworking in the Scrolls from Qumran', *CBQ* 49 (1987), pp. 45 and 48, sees a connection at Qumran between the Prince of Light and the personified hand of God.

conflict with the exodus from Egypt as they appear to do in 1QM 10–19. In the exodus, God delivered Israel with an outstretched arm. In Wis. 11.17-26, the text may connect this outstretched arm with Wisdom, perhaps God's powerful outstretched hand (v. 17), his power and arm (v. 21). In 1QM 17 the opponent of Satan is the hand of God. Similarly 4Q Cat^a frag. 12-13 1.9 states, 'The great hand of God will be with them to help them (לעוזרם)...]' which is something God's angel of truth will do in 1QS 3.24 using the same verb עזר.[84] According to 4Q Cat^a frag. 12-13 1.7 '[...] his angel of truth (מלאך אמתו) will help (יעזור) all the Children of Light from the power of (מיד) Belial [...].' Thus, Michael/the hand of God may be the angel of the LORD in the pillar of Cloud (Exod. 14.19).

There is some question as to whether a messianic herald proclaims the coming of Melchizedek. The majority opinion seems to be that the מבשר in v. 18 is not Melchizedek.[85] If Kobelski's reconstruction of 2.18 is right, this forerunner is a messianic figure, the prince of Dan. 9.25.[86] The result of this position is that a messianic figure proclaims the coming of Melchizedek who is 'your God' of Isa. 52.7. Others take Melchizedek as the herald in 2.15 and 18 and thus the anointed one who in turn proclaims God's reign in Isa. 52.7.[87] Melchizedek is clearly a herald (2.6). The question is how 2.6 relates to 2.16, 18, and 25 since v. 25 seems to demand that Melchizedek is the 'your God' of 2.16 and therefore not the herald mentioned in the same verse.

Kobelski, following Milik, suggests 11Q Melchizedek is part of the *Pesher on the Periods of History*.[88] This text associates angels with God's actions in the past.[89] 11Q Melchizedek assigns God's actions in

84.   The translation of 4Q Cata is that of F. du Toit Laubscher, 'God's Angel of Truth and Melchizedek. A Note on 11QMelch 13b', *JSJ* 3 (1972), p. 49.

85.   See van der Woude, 'Melchisedek', p. 367; de Jonge and van der Woude, '11Q Melchizedek', pp. 306-7; Horton, *Melchizedek*, pp. 78-79.

86.   See Kobelski, *Melchizedek*, p. 9, and his rendering of 11Q Melch 2.18; and B. Witherington III, *The Christology of Jesus* (Minneapolis: Fortress Press, 1990), p. 200, who sees this herald as performing a messianic function.

87.   See G.R. Beasley-Murray, *Jesus and the Kingdom of God* (Grand Rapids: Eerdmans; Exeter: Paternoster, 1986), p. 87. Miller, 'Isa 61', p. 468, takes Melchizedek as the herald of 2.18 and 2.6 and connects these verses with Isa. 61.1.

88.   Kobelski, *Melchizedek*, pp. 50-51, following Milik, 'Milkî-Sedeq', pp. 109-24.

89.   See Milik, 'Milkî-sedeq', p. 120, and his rendering of 4Q180 3-10. Kobelski, *Melchizedek*, p. 51, also points out that these texts speak of the sacrifice of Isaac

the future to Melchizedek. What one may have is a systematic rereading of problematic texts as rereadings about the angel of the LORD, or an angel. Since Philo provides evidence that he at times included the angel of the LORD in his concept of God, it does not follow that since Melchizedek is the angel Michael, he is thereby excluded from the writer's concept of God: the evidence is unclear.

Nearly all commentators agree that Melchizedek is a heavenly being. A clear support of this view is Melchizedek's contrasted position to Belial who is an angelic figure.[90] Beyond that conclusion it is unclear who Melchizedek is. He may or may not be the angel of the LORD. If he is the angel of the LORD, the text does not supply enough information to decide whether the writer included him in his concept of God. So again, I suggest this text gives a parallel to the New Testament application of texts about God to Jesus, but that the nature of the second figure here is so unclear that one may not with any confidence use it as an explanation of the New Testament application of passages about God to Jesus.

Other Second Figures from Qumran

4Q 166-67^b frag. 2 reads, '*For I will be like a lion [to E]ph[ra]im [and like a young lion to the house of Judah* (v, 14a). Its interpretation con]cerns the last Priest who shall stretch out his hand to strike Ephraim...' This text is a comment on Hos. 5.14, a passage about the LORD stretching forth his hand. In the commentary, this activity becomes that of the last Priest. Like the passages in 11Q Melchizedek, Hos. 5.15 speaks of God returning to his place. This 'returning' may be the impetus for its application to a second figure. The difficulty comes in identifying the last Priest: Is he the priestly messiah? If so, is he a heavenly or earthly figure? Is he the last heavenly priest Melchizedek? These questions for me have no convincing answer. Another parallel comes from the Habakkuk commentary which reads,

> [*But the righteous shall live by his faith*] (ii, 4b). Interpreted, this concerns all those who observe the Law in the House of Judah, whom God will deliver from the House of Judgement because of their suffering and because of their faith in the Teacher of Righteousness.[91]

and Gen. 22. The problem with the biblical text is that the angel answers from heaven (Gen. 22.11, 15).

90.   So Loader, *Sohn*, p. 218.

91.   Vermes, *Scrolls*, p. 283, dates the text to the late first century BCE.

Maurice Casey points out that in the biblical text, the object of 'faith' is most probably God.[92] Yet in 1Q Habakkuk Pesher, the object of faith may be the Teacher of righteousness. Casey implies that the Qumran writer took God as the object of faith in the biblical quotation and applied it to the Teacher of righteousness. Another example occurs in CD 5.17-18 which speaks of Moses and Aaron arising by the hand of the prince of lights while Satan raises up Jannes and his brother during the first exodus.[93] This passage contrasts the whole exodus narrative which points to the LORD or the angel of the LORD performing this function (e.g. Exod. 3.2-4). In Qumran, one has possibly two examples of apparently human figures to whom Qumran writers apply passages about God. These are the teacher of righteousness and perhaps the last priest, the priestly messiah.

Wisdom

Wisdom of Solomon, a document dating from between 200 BCE to 41 CE, applies a number of Old Testament passages about the divine to Wisdom[94] However, the concept 'Wisdom' raises many questions. Does 'Wisdom' always mean the same thing in Wisdom of Solomon? And is 'Wisdom' such a clear concept in the mind of the writer that a reader should always see it as a second figure with independent existence of the one God of monotheism? Before I attempt answers to these questions, I shall simply note the places where the writer mentions 'Wisdom' when referring to a biblical passage about God and his action in the world. I shall then discuss what these passages may have meant to the writer and his subsequent readers.

Wis. 10.1 associates Wisdom with the creation of mankind (Gen. 3.8-24) and attributes acts of God to her (Wis. 10.2, see Gen. 1.28 and 2.16).[95] Wisdom's association does not mean that God is not the creator

---

92.   M. Casey, 'Chronology and the Development of Pauline Christology', in *Paul and Paulinism. Essays in Honour of C.K. Barrett* (ed. M.D. Hooker and S.G. Wilson; London: SPCK, 1982), p. 128.

93.   Duhaime, 'Dualistic Reworking', p. 54, explains this passage by connecting the Prince of Lights with the angel of God in the exodus.

94.   For the date, see E. Schürer, *The History of the Jewish People in the Age of Jesus Christ (175 BC–AD 135)* (rev., ed. and trans. G. Vermes, F. Millar, and M. Goodman; Edinburgh: T. & T. Clark, 1986), 3.1, p. 572-73; Gilbert, 'Wisdom', p. 312, dates the book between 30 BCE and the first century CE.

95.   Some texts associate Wisdom and creation (9.9 [inactive]; 8.4 [associate in

of man (Wis. 2.23). Wis. 10.3 inserts a reference to Wisdom in the Cain and Abel episode where the biblical passage is about the LORD (Gen. 4.4-6). Wisdom saved Noah (Wis. 10.4 and Gen. 6–8). Wisdom saved Shem after the tower of Babel (Wis. 10.5 and Gen. 11.1-11 [though not explicitly attributed to God]). Wisdom rescued Lot (Wis. 10.6-8 and Gen. 18.22-19.24) where Wisdom may be the angel of the LORD. Wisdom guarded and appeared to Jacob.[96] Wisdom saved Joseph (Wis. 10.13 and Gen. 37.22–39.23) and brought him a sceptre (Wis. 10.14 and Gen. 40.1–41.45). Wisdom brought about the exodus (Wis. 10.15) and entered the soul of Moses (Wis. 10.16 and Exod. 3.12). Wisdom was or was in the starry flame which guided Israel on her exodus from Egypt.[97] The text associates Wisdom with God's intervention during the exodus (Wis. 10.18-19 and Exod. 14.14, 30 and 15.19). Wisdom prospered Israel through Moses (Wis. 11.1) and inspired the prophets (Wis. 7.27, a function of God's Spirit in the Old Testament).

The above texts have a common feature: in them, the Old Testament speaks of the visible presence of God, or the Old Testament text is problematic in that it alludes to some kind of plurality of figures as or around God. For instance, Wis. 10.1 may play off the possibly implied divine plurality of Gen. 1.26 or the anthropomorphism of 3.8-24. This theory explains Wis. 7.25-26 which speaks of Wisdom as the 'emanation of the glory', 'reflection', 'mirror', and 'image' of God. The same is true of the Cain incident with the implied anthropomorphism of Gen. 4.4-6. The problematic theophany of Genesis 18-19, likewise, may cause the introduction of Wisdom. Wis. 10.10-12 reinterprets the theophany and anthropomorphism in Gen. 28.13. Wis. 10.11 may reinterpret Gen. 31.13 (the angel of God, see v. 11). Wis. 10.12 in turn may refer to the theophany and anthropomorphism of Gen. 31.24 and 32.24-32. The same is true of the exodus (Wis. 10.15, 17 and Exod. 14.14-19) and the visible presence of God, perhaps the 'angel in whom God's name dwells.' Such a hypothesis explains why such acts are in turn simply attributed

God's works]; and 7.22). Perhaps Wisdom is the 'all powerful hand which created the world' (11.17).

96.   See Wis. 10.10-12; Gen. 27.41-45; 28.10-15; 29.1-30.43; 31.1-16, 24 and 32.1-32.

97.   Wis. 10.17; Exod. 13.21, 22; 14.14-19, 24; 33.9, 10; Num. 12.5; 14.14; Deut. 31.15; Neh. 9.12, 19; Ps. 99.7; cf. *2 Esd.* 1.14; Wis. 18.3 and Sir. 24.4. *1 En.* 42.3 also associates Wisdom with the exodus from Egypt.

to God later (Wis. 11.13 = the exodus; 19.9 = Red Sea incident; 3.7-8; 6.5 = future judgment).

The first question is, What was the author's understanding of Wisdom? The most convincing answer to me is that the data do not provide enough information to know. The second question is, What did the readers of Wisdom of Solomon understand by the idea Wisdom? Again the data are unclear. The writer affirms that Wisdom is with God (Wis. 9.9). This affirmation could mean either that she is an attribute of God or that she had independence from God. One could say the same about the affirmation that she knows God in an ultimate way (8.4 by implication). That is, a reader's understanding of these texts depends on his or her emphases. If the reader focuses on those data which seem to distinguish Wisdom from God, she will thus have some kind of independence from him. If the reader understands Wisdom as a simple metaphor for the immanence of God, that independence disappears. That she is God's messenger (8.21; 9.6, 10; 18.3 and 7.7 by implication) who comes from God's throne (9.10; 18.15-25; and see 9.4) might mean to some that she is an angel and to others that she is the Angel of the Lord. Other texts closely connect Wisdom with God. For instance, Wisdom is the Holy Spirit (9.17; 12.1 and perhaps 7.25). Wisdom possesses glory (9.11 [perhaps God's glory]). She is God's image (7.26). She is the Word of God (18.15-25; 9.1-2). She possesses attributes of God (7.22b). She has no separate will from God (18.15-25). The important point is that Wisdom does not violate monotheism according to the writer (12.13). That is, whatever Wisdom is, she is not a second God beside the one God of monotheism. Therefore, those who would read her as having independence from God nevertheless must square that independence with belief in only one God.

In Wisdom of Solomon, Wisdom has at least linguistic distinction from God. Beyond that observation, scholars hold differing opinions. That Wisdom is a second goddess beside the one God is not an attractive position.[98] Some scholars suggest that she is 'God's presence in the world' (1.7)[99] or that she is divine in an undefined way.[100] Others

---

98. Similarly see Gilbert, 'Wisdom', p. 311; and M. Casey, *From Jewish Prophet to Gentile God: The Origins and Development of New Testament Christology* (Cambridge: James Clarke, 1991), p. 90.

99. Gilbert, 'Wisdom', pp. 309-10. M. Delcor, 'The Apocrypha and Pseudepigrapha of the Hellenistic Period', in *CHJ*, II, p. 486.

100. G.W.E. Nickelsburg and M.E. Stone, *Faith and Piety in Early Judaism*.

suggest that Wisdom is an aspect of God or of God's activity,[101] or that she exists as a second figure *within* the one God of monotheism.[102] Still others suggest that she is distinct from and subordinate to God,[103] or that she occupies a midpoint between 'person' and 'personification'.[104] And others posit that she is God's epiphany and Shekinah.[105] Wisdom is divine in that she is an attribute of God, but the text does not indicate how far Wisdom has real distinction from God or within God. Here again one has a clear example of an Old Testament text about God applied to a second figure, yet again the nature of that figure is unclear.

Another work which mentions Wisdom is Sirach. The date of Sirach is problematic because of various forms of the work.[106] Parts of the text date to 190 BCE in Hebrew and 132 BCE in its Greek translation.[107] Sirach, like Wisdom of Solomon, ascribes several Old Testament passages about God to Wisdom, yet one must face the same questions as he or she did in Wisdom of Solomon. Does the author imply that Wisdom has personal existence apart from God? Or is Wisdom just a metaphor? Would Sirach's readers all have the same understanding of Wisdom which the author had? Before I attempt answers to these questions I shall notice one place where Wisdom in Sirach replaces reference to the divine in the biblical narrative. That is, Wisdom dwells in the pillar of cloud (Sir. 24.4; perhaps 14.27, alluding to Exod. 14.14-21). God's presence in the cloud is Wisdom according to Sirach.

In answering the above questions, several observations are important. First, the idea of Wisdom does not violate monotheism according to the author (1.8). That is, whatever Wisdom represents, she is not a second

Texts and Documents (Philadelphia: Fortress Press, 1983), pp. 219-20.

101. See Dunn, *Christology*, pp. 176 and xxxv n. 26; J.D.G. Dunn, 'Was Christianity a Monotheistic Faith from the Beginning?', *SJT* 35 (1982), p. 330.

102. See R.H. Fuller, 'The Theology of Jesus or Christology? An Evaluation of the Recent Discussion', *Semeia* 30 (1984), p. 109; and *idem*, 'Lower and Higher Christology in the Fourth Gospel', in *The Conversation Continues. Studies in Paul and John in Honor of J. Louis Martyn* (ed. R.T. Fortna and B.R. Gaventa; Nashville: Abingdon, 1990), p. 363.

103. It is unclear to me if Hurtado takes this position (Hurtado, *One God*, p. 44).

104. H. Ringgren, *Israelite Religion* (trans. D.E. Green; Philadelphia: Fortress Press, 1966), p. 309. On hypostatization see Hengel, *Judaism and Hellenism*, I, pp. 153-54; II, p. 98 n. 294, and the literature cited there.

105. So H. Gese, 'Wisdom Literature in the Persian Period', in *CHJ*, I, p. 204.

106. See Gilbert, 'Wisdom', pp. 290-92.

107. Gilbert, 'Wisdom', p. 291.

goddess beside the one God of monotheism. Secondly, Sirach has features
which both associate Wisdom with God and disassociate her from God.
For instance, those which associate include the following: Wisdom is an
attribute of God (42.20-21; 1.1 [eternally with him]; 1.6 [by implication—
God is the root of Wisdom]; perhaps 1.3; 15.18). Wisdom comes forth
from God's mouth (24.3). Wisdom alone has a type of omnipresence
(24.5). The following disassociates her from God: Wisdom is created
(1.4, 9, 14; 24.8-9). The question remains however whether God created
this attribute from nothing, or whether it is an emanation or generation
from God.[108] Interestingly, Wisdom praises herself in the presence of the
hosts and in the midst of her people (24.1-2). This passage may shed
light on the mysterious figure in 4Q 491 frag. 11, (identified with
Michael who praises himself in the midst of the gods).

Scholars hold different positions in regard to Wisdom in Sirach. It
appears unlikely that Wisdom is a second god, a goddess, beside the one
God of monotheism (see 1.8). Some hold that she is a personification of
a divine attribute with little real distinction from God.[109] Others suggest
that she is separate from God.[110] Others see her as having distinction
within the one God of monotheism.[111] Like Wisdom of Solomon, the
text furnishes evidence that Jews could apply texts about God to a
linguistic second figure. Also like Wisdom of Solomon, the text does not
furnish enough information to draw firm conclusions about the exact
nature of Wisdom. Scholars' disagreement over Wisdom in Wisdom of
Solomon and Sirach shows the ambiguity of the data. This ambiguity
means that it is difficult, if not impossible, to measure how pre-Christian
readers might have understood these texts. I thus note the phenomenon
of these texts applying passages about the divine to Wisdom, but it is
difficult to use these texts to explain the New Testament application of
passages about the divine to Jesus.

---

108. Cf. LXX Prov. 8.22 and 25b where creation and generation are the same.
Augustine, *Trinity* 6.1, notes the impossibility of God existing without his wisdom.

109. B.L. Mack and R.E. Murphy, 'Wisdom Literature', in *Early Judaism and its
Modern Interpreters* (ed. R.A. Kraft and G.W.E. Nickelsburg [BMI, 2; Philadelphia:
Fortress Press; Atlanta: Scholars Press, 1986), p. 377.

110. Casey, *Jewish Prophet*, p. 89.

111. See above n. 102.

Philo's Logos

Philo of Alexandria, who was between 60-70 years old in 40 CE, applies Old Testament passages about God to the Logos.[112] Part of the reason for this phenomenon has to do with Philo's view of biblical theophanies. Philo rules out the idea of seeing God as he is (*Fug.* 141), and in one place, Philo explains biblical theophanies as appearances of the Logos (*Som.* 1.228-30).[113] One intriguing explanation of theophany results from the appearance of the three men in Genesis 18 (*Abr.* 119-23). Philo allegorizes this theophany and explains it as a single figure casting two shadows which one may call 'God' loosely speaking. The central figure is the Father with two figures, the creative and the lordly potencies, at his sides.[114] The three stem from the one and are an alternative way of conceiving of God which Philo sees, though imperfect, as having biblical sanction.[115] Philo's explanation of theophany several times touches on the Red Sea incident. God sends an 'invincible help' which is nevertheless 'self sent' (*Vit. Mos.* 2.252). In still another record of this event, Philo mentions the Logos who rains forth wisdom from the cloud (*Rer. Div. Her.* 203-205). Philo further states, 'the cloud goes behind the travellers' rear to guide them on their way, and within is *the vision of the Godhead*, flashing rays of fire' (*Vit. Mos.* 2.254, my emphasis). Further along in the exodus event, the Logos distributes the manna (*Rer. Div. Her.* 191). Philo sees the Logos as the source of prophecy (*Rer. Div. Her.* 259). Since the idea of anthropomorphism to Philo is intolerable, the idea of the LORD coming down to see the Tower of Babel evokes an explanation referring to God's potencies (*Conf. Ling.* 134-39).

The question is Does Philo include or exclude the Logos from his concept of God? Philo does use 'angelic' language of the Logos which

---

112. On the age of Philo see *Leg. Gai.* 1, and the discussion in Williamson, *Philo*, I. On Philo's Logos, see S. Sandmel, *Philo of Alexandria. An Introduction* (Oxford: Oxford University Press, 1979), pp. 89-102; and E.R. Goodenough, *An Introduction to Philo Judaeus* (Oxford: Basil Blackwell, 2nd edn, 1962), pp. 91-111.

113. Another explanation in Philo is that such theophanies refer not to visible but mental perceptions of God (*Leg. All.* 3.100-103; cf. *Mut. Nom.* 14).

114. In Philo, *Quaest. in Gen.* 1.57, two Cherubim symbolize these two potencies.

115. See similarly Downing, 'Asymmetry', p. 430; and Fossum, 'Kyrios', p. 230, who connects one of the figures with the Logos. During the same event, Philo describes the activity of the Logos as κύριος (*Leg. All.* 3.218).

some readers might understand as separating the Logos and God. For example, Philo sees the Logos as holding 'the eldership among the angels' (*Conf. Ling.* 146). But the foundational idea here is that the Logos is the angel of the Lord. For example, *Conf. Ling.* 146 alludes to the theophany/angelophany of Gen. 16.7-13; 31.11-13 and 32.1-32 where Philo sees the Logos as the heavenly image of God citing Gen. 1.27 (*Rer. Div. Her.* 230-31). The angel of Exod. 23.20-21 is the Logos (*Migr. Abr.* 174). The question then is Does Philo distinguish the angel of the Lord from the one God? Philo addresses the relationship between the Logos and the one God of monotheism in several places; he places all focus on God (*Leg. All.* 2.86). For Philo, at times, the Logos is a half-way house between God and man neither uncreated like God nor created like man (*Rer. Div. Her.* 206). He is 'nearest, with no intervening distance, to the Alone truly existent One' (*Fug.* 101). From an inner voice, Philo divined, 'God is indeed one, His highest and chiefest powers are two, even goodness and sovereignty' (*Cher.* 27) uniting the two is Reason (28).[116] In several places Philo divides the Logos from the one God of monotheism (*Migr. Abr.* 175; *Rer. Div. Her.* 234, 236). On the other hand, the Logos is θεός in a derivative sense (*Som.* 1.230). Thus, the Word, as God's representation to man, accordingly is not a second God.[117] He nevertheless enjoys a certain undefined distinction from God.

Scholars take several positions regarding the Logos; some see the Logos as the immanence of God or his immanent activity[118] or God's mental activity in Creation.[119] Others suggest that he is a divine hypostasis[120] even representing a kind of binitarianism.[121] Still others suggest that Philo does not have a consistent view of the Logos.[122] Some further

---

116. See too *Rer. Div. Her.* 166; *Fug.* 97, 101; *Abr.* 121; and *Som.* 2.252-54.

117. Cf. Philo, *Quaest. in Gen.* 2.62; see Casey, *Jewish Prophet*, pp. 92-93.

118. See Williamson, *Philo*, p. 107; Hurtado, *One God*, pp. 45-47; Casey, *Jewish Prophet*, pp. 84-85; and Dunn, *Christology*, pp. 224-28. See too Sandmel, *Philo*, pp. 94-95.

119. P. Borgen, 'Philo of Alexandria', in *ABD*, V, p. 339.

120. See Segal, *Two Powers*, p. 162; D.T. Runia, *Philo of Alexandria and the Timaeus of Plato* (Philosophia Antiqua, 44; Leiden: Brill, 1986), p. 450; *idem*, 'God and Man in Philo of Alexandria', *JTS* 39 (1988), p. 72.

121. F. Young, 'Two Roots or a Tangled Mass', in *The Myth of God Incarnate* (ed. J. Hick; London: SCM Press, 1977), p. 114.

122. See literature cited in Mack and Murphy, 'Wisdom', p. 392. Cf. Williamson, *Philo*, p. 103, who aptly remarks, 'It is always, however, difficult for a modern mind to

question Philo's commitment to monotheism.[123] My position is that in some texts the Logos has a certain distinction from God who transcends the Logos and the powers.[124] In other texts, Philo includes the Logos in his concept of God.[125] I suggest that Philo applies Old Testament passages about God to the Logos because he has included him in his concept of the one God of monotheism though the nature of that inclusion is unclear.[126]

Ambiguous Second Figures in the Old Testament and Other Writings[127]

In some Old Testament and intertestamental texts, it is possible to see a certain distinction between God and his name, glory, wisdom, spirit and word. These phenomena are in certain cases interchangeable with God.[128] One Old Testament example is the idea of the LORD dwelling in his

grasp wholly what it is that an ancient writer—especially one who is avidly devoted to both scriptural Judaism and Greek philosophy—had in mind, and one suspects more than once that what looks like an inconsistency or a contradiction does so because of the intellectual and religious viewpoint of the (usually non-Jewish) reader of his works.'

123. See the implication of Dunn, *Christology*, p. 223; and Casey, *Jewish Prophet*, p. 85, though cf. pp. 92-93.

124. See similarly Downing, 'Ontological Asymmetry', p. 439. Downing's article (pp. 423-40) is a critique of Dunn's assessment of the evidence. See too Seyoon Kim, *The Origin of Paul's Gospel* (Grand Rapids: Eerdmans, 1982), p. 219.

125. Goodenough, *Philo*, p. 106, writes, 'That is, God and the Powers together constitute a sevenfold deity, with the One Being transcending the other six and ultimately alone having existence, just as the lower five are only aspects of the single radiation, the Logos itself'.

126. Philo's Alexandrian heritage makes possible influence of middle Platonism in his writings (see Borgen, 'Philo', p. 344). In middle Platonism, the Logos is the rational discourse and human rationality as well as the demiurgic aspect of divinity (see Thomas H. Tobin, 'Logos', in *ABD*, 4 pp. 348-49). Still Philo was committed to Jewish institutions (so Borgen, 'Philo', p. 341). See Tobin, 'Logos', p. 351, for the view that the explanation of the Logos in Philo remains unclear.

127. I shall not investigate those non-personal things which sometimes stand in the place of God (i.e. 'place', the Ark [1 Sam. 4.7]; the heavens etc.). Josephus, *Ant.* 9.15, rereads 2 Chron. 20.19 where the Israelites praise the LORD God as blessing the power of God.

128. On the question of their distinction, see G.F. Moore, *Judaism in the First Centuries of the Christian Era. The Age of the Tannaim* (Cambridge, MA: Harvard University Press, 1927), I, pp. 437-38.

temple while some Old Testament texts imply that the tabernacle or the temple is the place where God's name dwells.[129] The name of the LORD is in the temple, yet God hears from heaven (1 Kgs 8.34, 36 and by implication 29).[130] One could see distinction between God and his name in Exod. 23.20-21 which speaks of the angel in whom God's name dwells.[131] Although these texts may have implied a certain distinction between God and his name, many scholars see 'the name' as a way to speak of God's immanent presence.[132] Others see the name in more personal terms.[133] The idea of 'the name' being personally distinct from a god was a possibility many centuries before the rise of Christianity.[134] Moreover, Philo explicitly identifies 'the name' as the Logos (*Conf. Ling.* 146). Later Christian documents use 'the name' as a christological category.[135]

129. See for example Deut. 12.5, 11, 21; 14.23; 26.2, 29; 9.3; 1 Chron. 22.7; and 2 Chron. 2.1. See too Josephus, *Ant.* 8.114. Other texts speak simply of God's presence in the tabernacle or temple (2 Sam. 22.7; Ps. 11.49; 18.6[7]; Jon. 2.4, 7; Mic. 1.2 [cf. v. 3]; Hab. 2.20; see too Tob. 1.4; and Prayer of Azar. 1.31). 1 Kings speaks repeatedly of the name of the Lord in association with the temple (8.17, 29 and 9.3; see similarly 2 Chron. 22.7).

130. In this regard, 2 Kgs 21.7 contrasts the image of Asherah which should not be in the temple, with the name of the Lord which God placed there.

131. Cf. Philo's Logos as the name (see above). The LXX reads τὸ γὰρ ὄνομά μου ἐστιν ἐπ' αὐτῷ. The MT reads כִּי שְׁמִי בְּקִרְבּוֹ. Hurtado, *One God*, p. 160, suggests that this angel is not the Angel of the LORD. MacDonald, 'Christology', pp. 330-31, sees the phrase in question as 'he has my full authority.'

132. E.g. Rainbow, 'Monotheism', p. 88. In many places, the name compares with God (see Deut. 10.8; 21.5; 2 Sam. 22.50; Neh. 9.5; Ps. 7.17[18]; 18.49[50]; 34.3[4]; 86.9, 12; 99.6; 103.1; 116.17; Isa. 12.4; 25.1; by implication 30.27; Isa. 56.6; 60.9; Jer. 10.6; Zech. 10.12; 14.9; Mal. 3.16; Sir. 51.12; Prayer of Azar. 1.3; Tob. 3.11; 8.5; cf. Exod. 34.5 where the name is not a figure).

133. See R.N. Longenecker, *The Christology of Early Jewish Christianity* (London: SCM Press, 1970), pp. 41-46, and the literature cited there. See too J. Fossum, *The Name of God and the Angel of the Lord. Samaritan and Jewish Concepts of Intermediation and the Origin of Gnosticism* (WUNT, 36; Tübingen: Mohr [Siebeck], 1985).

134. In a text copied in the reign of Niqmadd, 2nd quarter of the 14th century BCE, *The Legend of King Keret* 6.56, says, 'May Horon [god of the nether world] break, O my son, May Horon break thy head, Ashtoreth name of Baal thy pate' (trans. H.L. Ginsberg in *ANET*, p. 149).

135. According to J. Daniélou, *The Theology of Jewish Christianity* (trans. J.A. Baker; Chicago: Regnery, 1964), pp. 151-57, *1 Clement* and *Hermas* identify 'the Name' as the Son. In Hellenistic Synagogue Prayers 1.2, a Christian interpolator

Some documents interpret Old Testament events and traditions about God as events of God's glory or vice versa. For instance, in Exod. 16.10, the glory of the LORD appears in the cloud, and in v. 9 the Israelites are to draw near to the LORD. In Exod. 24.15-18, the glory of the LORD appears on the Mountain, and in 25.1 (the next verse), the LORD speaks to Moses (see similarly Num. 14.10-11; 16.42-44; 20.6-7). Similar to the tradition above outlined over God's name, the glory of the LORD fills the temple (Exod. 40.14; 1 Kgs 8.11; 2 Chron. 5.14; and 7.1). In Lev. 9.4, Moses promises Aaron that the LORD will appear to him while in v. 6 this promise refers to the appearance of the glory of the LORD (see too v. 23). The glory is interchangeable with God in Ezek. 10.18-20. *Jub.* 1.1-6 interprets the theophany at Sinai as a revelation of the glory of the LORD. This interpretation continued to the time of the Rabbis who looked forward to the coming of the Shekinah.[136] Similarly, *1 En.* 77.1-2 interprets Ezek. 43.2 and the future return of the glory of God as a prediction that the Most High will descend and return from the east of the temple. Fossum suggests that Samaritanism amalgamated the angel of the LORD with the glory of the LORD, and then credited him with the destruction of the Egyptian army during the exodus.[137] Recent work on the esoteric tradition of some of the Tannaim suggests some distinction between God and his glory as well as the interchangeability between the two.[138]

The tradition in the Old Testament of God's transcendence makes it possible that some Jews could see a certain distinction between God and his glory. Some post-Christian writers saw such distinction. But in the Old Testament narrative, God's glory is an attribute of God and is not a completely distinct entity.[139] To stay within the limitations of this work, I

---

identifies Jesus as the name God caused to 'encamp among us.' *4 Ezra* 2.45-47 closely connects if not identifies the name as the Son of God. Nag Hammadi includes a similar understanding of 'the name' (see Valentinian Gospel of Truth 38.7–41.3).

136. See the tradition of bringing the Shekinah down to earth in *Gen. R.* §19.7, pointed out by Kim, *Origin*, p. 189. See too *Lev. R.* §1.14 pointed out by K.R. Snodgrass, 'Streams of Tradition Emerging from Isaiah 40.1-5 and their Adaptation in the New Testament', *JSNT* 8 (1980), p. 32.

137. Memar Marqah 111.5. Cf. Exod. 15.1; see Fossum, 'Kyrios', p. 242 n. 77 and *idem, Name*, pp. 227-28. I have not checked this Samaritan text first-hand.

138. Fossum, 'Religionsgeschichtliche Schule', p. 645, quoting and summarizing C.R.A. Morray-Jones, 'Merkabah Mysticism and Talmudic Tradition' (PhD thesis, Cambridge University, 1988). I have not consulted Morray-Jones' thesis first-hand.

139. See similarly Dunn, *Christology*, p. 128.

will omit investigation of the spirit and the word of the LORD which
point to the same kind of conclusions as the name, the glory and other
phenomena.[140] The name and the glory of God provide a number of
examples where an idea or text about God becomes a reference to the
name or glory of God. In such cases it is seldom clear what the nature of
the possible distinction between God and these things are. Since such
is the case, they provide little help in assessing the New Testament
hermeneutical axioms in applying Old Testament passages about God to
Jesus.

Other Data

I have omitted full-scale discussion of Rabbinic and Gnostic material for
two reasons: (1) it is notoriously difficult to determine what extent these
materials reflect pre-Christian Judaism, and (2) I have not attempted a
complete reading of these materials in the way which I have for the Old
Testament, Apocrypha, Pseudepigrapha, Qumran, Philo and Josephus.
Therefore, I simply note that Rabbinic and Gnostic materials contain
traditions where a writer applies a passage about God to a second figure
(e.g. the Shekinah, and Metatron), but the exact theological import of
such application remains obscure.[141]

I now turn to texts about God's agent. A number of Jewish traditions
interpret an Old Testament text about God as referring to the action of
God's agent. For example in *Jubilees* 48, Prince Mastema takes the
place of the LORD in Exod. 4.24-26 (*Jub.* 48.2).[142] Exod. 4.24-26 is
strange because the LORD in vv. 21-23 gives Moses instructions about

---

140. See similarly Rainbow, 'Monotheism', pp. 87-98; de Lacey, 'Jesus', p. 110;
and Casey, *Jewish Prophet*, p. 84. See too the *Isaiah Targum* 49.10-11. Josephus,
Ant. 7.92, rereads 2 Sam. 7.4 'The word of the LORD came...' as 'God appeared.'
Josephus, *Ant.* 6.166, interprets the Holy Spirit of 1 Sam. 16.14 as simply τὸ θεῖον;
see too *Ant.* 8.114-19, 333. In *Ant.* 8.240, he may interpret 1 Kgs 13.20 (about the
word of the LORD) simply as 'God'. In Gnosticism, *The Exegesis of the Soul* 129,
ascribes to the Holy Spirit the prophecies of Jer. 3.1-4; Hos. 2.2-7; and Ezek. 16.23-
26. The first and third quotations contain explicit statements that they were spoken by
the LORD.

141. On the Rabbinic texts, see E.E. Urbach, *The Sages. Their Concepts and
Beliefs* (trans. I. Abrahams; Cambridge, MA: Harvard University Press, 1975), pp. 1-
183. On Metatron, see P.S. Alexander, '2 (Hebrew Apocalypse of) Enoch', in *OTP*, I,
pp. 223, 235, 243-44.

142. Hayman, 'Monotheism', p. 8, also points out this text.

the exodus, yet in v. 24 after their meeting, the LORD tries to kill Moses. *Jub.* 48.2 removes this difficulty by making Mastema the one who tries to kill Moses. A similar phenomenon occurs in the Old Testament between 1 Chron. 21.1 and 2 Sam. 24.1. In 2 Sam. 24.1, the Lord incites David to count the people while 1 Chron. 21.1 relates that Satan incites David to number the people. A related phenomenon may occur in the New Testament where Acts 12.17 assigns Peter's release to ὁ κύριος who led him out of prison when the narrative affirms it was an angel who did this (12.7-11). The hermeneutical axiom allowing for these changes may be the belief that God's agent may act for God. God inciting David to act is in fact God using Satan to incite David to act. The Lord delivering Peter is in fact the Lord using an angel to deliver him. The important point is that these texts show that application of Old Testament texts about God to second figures does not necessitate the view that the writer included these second figures in their concept of God.

The Significance of Pre- and Post-Christian Parallels

I found that a number of pre- and post-Christian texts compare with the New Testament application of Old Testament passages about God to Jesus. These parallels included application of such texts to the angel of the LORD, Melchizedek, the last priest, the Teacher of righteousness, Wisdom, the Logos and Satan. One of my questions was How widespread was such application? Here caution must prevail because I have presented only some of the examples. I have omitted some for the sake of space. Others, no doubt, eluded my investigation. Yet it appears there was widespread application to Wisdom, the Word, the angel of the LORD and the glory of the LORD. I have pointed to the lack of consensus regarding these figures. Are they ways to speak metaphorically about God's immanence? Do they have independence from God? Are they divine? Repeatedly, I have come to the conclusion that the data are unclear on these issues. I suggested that if they are divine, it is still difficult to define that divinity more precisely in terms of the thoughts of the writer and pre-Christian Jewish readers. For those clearly non-divine figures to whom writers apply Old Testament passages about God, it appears that God's agent may indeed act for God who takes ultimate responsibility for his actions. Pre-Christian application to the messiah does not appear widespread. The question we raised over the significance of these parallels is a difficult one since the New Testament writers identify Jesus with both the Wisdom, Glory, Word of God on the one hand and as God's chief agent on the other. One could argue that it was either understanding which underlay the New Testament application of such Old Testament passages to Jesus. Application of such texts occurred both to divine and non-divine figures. I suggest therefore that the pre- and post-Christian parallels do not provide clear evidence to decide the New Testament writers' reasons for applying such passages to Jesus. The evidence does show that one cannot claim that application of such passages necessitates a view that Jesus was divine or that the early Christians worked with a Trinitarian view of God, nor can one claim such application necessarily depends on viewing Jesus as God's agent. Such may or may not have been the case; one must look at other New Testament data to decide.

Chapter 3

ISAIAH 40.3 IN THE NEW TESTAMENT

Isa. 40.3 proved very popular in first-century Christianity. The question is What did the 'way of the Lord' evoke for pre-Christian Jews? Furthermore, what was the relationship between the Lord Jesus and the 'way of the Lord' for the early Christians? My submission is (1) that Isa. 40.3 was part of a new exodus motif in its biblical context and in pre-Christian Judaism, (2) that this new exodus motif included the expectation of the glorious presence of God visibly manifest to the world, (3) that the evangelists have taken this promise and seen its fulfilment in Jesus, and (4) that the evangelists did not apply Isa. 40.3 to Jesus in a *strictly* messianic sense where the messiah is solely God's agent and nothing more.

Translation and Notes on Isa. 40.3-5, 10[1]

(3) A voice is crying out, 'In the wilderness, prepare the way of the LORD. Make straight in the desert a highway for our God. (4) Every valley shall be lifted up, and every mountain and hill shall become low. And the steep ground shall become a plain, and the impassable land shall become a broad valley. (5) And the glory of the LORD shall be revealed, and all flesh shall see it together. For the mouth of the LORD has spoken.' ... (10) Behold, the Lord GOD is coming in might, and his arm is ruling for him.

Before I examine the usage of Isa. 40.3 in the New Testament, it will be helpful to examine the verse in its Hebrew context. This examination is important since it may point out areas of difficulty in interpretation for pre-Christian Jews. This examination may also point out some of the different ways a pre-Christian Jew could have understood the Hebrew text.

---

1.   The following translation is my own.

Several elements in Isa. 40.3-5, 10 deserve attention. First, קוֹל קוֹרֵא of v. 3 has two possible translations, the first construing the two words as a nominal sentence, 'A voice is crying out',[2] and the second as in construct, 'A voice of one crying out'.[3] A question exists over the identity of the speaker of these words and the figures to whom he lifts his voice.[4] The diversity of scholarly views as to the identity of the voice and the figures whom he addresses only shows that the text says nothing explicit. The best solution is to leave them unidentified.[5] Also in v. 3, במדבר goes either with what precedes or what follows. Several factors indicate that this word in the MT should go with the following. First, 'In the wilderness, prepare...' mirrors 'make straight in the desert...'[6] Secondly, the verse would show remarkable balance and rhythm by forming four groups of two words each, each group with two stress accents. Thirdly, the Masoretic accentuation puts the most decisive break

---

2. See similarly R.N. Whybray, *Isaiah 40-66* (NCB; London: Oliphants, 1975), p. 50; NRSV; REB; NASB; and JB.

3. See Isa. 6.4; 13.4; 52.8; 66.6; the LXX; Vulgate; Peshitta; NIV; R.P. Merendino, *Der Erste und der Letze: Jes 40-48* (SVT, 31; Leiden: Brill, 1981), p. 31; F. Delitzsch, *Biblical Commentary on the Prophecies of Isaiah* (trans. J.S. Banks and James Kennedy (Edinburgh: T. & T. Clark, 4th edn, n.d.), p. 135.

4. Some of the choices are a heavenly being (Whybray, *Isaiah*, p. 48; J. Limburg, 'An Exposition of Isaiah 40.1-11,' *Int* 29 [1975], p. 407; and A.S. Herbert, *The Book of the Prophet Isaiah. Chapters 40-66* [Cambridge: Cambridge University Press, 1975], p. 18) or a human (E.J. Young, *The Book of Isaiah: The English Text, with Introduction, Exposition, and Notes* [Grand Rapids: Eerdmans, 1972], III, p. 26). Those who prepare the way may be heavenly powers (C. Westermann, *Isaiah 40–66: A Commentary* [trans. D.M.G. Stalker; London: SCM Press, 1969], p. 36; G.A.F. Knight, *Servant Theology. A Commentary on the Book of Isaiah 40-55* (ITC; Edinburgh: Handsel, rev. edn, 1984), p. 10; Herbert, *Isaiah*, 17; C.R. North, *The Second Isaiah: Introduction, Translation and Commentary to Chapter XL–LV* [Oxford: Clarendon Press, 1964], p. 74; U.E. Simon, *A Theology of Salvation: A Commentary on Isaiah 40–55* [London: SPCK, 1961], p. 38; and J. Skinner, *The Book of the Prophet Isaiah Chapter XL–LXVI* [Cambridge: Cambridge University Press, 1954], p. 3), a mission from the Babylonian exiles (J.D.W. Watts, *Isaiah 34–66* [WBC; Waco, TX: Word Books, 1987], p. 79), or the prophet and his company (Young, *Isaiah*, III, p. 18). Isa. 40.2 (LXX) refers to priests while the Targum at 40.1 speaks of the prophets.

5. See J.P. Fokkelman, 'Stylistic analysis of Isaiah 40.1-11', *OTS* 21 (1981), p. 77; and Delitzsch, *Isaiah*, p. 135.

6. Cf. D.L. Bock, *Proclamation from Prophecy and Pattern. Lucan Old Testament Christology* (JSNTSup, 12; Sheffield: JSOT Press, 1987), p. 95.

here possible after קוֹרֵא, a *Zaqep parvum*.[7] There is a question over the LXX reading a different text in which case במדבר would go with קוֹל קוֹרֵא since the omission of ערבה destroys both the metre and parallelism.[8] The Peshitta and Vulgate follow the reading in the LXX.[9] Scholars debate the rendering of the Targum at this point, but it apparently follows the MT in reading 'in the desert' with 'prepare'.[10] Some evidence of the LXX reading exists in the later Rabbinic material.[11] A further question is over the location implied by מדבר and ערבה. The basic issue is whether these words point to a highway straight from Babylon, one traversing the normal Babylonian roads to Jerusalem, or one unrelated to Babylon.[12] Within the last option it is possible to read the text metaphorically or literally. 'Making straight a path' in some contexts in the Old Testament points to a moral action and thus could point to a moral or a literal action.[13] Verse 4 brings forward a problem as to whether ינשא and ישפלו

---

7. See Westermann, *Isaiah*, p. 37, and Delitzsch, *Isaiah*, p. 135. Cf. W.F. Albright and C.S. Mann, *Matthew. Introduction, Translation, and Notes* (AB; Garden City, NY: Doubleday, 1971), p. 25, and the later Jewish tradition.

8. R.H. Gundry, *Matthew: A Commentary on his Literary and Theological Art* (Grand Rapids: Eerdmans, 1982), p. 44, supports the LXX. See too R.H. Gundry, *The Use of the Old Testament in St Matthew's Gospel* (NovTSup; Leiden: Brill, 1967), pp. 9-10. So also apparently Albright and Mann, *Matthew*, p. 25.

9. See Gundry, *Use*, pp. 9-10.

10. See B.D. Chilton, *The Isaiah Targum: Introduction, Translation, Apparatus and Notes* (ArB, 11; Edinburgh: T. & T. Clark, 1987), p. 77, and K. Stendahl, *The School of St Matthew and its Use of the Old Testament: With an Introduction by the Author* (Philadelphia: Fortress Press, 1968), p. 48, who understand the LXX as differing from the Targum. Bock, *Proclamation*, p. 95, notes the Targum is subject to dispute. W.D. Davies, and D.C. Allison, Jr, *A Critical and Exegetical Commentary on the Gospel according to Saint Matthew* (ICC; Edinburgh: T. & T. Clark, 1988), p. 293, follow Gundry, *Use*, pp. 9-10, who states the Targum follows the LXX. Gundry holds to his position in *Matthew* (1982), p. 44.

11. See Bock, *Proclamation*, p. 312 n. 15.

12. Compare Whybray, *Isaiah 40–66*, p. 50 (not the normal Babylonian route); Watts, *Isaiah 34–66*, p. 80 (the region as southeast of Jerusalem); Knight, *Servant Theology*, p. 11 (metaphorically chaos and disorder); Simon, *Theology*, p. 40 (separation of God and man).

13. Merendino, *Der Erste*, p. 34, points out that the Piel of ישר appears in 45.2 and 13 where God makes straight the way of Cyrus and in Prov. 3.6 where God makes straight the path of those who acknowledge him. Merendino himself sees the words in 40.3 together with 'raising a road' pointing to the eschatological nature of the new exodus (see 11.16; 19.23; 49.11; 62.10).

are imperfects or jussives.[14] If the words are jussives they continue the commands of v. 3b and c. If they are imperfects, they state what will take place when God comes. The mountains and hills are, according to some, metaphorical ways of speaking about the obstacles preventing Israel's return.[15] This understanding coincides with the metaphorical/ literal debate over these verses.[16]

The meaning of 'glory' in v. 5 is either the visible presence of God, or an adaptation of the 'glory' idea of the first exodus into 'majesty' or 'praise', or a revelation of God's activity.[17] I suggest below that the idea of God's visible presence is the probable meaning here. Also, there is minor debate on the meaning of יחדו and whether כי פי יהוה דבר functions as the direct object of וראו or is the ground of the whole of vv. 3-5.[18]

The key question in v. 10 is the meaning of the phrase בחזק. 1Q Isaᵃ reads בחוזק 'with strength' as does the LXX, μετὰ ἰσχύι. The MT reads חזק as an adjective functioning as a substantive, 'a strong one'. In Exod. 6.3, the text says, 'I appeared to Abraham, Isaac, and Jacob *as* God almighty...' (וארא אל אברהם אל־יצחק ואל יעקב באל שדי). The ב is a

---

14.   Young, *Isaiah*, p. 26, notes both possibilities. K. Elliger, *Deuterojesaja. Partone Jesaja 40,1-45,7* (BKAT; Neukirchen–Vluyn: Neukirchener Verlag, 1978), p. 7, points out that all the versions except Symmachus read the words as indicatives.

15.   E.W. Conrad, 'The "Fear Not" Oracles in Second Isaiah', *VT* 44 (1984), p. 142, sees a parallel to Zech. 4.7 and the obstacles in front of Zerubbabel where the הר becomes a מישר.

16.   Fokkelman, 'Stylistic Analysis', p. 78, suggests that the dichotomy literal/ symbolic is unhelpful. By way of contrast Merendino, *Der Erste*, p. 36, points out the comparison with Isa. 2.12-17 where the proud are abased.

17.   Those who see 'glory' as some kind of representation of God's visible presence include Watts, *Isaiah 34–66*, p. 81; O. Kaiser, *Isaiah 13–39: A Commentary* (London: SCM Press, 1974), p. 363; P.-E. Bonnard, *Le second Isaïe, son disciple et leurs éditeurs, Isaïe 40–66* (EB; Paris: Gabalda, 1972), p. 88; J.D. Smart, *History and Theology in Second Isaiah. A Commentary on Isaiah 35; 40–66* (Philadelphia: Westminster Press, 1965), p. 47; North, *Isaiah*, p. 76; Simon, *Theology*, p. 42; and Elliger, *Deuterojesaja*, p. 20. Cf. Knight, *Servant Theology*, p. 12 (redemptive, recreative and suffering love); Westermann, *Isaiah*, p. 38 (redemptive acts); and C.P. Staton, '"And Yahweh Appeared...": A Study of the Motif of "Seeing God" and of "God's Appearing" in the Old Testament Narratives' (DPhil thesis, Oxford University, 1988), p. 24.

18.   On the first point see Watts, *Isaiah*, 2 p. 81; cf. Knight, *Servant Theology*, p. 13.

Beth Essentiae.[19] If one reads the ב of Isa. 40.10 as a *Beth Essentiae* the verse would affirm the coming of God as a strong man. Lastly, scholars debate vv. 1-11 as either forming a prologue to chs. 40–55 or one to chs. 40–66.[20]

Context in the MT

Isaiah 40–66 appears in a book attributed to Isaiah, the son of Amoz, who prophesied between 740 (the year that King Uzziah died) until sometime in Hezekiah's reign (716–687 BCE.). Some see difficulty with attributing Isaiah 40–66 to such a prophet because many scholars suggest that these chapters are added to the original work by an unnamed redactor.[21] My interest, however, is in the understanding of the text as a whole, and the likely understanding of pre-Christian readers of the whole.[22] Therefore, for my purposes neither the date nor unity of Isaiah is a crucial issue.

In ch. 39, the prophet declares to Hezekiah that because he showed his treasures to the Babylonian envoys, his wealth would one day be in their hands (39.5-8). With ch. 40, the context shifts from a prediction of the Babylonian sack of Jerusalem to a situation where this prediction has

---

19. See W. Gesenius, *Gesenius' Hebrew Grammar* (rev. E. Kautzsch; trans. A.E. Cowley; Oxford: Clarendon Press, 2nd edn, 1985), § 119 i; Bonnard, *Isaïe*, p. 84 n. 10; Young, *Isaiah*, p. 38. Cf. North, *Isaiah*, p. 71; Skinner, *Isaiah*, p. 6. J.A. Alexander, *Commentary on the Prophecies of Isaiah* (ed. J. Eadie; Edinburgh: Andrew Eliot and James Thin, rev. edn, 1865), II, pp. 100-101, sees the phrase as a *Beth Essentiae* or more preferably denoting agency.

20. It is a prologue to 40–55 according to Herbert, *Isaiah*, p. 16; and E.A. Leslie, *Isaiah Chronologically Arranged, Translated and Interpreted* (New York: Abingdon, 1963), p. 139. See also Bonnard, *Isaïe*, p. 85. It is a prologue to 40–66 according to Westermann, *Isaiah*, p. 32; Delitzsch, *Isaiah*, p. 133; and K.R. Snodgrass, 'Streams of Tradition Emerging from Isaiah 40.1-5 and Their Adaptation in the New Testament', *JSNT* 8 (1980), p. 25.

21. J.A. Soggin, *Introduction to the Old Testament. From its Origins to the Closing of the Alexandrian Canon* (trans. J. Bowden; Philadelphia: Westminster Press, rev. edn, 1980), p. 310; cf. G.L. Robinson and R.K. Harrison, 'Isaiah', in *ISBE*, II, pp. 885-904.

22. On the legitimacy of reading Isaiah as a whole, see R. Rendtorff, 'The Book of Isaiah: A Complex Unity. Synchronic and Diachronic Reading', in *Society of Biblical Literature 1991 Seminar Papers* (ed. E.H. Lovering; Atlanta: Scholars Press, 1991), pp. 13-16; and A.T. Hanson, *The Prophetic Gospel. A Study of John and the Old Testament* (Edinburgh: T. & T. Clark, 1991), p. 95.

taken place (40.1).[23] Chapter 40, however, incites hope because God gives the command to comfort his people. This hope includes the expectation of God rescuing his people, an expectation which runs throughout chs. 40–66. As part of God's comfort to Israel, he has his herald shout, 'prepare the way of the Lord', 'make straight in the desert a highway for our God' (v. 3).[24]

These two phrases in Isa. 40.3 are the initial stages of a new exodus motif in Isaiah which points to the glorious presence of God. In the first exodus, God's glorious presence delivered his people:

> The LORD went in front of them in a pillar of cloud by day, to lead them along the way, and in a pillar of fire by night, to give them light, so that they might travel by day and by night. Neither the pillar of cloud by day nor the pillar of cloud by night left its place in front of the people (Exod. 13.21-22).

Moreover, in Exodus, this pillar of cloud and fire is the locus of the glory of God, even the LORD himself (see Exod. 16.10; 24.16; Num. 11.25; Deut. 4.37).[25] Isa. 63.9 possibly picks up this point saying, 'It was no messenger or angel but his presence that saved them'.[26] The book of Isaiah includes the idea of God's glory protecting Israel in ways which compare with God's actions in the first exodus. For instance, God's glory is a vanguard and rear guard (Isa. 58.8). This reference is similar to the description of God in the first exodus where the glory of God in the

23.   See Hezekiah's assumed safety and the implied position of the people in 40.1 where they have served hard service (v. 2) and are in need of divine comfort (v. 1).

24.   Those scholars who see some tie between this phrase and the Babylonian Marduk text include Merendino, *Der Erste*, p. 38; North, *Isaiah*, p. 74; and Herbert, *Isaiah*, p. 18; cf. Whybray, *Isaiah 40–66*, p. 50 (a military background); Young, *Isaiah*, III, p. 28 n. 14; and Elliger, *Deuterojesaja*, p. 17 (a way for dignitaries). Smart, *Isaiah*, pp. 45-46; and Simon, *Theology*, pp. 39-40, see an eschatological reference in the text; see too Merendino, *Der Erste*, p. 39. Herbert, *Isaiah*, p. 18, sees also exodus imagery as do Whybray, *Isaiah 40–66*, p. 50; Westermann, *Isaiah*, p. 33; North, *Isaiah*, pp. 74-75; Leslie, *Isaiah*, p. 140; Delitzsch, *Isaiah*, p. 136; Watts, *Isaiah*, II, pp. 80-81; and Skinner, *Isaiah*, p. 4.

25.   See too Josephus, *Ant.* 2.340; and *4 Ezra* 1.12-14. Cf. Num. 20.16.

26.   Isa. 63.9 has a textual problem. The choice is between 'It was no messenger or angel' (so NRSV, REB, NEB, JB, LXX) and 'there was distress to him and the angel of . . .' (see NRSV note, NASB, NIV, MT). The Qere is לוֹ צָר 'there was distress to him' (similarly see the Targum), but the Kethib is לֹא צָר 'there was no distress.' The LXX reads צִיר or צָר and the Kethib לֹא, οὐ πρέσβυς, 'no envoy.'

cloud moved from in front of Israel to behind to ward off the Egyptians (Exod. 14.19 and Isa. 52.12). Moreover, both Exodus and Isaiah 35 and 40 point to the visible glory of God (40.5; 35.2; Exod. 14.19-30). Both books include reference to the actual presence of God (Isa. 40.9; 35.4; and Exod. 14.24). These two books speak of strength given by the LORD to the weak (Isa. 40.28-31; 35.3-4; 52.12; and Exod. 14.11-14.). Both describe a way and a highway on which God and the people go.[27] Thus, according to Isaiah, God leading the people out of bondage will be similar to God leading Israel out of Egypt. The text describes God's promised coming as a physical manifestation of his glory (similar to the pillar of fire and the rear guard of the first exodus).[28] It is this comparison with the first exodus which suggests the author looked forward to a similar event in the new exodus.

The question is How might pre-Christian Jews have understood this coming of God's glory? It is possible that they thought of God's special presence visiting them. Pre-Christian or first-century Jews could take this interpretation in the light of the tradition of God's special presence accompanying the Israelites in the desert during the exodus and in the light of other biblical passages which speak of God moving from one place to the other. For instance, in Gen. 11.5 and 7, the LORD 'came down to see', and scattered the people building the tower of Babel. In 17.22, the text says, 'God went up from Abraham'. 18.21 repeats the idea of 11.5 by stating, 'I must go down and see', and this idea continues in 18.33, 'the LORD went his way'. Gen. 46.4 states, 'I myself will go down with you to Egypt'. All these verses give the impression of God's particularized earthly presence moving from one place to another.[29] In these verses, God's presence may be visible (17.1-22 and 18.1-33) or invisible (46.4). This idea of God's presence moving is not

---

27.　See Isa. 35.8 which uses דרך and מסלול while Isa. 40.3 has דרך and מסלה. The difference in the ways and highways of the two passages is more apparent than real. In 35.8, the way and the highway are the means by which God's people travel while 40.3 is the way of the LORD. However, if 35 points to the exodus, the way the people travel is the same way which the LORD forges at their head. Compare Exod. 13.21 and Isa. 35.1-2.

28.　Similarly see Watts, *Isaiah 34–66*, p. 80. Cf. Knight, *Servant Theology*, pp. 10-11, and Westermann, *Isaiah*, 33, pp. 38-45.

29.　The Old Testament includes reference to belief in God's omnipresence (1 Kgs 8.27; Ps. 139.7-12); however, if a reader reads the Old Testament read as a whole, he or she will find that the Old Testament also represents a particularised presence of God which inhabits special places (1 Kgs 9.2).

limited to Genesis. It is present in the rest of the Old Testament, Apocrypha and Pseudepigrapha.[30] Examples in the footnote from these sources show that belief in the coming of God's presence to earth was one which spanned the centuries. There is also a tradition that God's coming would not be visible.[31] However, since the biblical narrative includes the idea of God's invisible visitation, there is little reason to argue that God's coming in punishment through war did not include the idea of his actual presence.

A similar new exodus theme occurs in Mic. 2.13 which states, 'The one who breaks out will go up before them; they will break through and pass the gate, going out by it. Their king will pass on before them, the LORD at their head.' Against this verse, Mic. 7.15 contrasts, 'As in the days when you came out of the land of Egypt, show us marvellous things'.[32] Thus, God at the head of his people means, according to Micah, a new exodus *in continuity with but surpassing the old.* 'As he did for...' is similar to Deut. 1.30 where Moses promises Israel on the eve of the conquest that the LORD will again fight for them, before their very eyes. This text makes it clear that one may perceive God in his actions, but it also suggest God's own presence.

There are at least two problems with reading Isa. 40.3 as pointing to a literal coming of God. The first concerns the historical situation of the Babylonian exiles. The second concerns the negative assessment of

30.   See Exod. 3.8; 11.4; 12.23; 13.21; 19.11, 18; 20.25; 33.3; 34.5; Lev. 26.12; Num. 11.17; 12.5; 22.9, 20; Deut. 1.30; 9.3; 23.14; 29.5; 31.3; 31.6; 33.2; Judg. 5.4; 1 Sam. 3.10; 2 Sam. 22.10; 1 Kgs 19.11; 1 Chron. 17.5; Neh. 9.12; Job 9.11; Isa. 50.1; Mic. 1.3, 15; 2.13; 7.15; Hab. 3.3; and Zech. 14.5. In the Apocrypha, see Jdt. 16.2; *4 Macc.* 10.21; and Wis. 6.5. In the Pseudepigrapha, see *1 En.* 1.3-4; 25.3; 77.2, 89.16, 20; *2 En.* 58.1 [J and A]; 2 Esd. 5.56; 6.6; 9.25; *Jos. Asen.* 17.9; *Jub.* 1.26; *LAE* [Apocalypse] 22.3; *Mart.* and *Asc. Isa.* 9.13; *T. Adam* 3.1; *T. Job* 43.14. It is possible that some would have seen the promise of God's coming as just that. Josephus, *Apion* 2.117, relates that some pagans expected Apollo to visit the earth. J.D.G. Dunn, *Christology in the Making. A New Testament Inquiry into the Origins of the Doctrine of the Incarnation* (London: SCM, 2nd edn, 1989), p. 20, notes Ovid, *Metamorphoses* 8.626-721, where Baucis and Philemon entertain gods disguised as men. For a further discussion of the idea of a god coming to earth, see F. Young, 'Two Roots or a Tangled Mass', in *The Myth of God Incarnate* (ed. J. Hick; London: SCM Press, 1977), pp. 87-121. See too Euripides, *Alcestis* 1-10, where Apollo comes to earth.

31.   E.g. 1QM 12.7-10 indicates that God will visit through war.

32.   Cf. Hab. 3.3-6 where the everlasting hills sink low when God in his glory comes to punish Israel's enemies.

seeing God in the Old Testament (see Exod. 33.20). However, the answer to these criticisms may lie in the remaining chapters of Isaiah 40–66. These chapters may present this new exodus as postponed.[33] This explanation of the historical difficulty coincides with the view of Isa. 40.3 in later Judaism in general which saw the promise of that verse as awaiting a still future fulfilment.[34] Moreover, if Isa. 40.1-11 is a prologue, perhaps these verses indicate the promise of Isaiah 40–66 as a whole. In other words, comfort of the people in returning from Babylon may not coincide temporally with God's glorious theophany. On the second score, Old Testament writers indeed believed in the invisibility of God: Exod. 33.20 states, 'no one shall see me and live'. Thus, for a reader who worked within a biblical framework, the idea of seeing God in a certain sense was impossible. However, the warning of God in Exodus has to do with seeing God's face or God in the fullness of his glory. The idea that no one ever could see God partially and live is one foreign to the Old Testament narrative as well as a representative sample of extra-canonical Jewish works.[35] Therefore, if a reader expected a new exodus in continuity with but surpassing the old, such a reader would understand Isa. 40.3-5 as pointing to the revelation of God. Thus, for readers of the Old Testament as a whole, Isa. 40.3-5 points at least to a partial revelation of God when read against the background of the first exodus. In 40.10, the readers could see this revelation in the phrase בחזק, 'as a strong one'. This idea may go back to the mysterious figure of Exod. 23.21, the angel of whom God says, 'my name is in him'.[36]

---

33. See R.E. Watts, 'Consolation or Confrontation? Isaiah 40–55 and the Delay of the New Exodus', *TB* 41 (1990), pp. 31-59, for an explanation of the delay of the new exodus.

34. However, there is a post-Christian tradition which describes an appearance of God in the return of the Exiles (*4 Bar.* 7.19).

35. See Gen. 12.7; 17.1; 18.1; 26.2; 23.23; 26.24; 28.13; 32.30. 35.7, 9; 46.2; 48.3; Exod. 3.6; 4.1, 24; 6.3; 17.6; 24.10; 33.20; Lev. 9.24; 16.2; Num. 12.8; 14.10; 16.19, 42; 20.6; Deut. 31.15; Judg. 6.23; 13.3-22; 1 Sam. 3.21; 1 Kgs 3.5; 9.2; 11.9; 2 Chron. 1.7; Ps. 17.15; 63.21; 77.16; 84.7; Zech. 9.14; 2 Macc. 3.30; *1 En.* 14.20; *2 En.* 20.3; 39.5; *Jub.* 1.28; *LAE* 25.1-3; *Pseudo-Philo* 8.3; 11.15; *Sib. Or.* 1.200; 4.30; *T. Isaac* 6.27; *T. Jac.* 2.14-15; 3.5; 7.8; *T. Job* 42.1; and CD 8 (cf. *Sib. Or.* frag. one; in Philo, see *De Post. Cain.* 5-7; in Gnosticism, see Trip. Tract. 1, 54, 18; and 1, 56, 28).

36. Scholars debate the meaning of this last phrase. Compare U. Cassuto, *A Commentary on the Book of Exodus* (trans. I. Abrahams; Jerusalem: Magnes, 1967), p. 306; J.P. Hyatt, *A Commentary on Exodus* (NCB; London: Oliphants, 1971),

This angel is perhaps the one of Exod. 14.19 whom the pillar of cloud accompanies. One of the later Rabbinic debates centred upon the description of God as a fighting man referring to this angel.[37]

In summary, Isa. 40.3-5, read as a whole, points to a theophany of God, which in its context means a revelation of God resulting in salvation for his people. The setting of Isa. 40.3-5 in Isaiah 40–66 presents this event as part of the future deliverance of God. Isa. 40.3 in its present context is part of a new exodus motif with the idea that God's glory would appear at the head of his people and lead them to victory over their enemies.[38]

Context in the LXX

There are a few differences between the MT and the LXX in Isa. 40.1-5.[39] The first change is the LXX reading 'God' (ὁ θεός) for the MT's 'your God' (אלהיכם) in v. 1. In v. 2, the LXX reads 'priests' (ἱερεῖς) for which the MT has no equivalent. The LXX, furthermore, changes the MT 'and cry to her' (וקראו אליה), to 'comfort her' (παρακαλέσατε αὐτήν). The LXX has 'humiliation' (ταπείνωσις) for the MT 'hard service' (צבא). The phrase 'her punishment has been accepted [as satisfactory]' (נרצה עונה) becomes in the LXX 'her sin has been forgiven' (λέλυται αὐτῆς ἡ ἁμαρτία).[40] The LXX translators leave out the 'on account of' with 'sins' (ב) at the end of v. 2.[41] In v. 3, the LXX takes 'in the desert' (במדבר) with 'a voice is crying out' (קול קורא).[42] The LXX reads the MT

---

p. 250; and J.I. Durham, *Exodus* (WBC; Waco, TX: Word Books, 1987), p. 310.

37.   See Segal, *Two Powers*, pp. 33-56.

38.   On the relationship to the Babylonian captivity see E. Haenchen, *Der Weg Jesu. Eine Erklärung des Markus-Evangeliums und der kanonischen Parallelen* (Berlin: Alfred Töpelmann, 1966), p. 40 n. 5; and F. Godet, *A Commentary on the Gospel of St Luke* (trans. E.W. Shalders; Edinburgh: T. & T. Clark, 5th edn, 1870), I, p. 173.

39.   See chart below.

40.   BDB, p. 953b 2. Lev. 26.41 and 43 use the same verb in the Q meaning 'make amends for iniquity'.

41.   See BDB, p. 308, for this definition of ב.

42.   Reading the LXX this way keeps the parallelism between 'Prepare a way' and 'make straight the paths' since neither clause would then include a phrase regarding location. See Alfred Rahlfs, *Septuaginta* (Stuttgart: Deutsche Bibelgesellschaft, 1979), II, p. 619.

'highway' (מסלה) as the plural 'footpaths' (τρίβους).[43] The LXX omits 'in the wilderness' (בערבה). The LXX also has 'the crooked [places]' (τὰ σκολία) while the MT has 'steep' (עקב). The LXX reads a singular for the MT 'rough places' (רכסים). The MT has 'a plain' (בקעה) where the LXX reads the plural. The last change is from 'together' (יחדו) to 'the salvation of God' (τὸ σωτήριον τοῦ θεοῦ). The last change creates parallelism in the LXX between 'The glory of the Lord will be seen', and 'All flesh will see the salvation of God'.[44] Overall, however, the LXX presents the same idea as the MT.

One of the key questions regarding the LXX here is, How do the translators understand σωτήριον and δόξα in v. 5? One reason this question is key is because σωτήριον may have a connection for Luke with the messiah since according to Lk. 2.30, Simeon takes Jesus in his arms and says to God, 'My eyes have seen your σωτήριον'. Does the LXX take away the idea of God's visible manifestation? The phrase τὸ σωτήριον τοῦ θεοῦ/κυρίου has no clear messianic overtone—such as being a name of the messiah. But in several instances τὸ σωτήριον occurs with the acts of God and the arm of the Lord in Isaiah. For instance, in Isa. 51.5, the LXX says, 'My righteousness speedily draws near, and my salvation shall go forth as light, and on my arm shall the Gentiles trust: the islands shall wait for me, and on my arm shall they trust'.[45] In two places, the LXX translators associate τὸ σωτήριον with the walls of Jerusalem. It is possible that the author has some idea of God himself being the protection of Jerusalem, although connection with the messiah is also possible.

The phrase 'glory of the Lord' and its equivalents deal primarily with the idea of the theophany of God. This equation is clear from passages like Isa. 4.2-6[LXX] which indicate the appearance of the glory of God over Israel in a new exodus:

> (2) And on that day God will shine in counsel with glory on the earth in order to exalt and glorify the remnant of Israel, (3) and there will be a

---

43. Elliger, *Deuterojesaja*, p. 2, suggests that the change to the plural implies the translator was thinking of the return from many lands.

44. Elliger, *Deuterojesaja*, p. 2, states that καὶ ὀφθήσεται almost always translates ונראה. Furthermore, he sees the phrase stemming from 52.10.

45. See J.M. Baumgarten, 'The Heavenly Tribunal and the Personification of Sedeq in Jewish Apocalyptic', in *ANRW*, II.19.1, pp. 219-39. Snodgrass, 'Streams', p. 27, sees a connection between σωτήριον and the 'arm of the Lord.' See too Jn 12.38.

group left in Zion, and that left in Jerusalem will be called holy—all those
having been written for life in Jerusalem. (4) Because the Lord will wash
away the filth of the sons and daughters of Zion, and he will cleanse the
blood from their midst with a spirit of judgment and a spirit of burning.
(5) And he will be present, and a cloud will overshadow every place of
Mount Zion and everything surrounding it, by day like a cloud of smoke
and at night like a cloud of the light of a burning fire. (6) And it will be
covered in all glory. And it will be a shade from the heat and a shelter and
covering from the harshness and the rain.[46]

The connection between δόξα and the glory of God which led the
Israelites out of Egypt is clear in vv. 5-6 where a cloud will overshadow
the region by day and smoke and the light of fire by night (see Exod.
13.21-22). Isa. 6.1[LXX] also ties God's glory with theophany: 'And it
came about in the year that Uzziah, the king, died that I saw the Lord
sitting on a throne, high and lifted up. And the house was full of his
glory.' Again in 60.2[LXX], God's glory means theophany: 'And the
Lord will appear over you, and his glory will be seen over you.' Thus, in
the LXX there is no clear evidence that the translators connected δόξα
with the messiah. This lack of connection is also clear from Isa. 42.8
which promises that God will not share his glory with another.

Interpretation in Extracanonical Jewish Literature

Apocrypha and Pseudepigrapha
Some texts in the Apocrypha include ideas related to those found in Isa.
40.3-5. For instance, Jdt. 16.15, dating from the Maccabean era says,
'For the mountains shall be shaken to their foundations with the waters;
before your glance the rocks shall melt like wax'.[47] Sir. 16.18-19,
written between 190–170 BCE, similarly reads, 'Lo, heaven and the
highest heaven, the abyss and the earth, tremble at his visitation! The
very mountains and the foundations of the earth quiver and quake when
he looks upon them.'[48] Also Sir. 43.16 states, 'when he appears, the

46.   This LXX translation is my own.
47.   For the date of Judith, see E. Schürer, *The History of the Jewish People in
the Age of Jesus Christ 175 BC–AD 135* (rev., ed. and trans. G. Vermes, F. Millar, and
M. Goodman; Edinburgh: T. & T. Clark, 1986), III, pp. 217-19. Charles, *APOT*, I,
pp. 266 n. 16, notes that the allusion is to Ps. 97.5. I cite the text here because of the
similarities between Ps. 97.5 and Isa. 40.3-11.
48.   On the date of Sirach, see Schürer, *History*, III.1, p. 202. This text points to
God's coming but does not state the surrounding circumstances.

mountains shake'.[49] Perhaps one of the earliest allusions to Isa. 40.3-5 occurs in Bar. 5.6-9, which according to some recent researchers dates between 164 and 116 BCE (the date of the Greek translation of Jeremiah).[50] The unity of this text, however, is in question with this section possibly dating later.[51]

> (6) *For they [your children] went out from you on foot, led away by their enemies;* but *God will bring them back to you, carried in glory,* as on a royal throne. (7) For *God has ordered that every high mountain and the everlasting hills be made low and the valleys filled up, to make level ground, so that Israel may walk safely in the glory of God.* (8) The woods and every fragrant tree have shaded Israel at God's command. (9) For *God will lead Israel with joy, in the light of his glory, with the mercy and righteousness that come from him.*

My italics indicate connections between this text and the larger context of Isaiah 40.[52] According to Baruch, God's glory will come and deliver captive Israel. Furthermore, there is connection in this glorious manifestation with Israel's coming out of captivity. God's glory will surround Israel and usher them into the promised land.[53] It is difficult to know how the author of Baruch 5 or pre-Christian readers understood Isa. 40.3-5 in regard to the return from the Babylonian exile. Since the author is writing under the guise of a pseudonym, he may assume the perspective of the original person Baruch, the amanuensis of Jeremiah. If so, the author may want his readers to assume that the second exodus, the return from Babylon, was like the first. If the writer is thinly disguising his own times (perhaps the Maccabean revolt), he is perhaps expecting a similar manifestation of God in saving help for the Jews of his day. Whatever the proper interpretation, the writer applied Isa. 40.3-5 to God alone. At the time of the writing of Baruch, there is no suggestion here of a messianic application of this verse.

According to 2 Macc. 2.1-8 dating from as early as 125 BCE to as late

49. Charles, *APOT*, I, p. 476 n. 17, points out that this passage is an allusion to Ps. 29.8.

50. See G.W.E. Nickelsburg, 'The Bible Rewritten and Expanded', in *JWSTP*, pp. 140-46.

51. See Schürer, *History*, III.2, pp. 736-38, who argues for no fixed date for the second half of Bar. 3.9–5.9.

52. See Isa. 39.7; 40.4 [read as jussives] and 5. See too Charles, *APOT*, II, p. 595 nm. 6-7. The italics in this and the following quotations note allusions to Isa. 40 and its larger context.

53. Similarly see Snodgrass, 'Streams', p. 31.

as the date of Nero, the prophet Jeremiah hides some of the altar fire, the tent and the ark in order for God to gather them at a later time.[54] The text reads,

> (6) Some of those who followed him came up intending to mark the way, but could not find it. (7) When Jeremiah learned of it, he rebuked them and declared: 'The place shall remain unknown until God gathers his people together again and shows his mercy. (8) Then the Lord will disclose these things, and the glory of the Lord and the cloud will appear, as they were shown in the case of Moses, and as Solomon asked that the place should be specially consecrated.'

The text associates God's gathering his people with the appearance of the glory of the Lord and the cloud. It also speaks of the special consecration which Solomon saw (2 Chron. 7.1-2) and the revelation of God's glory to Moses (Exod. 14.14-20). The text implies a second exodus associated with the gathering of the exiles. Furthermore, this second exodus includes the idea of the manifestation of God's glory in a way similar to the first. Thus, if the text of 2 Maccabees alludes to Isa. 40.3-5 or a similar tradition, it interprets 'the way of the Lord' as implying God's coming in a way reminiscent of the exodus with a visible manifestation of God's glory in the cloud. Again, there is no mention of the application of the second exodus idea to the messiah or anyone else.

Another allusion to Isa. 40.3-5 occurs in the *T. Mos.* 10.1-7, a fragmentary text dating from sometime between the Maccabean revolt and 30 CE, which reads,[55]

> (1) Then his kingdom will appear throughout his whole creation. Then the devil will have an end. Yea, sorrow will be led away with him. (2) Then will be filled the hands of the messenger, who is in the highest place appointed. Yea, he will at once avenge them of their enemies. (3) For the Heavenly One will arise from his kingly throne. Yea, he will go forth from his holy habitation with indignation and wrath on behalf of his sons. (4) And the

---

54. 2 Macc. 1.1–2.18 consists of two letters added to the rest of the book which dates from 124 BCE according to Schürer, *History*, III.1, pp. 532-33. The second letter, 1.10–2.18, in his opinion, could date up to 67 BCE. H.W. Attridge, 'Historiography', in *JWSTP*, pp. 176-79, dates the second letter between 77 BCE and the reign of Nero.

55. See J. Priest, 'The Testament of Moses', in *OTP*, I, pp. 920-21. See too Schürer, *History*, III.1, pp. 281-83, for possible redactional stages of this document. J.J. Collins, 'Testaments', in *JWSTP*, pp. 347-48, sees a date of the final form around the turn of the era. Snodgrass, 'Streams of Tradition', p. 31, sees an allusion to Isa. 40.3-5 in this text.

earth will tremble, even to its ends shall it be shaken. And the high mountains will be made low. Yea, they will be shaken, as enclosed valleys will
they fall. (5) The sun will not give light. And in darkness the horns of the
moon will flee. Yea, they will be broken in pieces. It will be turned into
blood. Yea, even the circle of the stars will be thrown into disarray. (6) And
the sea all the way to the abyss will retire, to the sources of waters which
fail. Yea, the rivers will vanish away. (7) For God Most High will surge
forth, the Eternal One alone. In full view will he come to work vengeance
on the nations. Yea, all their idols will he destroy.

There is a allusion to Isa. 40.4 in *T. Mos.* 10.4. Furthermore, the idea of
the mountains falling provides an image of levelling the land. The
expression of God coming in full view echoes Isa. 40.5b. Here, the
Testament associates this text with the coming of God. However, in v. 2,
the text mentions the messenger who is a priest, and this priest is also
present during the cataclysmic events.[56] The presence of a priest in this
passage may be an interpretation of Mal. 3.1 which promises that God
will send his messenger (perhaps a priest according to 2.7) before
himself. In the *Testament of Moses*, God however comes (vv. 3, 7), and
he comes alone (v. 7). The statement that God will come alone suggests
that God will not use an agent in his place (v. 7). Moreover, the author
of the Testament apparently understands the coming of the LORD
literally as the eschatological manifestation of God on earth. However, it
is possible that the priest in v. 2 is Michael, who in turn may be 'the
angel of the LORD'. This idea would explain the phrase, 'in the highest
place appointed' and why the 'he' of the next verse should be Michael
but apparently refers to God given the comment in v. 7. On either view,
God comes himself, or God as 'the angel of God' comes.

Another allusion to Isa. 40.3-5 occurs in *1 En.* 1.6, a text which dates
from between the second century BCE and the first century CE.[57]

(1) The blessing of Enoch: with which he blessed the elect and the righteous who would be present on the day of tribulation at (the time of) the

56. Priest, 'Testament', I, p. 932 n. 10a, sees 'filling the hands' as a technical
term for ordination to the priesthood. He states that scholars usually identify the
messenger as Michael. See 1 Kgs 13.33 for an Old Testament example of the phrase.
Noll, 'Angelology', p. 67, suggests here 'filling the hands' is figurative in the context
of holy war. Schürer, *History*, III.1, pp. 284 n.21, points out that *Targ. Ps.-J.* on
Deut. 34.1-3 has the eschatological vision culminate with Michael. I have not checked
this Rabbinic text first-hand.
57. So Snodgrass, 'Streams of Tradition', p. 31. Schürer, *History*, III.2
pp. 254-55, dates the text between 200 and 160 BCE.

removal of all the ungodly ones. (2) And Enoch, the blessed and righteous man of the Lord, took up (his parable) while his eyes were open and he saw, and said, '(This is) a holy vision from the heavens which the angels showed me: and I heard from them everything and I understood. I look not for this generation but for the distant one that is coming. I speak about the elect ones and concerning them.' (3) And I took up with a parable (saying), 'The God of the universe, the Holy Great One, will come forth from his dwelling. (4) And from there he will march upon Mount Sinai and appear in his camp emerging from heaven with a mighty power. And everyone shall be afraid, and Watchers shall quiver. (5) And great fear and trembling shall seize them unto the ends of the earth. (6) Mountains and high places will fall down and be frightened. And high hills shall be made low; and they shall melt like a honeycomb before the flame. (7) And the earth shall be rent asunder; and all that is upon the earth shall perish. And there shall be a judgment upon all, (including) the righteous. (8) And to all the righteous he will grant peace. He will preserve the elect, and kindness shall be upon them. They shall all belong to God and they shall prosper and be blessed; and the light of God shall shine unto them. (9) Behold, he will arrive with ten million of the holy ones in order to execute judgment upon all. He will destroy the wicked ones and censure all flesh on account of everything that they have done, that which the sinners and the wicked ones committed against him.'

This text refers to the day of tribulation (v. 1), which will mean an appearance of God from heaven echoing God's Sinai theophany (v. 4).[58] According to v. 6, the mountains and high places will flatten out (see Isa. 40.4). 'Before the flame' may be a reference to the full blaze of God's glory (v. 6). Verse 9 is perhaps an allusion to Zech. 14.5. Thus, *1 Enoch* 1 points to the glorious manifestation of God which will mean judgment for the ungodly. With the reference to Sinai, the text may imply a second exodus for the righteous people of God. However, there is a similar tradition where the mountains will flatten out before the Elect One, the Son of Man. In *1 En.* 52.6-9 dating perhaps from the last quarter of the first century, the writer states,[59]

As for these mountains which you have seen with your own eyes—the mountain of iron, the mountain of copper, the mountain of silver, the mountain of gold, the mountain of colored metal, and the mountain of lead—

58.   On v. 4, see J. VanderKam, 'The Theophany of Enoch 1,3b-7,9', *VT* 23 (1973), pp. 129-50, particularly pp. 132-33. See too M.E. Stone, 'Apocalyptic Literature', in *JWSTP*, p. 400, who sees ch. 1 pointing to an epiphany.

59.   Schürer, *History*, III.1, pp. 256-59, favours the last quarter of the first century for the date of the Similitudes.

all of them, in the presence of the Elect One, *will become like a honeycomb (that melts) before fire*, like water that gushes down from the top of such mountains, and become helpless by his feet. It shall happen in those days that no one shall be saved either by gold or by silver; and no one shall be able to escape... All these substances will be removed and destroyed from the surface of the earth when the Elect One shall appear before the face of the Lord of Spirits.

The italicized text is very similar to *1 En.* 1.6 and thus introduces a second figure into the eschatological scheme of *1 Enoch* 1. The text makes clear that the Son of man is distinct from the Lord of Spirits. Thus, there are two possible interpretations: (1) It may be that this second figure is the 'mighty power' of *1 En.* 1.4. If such is the case, this power, the son of Man, comes *in addition to* God. (2) Equally possible is the interpretation that *1 En.* 52.6-9 interprets *1 Enoch* 1 replacing the coming theophany with a strictly human figure. If such interpretation is correct, *1 En.* 52.6-9 is the first reference I have found to the coming of a figure instead of God.

Psalms of Solomon 8, a document dating from the first century BCE, alludes to Isa. 40.3.[60] In this document, the text reads as follows:

(2) The sound of many people as of a violent storm, as a raging fire storm sweeping through the wilderness...(14) Because of this God mixed them (a drink) of a wavering spirit, and gave them a cup of undiluted wine to make them drunk. (15) He brought someone from the end of the earth, one who attacks in strength; he declared war against Jerusalem, and her land. (16) The leaders of the country met him with joy. They said to him, 'May your way be blessed. Come, enter in peace.' (17) They graded the rough roads before his coming; they opened the gates to Jerusalem, they crowned her city walls.

The writer of the psalm applies to Pompey the kingly preparation implied in Isaiah.[61] Furthermore, v. 2 perhaps applies 'people' to Pompey's army. Originally Isaiah pointed to the people of God coming in a second exodus; now the ones whom God leads are Israel's enemies.[62] What is the theological import of this application? This reference is perhaps an

60.   See R.B. Wright, 'Psalms of Solomon', in *OTP*, 2 pp. 640-41. Schürer, *History*, III.1, p. 194, dates *Ps. Sol.* 8 between 63 and 48 BCE. Similarly see D. Flusser, 'Psalms, Hymns and Prayers', in *JWSTP*, p. 573.

61.   G.B. Gray, 'The Psalms of Solomon', in *APOT*, I, p. 641 n. 18 ff., notes that others identify the coming figure as Antiochus Epiphanes.

62.   See Wright, 'Psalms', p. 659 n. k, who points out that one ms reads 'their coming' in v. 17.

ironic use of Isa. 40.3. It is also possible that the writer used biblical language without meaning to replace God's coming with Pompey's. If he did intend to replace God's coming with Pompey's, it is unclear from the text what that replacement meant to the writer theologically. Rev. 16.12 may use language similar to Isa. 40.3 and *Ps. Sol.* 8.17 when the writer of the Apocalypse writes the words, 'in order to prepare the way for the kings of the east' (ἵνα ἑτοιμασθῇ ἡ ὁδὸς τῶν βασιλέων τῶν ἀπὸ ἀνατολῆς ἡλίου). The writer of *Psalms of Solomon* may have had in mind a comparison between Cyrus before whom God made straight ways, and Pompey before whom the priests made straight ways (compare *Ps. Sol.* 8.1-17 and Isa. 45.1-2). The text goes on to say in *Ps. Sol.* 8.19, 'He captured the fortified towers and the wall of Jerusalem, *for God led him in securely while they wavered.*' Thus, the writer still underscores God's activity during Pompey's actions. The text furnishes no further information about God's coming either himself or through an intermediary.

Qumran

Isa. 40.3-5 occurs several times at Qumran.[63] For instance, 1QS 8.12-15, which dates from about 130–50 BCE, reads,[64]

> And when these become members of the Community in Israel according to all these rules, they shall separate from the habitation of ungodly men and shall go into the wilderness to prepare the way of Him; as it is written, *Prepare in the wilderness the way of . . . [.], make straight in the desert a path for our God.*

This section associates Isa. 40.3-5 with the Qumran community's withdrawal into the desert.[65] In the context, 'him' refers to God. This identification is clear from the parallel words 'a path for our God'. The

63. See A. Chester, 'Citing the OT', in *It is Written: Scripture Citing Scripture. Essays in Honour of Barnabas Lindars, SSF* (ed. D.A. Carson and H.G.M. Williamson; Cambridge: Cambridge University Press, 1988), pp. 144-45, for some of the finer points of Isa. 40.3 at Qumran.

64. See G. Vermes, *The Dead Sea Scrolls in English*, (London: Penguin Books, 3rd edn, 1987), p. 61; and Schürer, *History*, III.1 pp. 381-82. D. Dimant, 'Qumran Sectarian Literature', in *JWSTP*, pp. 498, 501 n. 90, supports a date in the second half of the second century BCE.

65. Concerning the composite nature of this document see Schürer, *History*, III.1, p. 383; C. Dohmen, 'Zur Gründung der Gemeinde von Qumran (1QS VIII–IX)', *RevQ* 41 (1982), pp. 81-96; Dimant, 'Qumran', p. 501.

four dots instead of the 'LORD' is perhaps due to a reverence for God's name.[66] This text is less clear about the implication of the way of the Lord. The author may include an ethical interpretation while at the same time implying a human exodus from Jerusalem to the wilderness where they await God's decisive intervention.[67] God's coming here may imply a literal coming or simply a figurative one in the granting knowledge. The later is possible since their preparation involved study of Torah. In 1QS 9.18-21, the document associates preparing the way with ethics. The text reads,

> He [the Master] shall guide them all in knowledge according to the spirit of each and according to the rule of the age, and shall thus instruct them in the mysteries of marvellous truth that in the midst of the men of the Community they may walk perfectly together in all that has been revealed to them. This is the time for the preparation of the way into the wilderness, and he shall teach them to do all that is required at that time and to separate from all those who have not turned aside from all ungodliness.

Elsewhere, 1QS points to a coming day in which God will obliterate evil (1QS 3.13-15, 17-19; 4.6-8, 11-13, 18-19, 25-26; and 5.12-13). According to 1QS, the Qumran sectarians were preparing for the eschatological day when God would judge the wicked and vindicate the righteous. This preparation also anticipated the coming of three figures, the prophet, the messiah of Israel, and the messiah of Aaron (1QS 9.11). So in preparing for the eschatological day, the Qumran sect expected a coming of the two messiahs in the meantime. God's angel of truth will also appear in the cause of the righteous (1QS 3.24). If this text points to the final victory of the sons of light, either God and the angel will come, or God as the angel. The coming of this angel and God probably is not a non-literal coming through intermediaries since otherwise there would be no need for the reference to the angel at all. Another possibility is 'God even the angel' (cf. Gen. 48.15-16). Thus, reading 1QS as a whole, the expectation surrounding Isa. 40.3 included the two messiahs, and the prophet. It also includes an angel and God.

1QM 11.7c-10a, dating from the second half of the second century

---

66. For a discussion of the rendering of the divine name at Qumran see P. Skehan, 'The Divine Name at Qumran, in the Masada Scroll, and in the Septuagint', *BIOSCS* 13 (1980), pp. 14-44.

67. On 'in the desert', see J.A. Fitzmyer, *The Gospel according to Luke* (AB; Garden City, NY: Doubleday, 1981), I, p. 460, who states that Qumran uses Isa. 40.3 to explain why the community is in the desert.

BCE to the first decades of the CE, emphasizes continuity between God's past actions and his future ones.[68] The author also writes, 'For Thou wilt fight with them from heaven' (1QM 11.17). According to 12.10, the Hero of War is with the congregation who will fill the land with his glory (1QM 12.12). If 1QM as a whole points to the final eschatological battle, the expectation of the coming of angelic figures might be included in Qumran's eschatological expectation.[69] There could be a connection between Michael and God's mighty hand (13.1-14.1). Several smaller documents from Qumran include citations of or allusions to Isa. 40.3. 4Q 176 reads,

> From the Book of Isaiah: Consolations *[Comfort, comfort my people]—*
> *says your God—speak to the heart of Jerusalem and c[ry to her that] her*
> *[bondage is completed], that her punishment is accepted, that she has*
> *received from the hand of **** double for all her sins...*A voice calls, 'In
> the wilderness, prepare the way of **** make straight in [the desert a
> h]ighway for our God, [...] every valley shall be exalted [...and hil]l be
> made low, and the steep ground shall become a [p]lain [...a val]ley
> [...the g]lory of **** [...[70]

4Q 176 quotes Isa. 40.1-5 with only orthographic changes from the MT in the extant portions. This text also joins Ps. 79.2-3 and Isa. 40.1-5 which suggests the author of 4Q 176 looked forward to Isa. 40.1-5 reversing the situation of Ps. 79.2-3. Interestingly, it also contains Zech. 13.9 which is the climax of the covenant when God's people shall call upon his name. This fragmentary document also speaks of a figure, 'And he shall accomplish Thy miracles and Thy righteousness among Thy people'. It is unclear, however, how this figure relates to Isa. 40.3.

---

68.   On the date, see Dimant, 'Qumran', pp. 516-17 (second half second century BCE); Schürer, *History*, III.1, pp. 402-404 (first century BCE or early decades of the CE). Garrett, 'Exodus', p. 665, points out this text as showing continuity between actions in the past and in the eschaton in that the camp arrangement conforms to the first exodus (see Exod. 18.25 and Dimant, 'Qumran', p. 516).

69.   See 1QM 7.3-7; 9.10-18. This expectation may be due to Dan. 11.40–12.3 which includes the idea of Michael coming in a period of deliverance. See Schürer, *History*, III.1, p. 401.

70.   Vermes, *Scrolls*, p. 302, translates vv. 1-2. The remaining verses are my translation. Schürer, *History*, III.1, p. 448, hazards no guess for the date of this fragment. J.A. Fitzmyer, *The Dead Sea Scrolls: Major Publications and Tools for Study* (SBLRBS, 20; Atlanta: Scholars Press, rev. ed. 1990), p. 64, states that this text includes Isa. 40.1-5; 41.8-9; 49.7, 13-17; 43.1-2, 4-6; 51.22-23; 52.12; Zech. 13.9.

The four asterisks represent an alternative to the Tetragram.[71] 4Q 162 interprets Isa. 5.24-25 as the Lord stretching out his arm again in the visitation of the last days. This text may tie into the idea of God stretching out his arm and the first exodus (Exod. 6.6; Isa. 40.10). Thus, this document may tie the idea of mountains quaking with the visitation of the arm of the Lord (see Isa. 5.25). 4Q 504 fr. 6 reads,

> And like an eagle which rouses its nestlings and hovers over [its young], spreads out its wings, takes one and carries it on [its pinions], so we dwell apart and are not reckoned among the nations and... Thou art in our midst in the pillar of fire and the cloud [of] Thy [holi]ness walking before us, and as it were Thy glory in our mid[st]....

The text, with its reference to the pillar of fire and cloud, recalls exodus imagery (Exod. 13.21). Thus, this text interprets God's new exodus presence as something which invisibly resides with the Qumran community. This text may support the idea of God's invisible presence in the new exodus or may point to an anticipation of what will fully take place in the end.

A last interesting Qumran text related to Isa. 40.3 is 11Q Melchizedek, which dates from late Hasmonean to early Herodian times.[72] 11QMelch 2.15-16, 24-25 states,

> This is the day [of salvation about w]hich [God] spoke [through the mouth of Isa]iah the prophet who said, ['How] beautiful [16]on (the) mountains are the feet of the heral[d who pro]claims peace, the her[ald of good who proclaims salvati]on, saying to Zion, "Your God [is king."']...'Your G[o]d is [25][Melchizedek...[73]

This document apparently applies to Melchizedek Isa. 52.7 which is similar in idea to Isa. 40.9 which says, '[L]ift up your voice with strength, O Jerusalem, herald of good tidings...say to the cities of Judah, "Here is your God!"' The writer of 11Q Melchizedek could thus connect Isa. 40.3, conceptually related to 40.9, with Isa. 52.7 and thus connect Isa. 40.3 with the coming of Melchizedek. The identification of Melchizedek here with the archangel Michael has justification in some Qumran

---

71. See Vermes, *Scrolls*, p. 302.

72. See Schürer, *History*, III.1, p. 449.

73. The above translation is that of P.J. Kobelski, *Melchizedek and Melchiresa* (CBQMS, 10; Washington, DC: Catholic Biblical Association of America, 1981), pp. 8-9.

documents.[74] The text of 11Q Melchizedek, thus, perhaps points to Michael's coming as part of the eschatological renewal. It is unclear whether God will come in addition to this angel, or whether the angel Michael is here the angel of the LORD.

Post-Christian Jewish Literature

Another interesting interpretation of Isa. 40.3-5 occurs in *Targum Jonathan*, the precise date of which is unknown.[75] The targum makes several interpretative changes to the text of Isa. 40.1-5. In v. 3, 'the way of the Lord' becomes 'the way before the people of the Lord'. 'Before our God' becomes 'before the congregation of our God'. In v. 9, 'Do not fear to say to the cities of Judah, "Here is your God!"' becomes 'fear not; say to the cities of the house of Judah, "The kingdom of your God is revealed!"'[76] In these three cases, what in the MT was a reference to God's manifestation has a translation which lessens this idea and instead emphasizes God's people. The translators of the Targum thus connect the idea of God's coming with the people returning from exile. This connection has justification in the MT in that 'the way' elsewhere in Isaiah 40–66 is a way for the people.[77] The change from 'here is your God' is a little more difficult to understand. According to Chilton the kingdom of God in the Isaiah Targum is 'God's intervention on behalf

74. Schürer, *History*, III.1, p. 450, equates Melchizedek and the Prince of Light in 1QS 3.20; CD 5.18; and 1QM 13.10 and Michael in 1QM 17.6-7. Also Melchiresha', the name of Belial/Satan, further supports this equation (4Q Amram and 4Q 280-82). Dimant, 'Qumran', p. 521, adds 4Q 177 12–13 1.7 as evidence of Melchizedek's association with God's 'Angel of his Truth'. Vermes, *Dead Sea Scrolls*, pp. 160-61, 262-63, and 300-301, sees Melchizedek as the archangel Michael. CD 5.17-18 identifies the Prince of Lights as the one who raised up Moses and Aaron at the time of Israel's first deliverance.

75. Chilton, *Isaiah*, pp. xx-xxv, classifies this chapter as belonging theologically to either the Tannaitic (late first and second century AD) or the Amoraic (third and following) periods.

76. A similar change occurs in Isa. 31.4-5 and 52.7.

77. In 45.2, God promises Cyrus that he will go before him levelling mountains and removing all objects which might deter Cyrus's way. In v. 13, God promises to make his paths straight. In 49.11, God promises redeemed Israel, 'I will turn all my mountains into a road, and my highway shall be raised up'. The idea then, according to the MT is that God will prepare Cyrus's way who in turn is preparing a way and leading Israel along this way. Thus, the inference is logical that 'the way of the Lord' is 'the way of the people of the Lord'.

of his people'.[78] In the Isaiah Targum, the idea of God bringing about a new exodus is still present (41.18; 42.15; 43.16, 19). In 51.11, the translator perhaps thinks of the cloud of glory which accompanied Israel in the first exodus. The Targum, however, presents little evidence of a messianic application of Isa. 40.3.

According to the major indexes of the Mishna, Isa. 40.3 does not occur in this literature.[79] This absence also occurs in the Babylonian and Jerusalem Talmuds.[80] The Babylonian Talmud does however in Sanhedrin 110b and 91b attribute Isaiah 35 to the future world, and since chapter 35 and 40 are contextually related, the probable understanding of Isa. 40.3 would also relate to the future.

The Midrashim well attest Isa. 40.3.[81] The first example comes from the *Midrash Rabbah on Genesis* where R. Simlai associates Isa. 40.1 and God's future comfort of Jerusalem (*Gen. R.* 50.9). The text states,

> If Joseph could thus comfort the tribal ancestors by speaking soothing words to them, how much more when the Holy One, blessed be He, comes to comfort Jerusalem! Thus it says, *Comfort ye, comfort ye My people, saith your God.*[82]

Another text is *Num. R.* 1.2,

> If there was a low place, the cloud raised it; a high place it lowered, making all level; as it is said, *Every valley shall be lifted up and every mountain and hill shall be made low.*[83]

Here, R. Hoshaya works with the idea that all that will occur in the second exodus must also have occurred in the first and uses Isa. 40.4 to describe what must have happened in the first exodus. This text shows just how literally some Jews took the promise in Isa. 40.3-5. It also

---

78.   Chilton, *Isaiah*, p. 49.

79.   See P. Blackman, *Mishnayoth* (7 vols.; New York: Judaica Press, 2nd edn, 1964), and H. Danby, *The Mishnah. Translated from the Hebrew with Introduction and Brief Explanatory Notes* (London: Oxford University Press, 1933).

80.   See I. Epstein, *The Babylonian Talmud* (39 vols.; London: Soncino, 1948), and M. Schwab, *Le Talmud de Jérusalem* (6 vols.; Paris: Besson & Chantemerle, 1960); A. Cohen, *The Minor Tractates of the Talmud: Massektoth Ketannoth* (2 vols.; London: Soncino, 1965).

81.   See J.J. Slotki, *Index Volume*, in *Midr. R.*, 10 p. 243.

82.   H. Freedman, *Genesis*, in *Midr. R.*, 2 p. 1000. See too *Deut. R.* 4.11 which describes the event of Isa. 40.4 as future.

83.   J.J. Slotki, *Numbers*, in *Midr. R.*, 5 pp. 3-4.

shows that Jews understood the future exodus of Isaiah in terms of the first exodus. *Lev. R.* 1.15 also underscores these points:

> In this world the *Shekinah* manifests itself only to chosen individuals; in the Time to Come, however, *The glory of the Lord shall be revealed, and all the flesh shall see it together; for the mouth of the Lord hath spoken it.*[84]

That is, this text reflects the understanding of Isa. 40.5 as pointing to the universal theophany of God's Shekinah.[85]

In the Leqach Tob, Isa. 40.3 refers to the fourth in a series of ten voices which announce certain end time events.[86] This voice cries out after the messiah receives tribute in Rome. After the seventh voice, Elijah brings news that their God has become King. The context does not inform readers whether the writers and/or the first readers thought of Isa. 40.3 as a theophany in regard to God and the messiah. The difficulty of this text is its understanding of the eschatological scheme: the messiah arrives with the fourth voice. Then the text switches to God's coming and then again in the tenth voice to the messianic star.[87] A last example of Isa. 40.3 in Rabbinic material occurs in the Pesikta.[88] Here again, however, it is unclear how the eschatological thought of the writer worked itself out.

84.   J. Israelstam and J.J. Slotki, *Leviticus*, in *Midr. R.*, 4 p. 17. I have changed the spelling of Shekinah in this quote (originally Shechinah) to present a consistent spelling in the text of this work.

85.   P.S. Alexander, 'Shekhinah', in *DBI*, p. 633, writes, 'There can be little doubt that in certain contexts the idea of the Shekhinah implies a dichotomy or bi-polarity within God. In two of these contexts the nature of that dichotomy is reasonably clear. 1. The Shekhinah occurs in contexts concerned with prophecy or revelation. When the prophets have a vision of God, what they are said to see is the Shekhinah (Deuteronomy Rabbah 11.3). When they receive a verbal communication from God, it is the Shekhinah which communicates with them (Mekhilta de-Rabbi Ishmael, Pisha 1)...2. According to one tradition "primarily the Shekhinah dwells among the inhabitants of the earth" (Pesiqta de-Rav Kahana 1.1; Genesis Rabbah 19.7) as opposed to being in heaven. Implied here is a dichotomy between God as immanent and God as transcendent: the Shekhinah represents God as immanent, and so strictly speaking is not appropriate to God in heaven.'

86.   H.L. Strack and P. Billerbeck, *Kommentar zum Neuen Testament aus Talmud und Midrasch* (Munich: Beck, 1961), I, pp. 96-97. I did not have access to Leqach Tob, and therefore I must depend on Strack and Billerbeck for the context.

87.   The tradition here is late, R. Levi (AD 300) and R. Huna (AD 360).

88.   W.G. Braude and I.J. Kapstein, *Pesikta de Rab- Kahaana. Rab Kahana's Compilation of Discourses for Sabbaths and Festal Days* (Philadelphia: Jewish Publication Society of America, 1975), § 16.

Justin Martyr (114–165 CE), *Dialogue with Trypho* 8, associates Elijah with the forerunner of the messiah. This position would be logical if one believed that Mal. 4.5 [3.23] pointed to Elijah coming before the great and terrible Day of the Lord. If Elijah preceded the final visitation of God, he must also precede the messiah, if the messiah was to come before the coming of the day of the Lord. In *Dialogue with Trypho* 50, Trypho asks Justin to prove that there is another God and that he submitted to be born of a virgin. Justin replies by asking first to quote Isa. 40.1-17. It is unclear if this quotation refers to Justin's previous point that John came in the Spirit of Elijah or refers to Justin's proving that there is 'another God'.

Further Related Data

Several documents present an eschatological scheme in which after the coming of the messiah, God comes. For instance, *Ladder of Jacob* is a first-century CE document which is an interpretation of Jacob's dream at Bethel.[89] In this dream, God promises a final vengeance which will take place after 'the king' has arisen (see 6.1). In 6.9, the text relates that the Lord will then fight for Jacob's tribe. If this text is modelling God's final deliverance on the biblical exodus, the text points to God's actions after the coming of the messiah. Similarly *1 En.* 90.10-14 includes the idea of the messiah coming and then help from God. Conversely, *1 En.* 91.7-10 presents the Lord coming before the messiah. A possible New Testament example of this scheme may be Lk. 1.68-79.[90] There, Zechariah blesses God's visitation in raising up the messiah in vv. 68-75. In 1.76, he blesses John who will forerun the Most High. Then, at a future time, the ἀνατολή from the heights will visit. It is possible that v. 78 looks to Isa. 60.1-2 and the eschatological visitation of God.[91] One last set of passages interprets the exodus event as the revelation of some aspect of God. For instance in Sir. 24.3-4, Wisdom states, 'I came forth from the mouth of the Most High, and covered the earth like a midst. I dwelt in the highest heavens, and my throne was in a pillar of cloud'.[92] The allusion here is

89. See H.G. Lunt, 'Ladder of Jacob', in *OTP*, II, pp. 401, 403.

90. Cf. I.H. Marshall, *Luke. Historian and Theologian* (Grand Rapids: Baker, 1970), p. 99, who suggests 1.68 may be a prophetic perfect.

91. See too Mt. 21.33-46; Mk 12.1-12 and Lk. 20.9-19 which point to the Owner coming in vengeance against those who killed his Son.

92. Charles, *APOT*, I, p. 397 n. 4, also recognises this passage as an allusion to the exodus.

to the pillar of cloud in the exodus which housed the glory of God (see Exod. 14.19).

A similar tradition about Wisdom occurs in Wis. 10.17, dating from 200 BCE to 41 CE, where Wisdom again is in the pillar of cloud.[93] The text reads,

> She gave to holy people the reward of their labors; she guided them along a marvelous way, and became a shelter to them by day and a starry flame through the night. (18) She brought them over the Red Sea, and led them through deep waters; (19) but she drowned their enemies, and cast them up from the depth of the sea.

Here again Wisdom takes the place of God's glory in the exodus event which the text of Wisdom of Solomon interprets as a revelation of God.[94] Moreover, 16.16 interprets the hail plague of the exodus as 'the ungodly, refusing to know you, were flogged by the strength of your arm'. This phrase opens the possibility that God's Wisdom is his 'arm' and thus points to a possible connection with Isa. 40.10 and God's arm ruling for him. The identification of Wisdom and the pillar of cloud is possible in Philo who identifies some Old Testament theophanies as appearances of the Word (*All. Int.* 3.208) and perhaps the Wisdom of God (*All. Int.* 1.43). These texts make it possible for pre-Christian readers of the new exodus prophecy to expect a revelation of God's Wisdom.

Summary of the Background Material
According to the background material, the context of Isa. 40.3 points to a new exodus for the people of God. The interpretation of Isa. 40.3 in the LXX agrees with the MT in pointing to a theophany. Some extra-canonical Jewish texts understand Isa. 40.3 as referring to a theophany in general although various nuances of the verse are found in different traditions. Some texts use the passage to point to a coming of God without mentioning anyone else. Other texts point to the coming of the archangel Michael, or the Son of Man and are unclear if these figures are expressions of the divine or strictly creatures. Still other passages suggest that Isa. 40.3 implied the coming of the messiah without explicitly identifying how the messiah related to the coming of God. Also, some evidence exists that Jews would interpret the future exodus by comparing it to the past. While it is possible pre-Christian Jews interpreted

93.   See Schürer, *History*, III.1, pp. 572-73.
94.   See Schürer, *History*, III.1, pp. 570.

Isa. 40.3 as God sending an agent the messiah, such explanation hardly explains the continued belief in the coming of God's Shekinah which surrounded Isa. 40.3 in post-Christian literature. A last set of passages interprets the first exodus as the revelation of God's Wisdom. Thus, examination of the pre-Christian Jewish literature allows several possibilities from which to choose in determining the Evangelists' understanding of Jesus.

New Testament Data

A look at the details of Isa. 40.3 in the Gospels is necessary. Since Mark begins his Gospel with a conflate quote from Exod. 23.20/Mal. 3.1 and Isa. 40.3, I include these verses in my comparison (see following chart).

Matthew, Mark and Luke include a quotation of Mal. 3.1/Exod. 23.20 in their Gospels which Matthew and Luke agree in separating from their Markan context and inserting into the pericope of Jesus' testimony concerning John (Mt. 11.7-19 and Lk. 7.24-35).[95] The close verbal agreement of these two passages suggests that Matthew and Luke took their quotation from Q, as does the added 'before you' (ἔμπροσθέν σου) which is absent from the Markan quotation.[96] Q and the pre-Marcan tradition agree in the other details of the quotation.[97]

The Old Testament source of Mk 1.2 and parallels resists identification. Mark attributes both 1.2 and 3 to Isaiah while Matthew and Luke use 'This is the one about whom it is written' (Mt. 11.10 and Lk. 7.27).[98] There is no text extant in Isaiah which matches 1.2b and c. When one searches for possible sources outside Isaiah, two appear, Mal. 3.1 and Exod. 23.20. Mk 1.2b and parallels are virtually identical to both these

95. So Gundry, *Matthew* (1982), p. 44.

96. So A. Suhl, *Die Funktion der alttestamentlichen Zitate und Anspielungen im Markusevangelium* (Gütersloh: Mohn, 1965), p. 135; and D.L. Tiede, *Luke* (ACNT; Minneapolis: Augsburg, 1988), p. 86. Cf. J. Nolland, *Luke 1–9.20* (WBC; Dallas: Word Books, 1989), I, p. 138.

97. Cf. C.T. Ruddick, 'Behold, I send My Messenger', *JBL* 88 (1969), p. 382, who sees Mk 1.1, 2, 3, 7, and 8 as coming from the evangelist's own pen.

98. See R.A. Guelich, *Mark 1–8.26* (WBC; Dallas: Word Books, 1989), p. 10, who discusses 1.2b as a gloss, as imprecision common in testimonia, and as the preponderance of Isaiah and the messianic age. Guelich understands 'by Isaiah the prophet' as referring to the whole complex of events in 1.2b-15, including Isa. 42.1; 52.7 and 61.1.

Comparison of Sources

The way-preparation saying (Mal. 3.1 / Exod. 23.20)

Greek

Mt. 11.10	ἰδοὺ ἐγὼ ἀποστέλλω τὸν ἄγγελόν μου πρὸ προσώπου σου, ὃς κατασκευάσει τὴν ὁδόν σου ἔμπροσθέν σου.
Mk. 1.2	ἰδοὺ ἀποστέλλω τὸν ἄγγελόν μου πρὸ προσώπου σου, ὃς κατασκευάσει τὴν ὁδόν σου· ἔμπροσθέν σου.
Lk. 7.27	ἰδοὺ ἀποστέλλω τὸν ἄγγελόν μου πρὸ προσώπου σου, ὃς κατασκευάσει τὴν ὁδόν σου ἔμπροσθέν σου.
Mal. 3.1	ἰδοὺ ἐγὼ ἐξαποστέλλω τὸν ἄγγελόν μου καὶ ἐπιβλέψεται ὁδόν πρὸ προσώπου μου
Exod. 23.20	ἰδοὺ ἐγὼ ἀποστέλλω τὸν ἄγγελόν μου πρὸ προσώπου σου, ἵνα φυλάξῃ σε ἐν τῇ ὁδῷ,
Mal. 3.1	הנני שלח מלאכי ופנה־דרך לפני
Exod. 23.20	הנה אנכי שלח מלאך לפניך לשמרך בדרך

English

Mt. 11.10	See, I myself am sending my messenger before you who will prepare your way in front of you
Mk. 1.2	See, I am sending my messenger before you who will prepare your way in front of you
Lk. 7.27	See, I am sending my messenger before you who will prepare your way before me
Mal. 3.1	See, I myself am sending my messenger and he will make a way before me
Exod. 23.20	See, I myself am sending a messenger before you in order to guard you in the way.

The voice in the wilderness (Isa. 40.3)

Greek

Mt. 3.3	φωνὴ βοῶντος ἐν τῇ ἐρήμῳ· ἑτοιμάσατε τὴν ὁδὸν κυρίου, εὐθείας ποιεῖτε τὰς τρίβους αὐτοῦ·
Mk. 1.3	φωνὴ βοῶντος ἐν τῇ ἐρήμῳ· ἑτοιμάσατε τὴν ὁδὸν κυρίου, εὐθείας ποιεῖτε τὰς τρίβους αὐτοῦ·
Lk. 3.4	φωνὴ βοῶντος ἐν τῇ ἐρήμῳ· ἑτοιμάσατε τὴν ὁδὸν κυρίου, εὐθείας ποιεῖτε τὰς τρίβους αὐτοῦ·
Jn 1.23	φωνὴ βοῶντος ἐν τῇ ἐρήμῳ· εὐθύνατε τὴν ὁδὸν κυρίου,
Isa. 40.3	φωνὴ βοῶντος ἐν τῇ ἐρήμῳ· ἑτοιμάσατε² τὴν ὁδὸν κυρίου,³ εὐθείας ποιεῖτε τὰς τρίβους τοῦ θεοῦ ἡμῶν.
Isa. 40.3	קול קורא במדבר פנו דרך יהוה ישרו בערבה מסלה לאלהינו

English

Mt. 3.3	A voice of one crying out in the wilderness, 'Prepare the way of the Lord, make straight his paths.
Mk. 1.3	A voice of one crying out in the wilderness, 'Prepare the way of the Lord, make straight his paths.
Lk. 3.4	A voice of one crying out in the wilderness, 'Prepare the way of the Lord, make straight his paths.
Jn 1.23	A voice of one crying out in the wilderness, 'Make straight the way of the Lord,
Isa. 40.3	A voice crying out in the wilderness 'Prepare the way of the Lord, make straight the paths of our God.
Isa. 40.3	A voice crying out, 'In the wilderness prepare the way of the Lord, make straight in the desert a highway for our God.

1. The Samaritan Pentateuch, the Vulgate, and perhaps the Hebrew text behind the LXX, read מלאך instead of מלאכי which is also the reading of the MT at Exod. 23.23.
2. The Isaiah text is according to J. Ziegler, *Isaias* (SVT, 14; Göttingen: Vandenhoeck & Ruprecht, 1967).
3. Aquila reads εὐθύνατε ἐν ὁμαλῇ 'make straight in the even *way*'. Symmachus adds ἐν ἀβάτῳ 'in the impassible *place/way*'.

Ref		
Lk. 3.5	πᾶσα φάραγξ πληρωθήσεται και	πᾶν ὄρος και βουνός ταπεινωθήσεται,
Isa. 40.4	πᾶσα φάραγξ πληρωθήσεται και	πᾶν ὄρος και βουνός ταπεινωθήσεται,
Isa. 40.4	וְכָל־הָ֤ר וְגִבְעָה֙ יִשְׁפָּ֔לוּ וְכָל־גֶּיא֙ יִנָּשֵׂ֔א	

Ref	
Lk. 3.5	Every valley shall be filled, and every mountain and hill shall be humbled,
Isa. 40.4	Every valley shall be filled, and every mountain and hill shall be humbled,
Isa. 40.4	Every valley shall be lifted up, and every mountain and hill shall be made low,

Ref					
Lk. 3.5	και ἔσται τὰ σκολιὰ εἰς εὐθεῖαν	και αἱ	τραχεῖα	εἰς ὁδοὺς λείας	
Isa. 40.4	και ἔσται πάντα τὰ σκολιὰ εἰς εὐθεῖαν	και ἡ	τραχεῖα	εἰς ὁδοὺς λείας[4]	
Isa. 40.4	וְהָיָ֤ה הֶֽעָקֹב֙ לְמִישׁ֔וֹר וְהָרְכָסִ֖ים לְבִקְעָֽה				

Ref	
Lk. 3.5	the crooked shall be straight and the rough ways smooth ways;
Isa. 40.4	and all the crooked shall be straight and the rough way smooth ways
Isa. 40.4	and the uneven shall be ground level and the rough places a valley

Ref	
Lk. 3.6	και ὀφθήσεται ἡ δόξα κυρίου,
Isa. 40.5	και ὀφθήσεται ἡ δόξα κυρίου,
Isa. 40.5	וְנִגְלָ֖ה כְּב֣וֹד יְהוָ֑ה

Ref	
Lk. 3.6	And the glory of the Lord
Isa. 40.5	And the glory of the Lord

Ref						
Lk. 3.6	και ὄψεται	πᾶσα	σάρξ	τὸ	σωτήριον	τοῦ θεοῦ.
Isa. 40.5	και ὄψεται	πᾶσα	σάρξ	τὸ	σωτήριον	του θεοῦ.

Ref	
Lk. 3.6	And all flesh shall see the salvation of God.
Isa. 40.5	shall be seen, And all flesh shall see the salvation of God.
Isa. 40.5	shall be revealed, And all flesh shall see it together.

4. Rahlfs reads εἰς πεδία 'plains' for εἰς ὁδοὺς λείας 'smooth ways.' Aquila and Symmachus read εἰς πεδίον 'a plain'.

LXX verses.[99] Thus, in 1.2b it is virtually impossible to decide which verse is the source of this part of the quotation.[100] In Mk 1.2c, the task is somewhat easier. There, the text of Exod. 23.20 in both the MT and LXX differs significantly from that of Mk 1.2c. For Mal. 3.1, the LXX text differs from Mark, but the underlying Hebrew text of Malachi is closer to that of Mark since κατασκευάσει in Mk 1.2 and parallels is closer to פָּנָּה of Mal. 3.1 than to the other translations.[101] Mark, however, transposes and alters πρὸ προσώπου μου of Mal. 3.1 to πρὸ προσώπου σου perhaps under the influence of Exod. 23.20. σου appears in the Synoptic Gospels in disagreement with the LXX and MT, although again the σε / ךָ of Exod. 23.20 may have influenced the writers of Q and the pre-Marcan tradition. The addition of πρὸ προσώπου σου/ἔμπροσθέν is perhaps due to Exod. 23.20 but positionally due to Mal. 3.1. The four Gospels agree remarkably in their use of Isa. 40.3. The only deviation in the section commonly quoted is in John who differs in translating פַּנּוּ with εὐθύνατε instead of ἑτοιμάσατε. This change is perhaps due to the influence of εὐθείας ποιεῖτε in the section unquoted by John.[102]

Major Changes of the LXX/MT

There are two major changes of the LXX and MT in the Gospels. First is the translation of יהוה as κυρίου following the LXX, and the second is the replacement of 'of our God' (LXX and MT) with 'his' (Matthew, Mark and Luke). An explanation of the first change is in order. The phrase τὴν ὁδὸν κυρίου in all four Gospels and the LXX violates the Canon of Apollonius which states that two nouns in regimen should both have the definite article or both lack it.[103] According to the Canon, one should

---

99.   Both Malachi and Exodus add ἐγώ although the Hebrew of Exodus is slightly more emphatic with אָנֹכִי. Malachi transposes the phrase πρὸ προσώπου μου until after 3.1b. In addition, the first person of Malachi is second person in Exodus and Mark.

100.   Cf. Guelich, *Mark*, I, pp. 7-8; and J.D. Kingsbury, *The Christology of Mark's Gospel* (Philadelphia: Fortress Press, 1983), p. 59 n. 58.

101.   See Stendahl, *Matthew*, p. 51 n. 4, who points out that ἐπιβλέπειν is the usual reading in the LXX for the Qal of פָּנָה. Suhl, *Funktion*, p. 135 n. 217, points out that Theodotion has ἑτοιμάσει which presupposes the Piel. Symmachus, according to Suhl, has ἀποσκευάσει which also presupposes the Piel.

102.   Contrast Stendahl, *Matthew*, p. 52, who sees εὐθύνατε as another synonym for פָּנָה.

103.   C.F.D. Moule, *An Idiom Book of New Testament Greek* (Cambridge: Cambridge University Press, 2nd edn, 1959), pp. 114-15.

expect τὴν ὁδὸν τοῦ κυρίου, which occurs in Acts 13.10 in the plural (note variant), or ὁδὸν κυρίου but not τὴν ὁδὸν κυρίου or ὁδὸν τοῦ κυρίου.[104] The usual exceptions to the Canon occur when the first noun, the *nomen regens*, is anarthrous.[105] Here, however, the second noun, the *nomen rectum*, is anarthrous and falls into a pattern usually reserved in the New Testament for proper nouns.[106] There are at least 218 examples in the New Testament which break the Canon of Apollonius in this way. Of these, 178 are proper nouns,[107] 22 are phrases with κύριος,[108] 2 are

104. The textual variant in Acts 13.10 omits the article. The earliest attestation is for its inclusion (see the original hand of ℵ and B). The omission of the article in the lesser Alexandrian witnesses A, C and Y, the Western D and E, and the Byzantine text is perhaps due to scribal assimilation to Isa. 40.3 quoted in Mt. 3.3, Mk 1.3, Lk. 3.4 and Jn 1.23.

105. For a discussion of the exceptions to the Canon of Apollonius, see Moule, *Idiom Book*, p. 115, and S.D. Hull, 'Exceptions to Apollonius' Canon in the New Testament: A Grammatical Study', *Trinity Journal* 7 (1986), pp. 3-16.

106. See Hull, 'Exceptions', pp. 6-7, 11, who finds 185 examples of proper nouns breaking the Canon in this way with 21 examples of κυρίου and two adjectival exceptions. He leaves another 7 unexplained. See too Moule, *Idiom Book*, pp. 114-15.

107. Aaron (Lk. 1.5; Heb. 7.11; 9.4); Abel (Mt. 15.21); Abraham (Mt. 22.32; Mk 12.26; Lk. 16.22; 20.37; Acts 3.13; 7.32. Heb. 7.5); Adam (Rom. 5.14); Alexander (Mk 15.21); Andrew (Jn 1.44); Aretas (2 Cor. 11.32); Balaam (Rev. 2.14); Barnabas (Col. 4.10); Babylon (Mt. 1.11, 12, 17 [2×]); Gamaliel (Acts 22.3); Gennesaret (Lk. 5.1); Dalmanutha (Mk 8.10); David (Mt. 12.23; 21.19, 15; Lk. 1.32; Jn 7.42; Acts 7.45; 15.16; Rev. 3.7; 5.5; 22.16); Decapolis (Mk 7.13); Hamor (Acts 7.16); Zechariah (Mt. 23.35; Lk. 1.40); Zebedee (Mt. 20.20; 26.37; 27.56; Mk 10.35); Elijah (Lk. 4.25); Herod (Mt. 2.15; Mk 8.15; Lk. 1.5; 23.7); Isaiah (Mt. 13.14; 12.38); Thessalonians (1 Thess. 1.1; 2 Thess. 1.1); James (Mt. 22.32; Mk 5.37; 12.26; Lk. 1.33); Jason (Acts 17.5); Jericho (Heb. 10.30); Jesus (Mt. 14.1; 26.75; Mk 1.1; Lk. 5.8; Acts 2.38; 3.6; 4.10; 8.12; 10.40; 16.7; 26.9; Phil. 1.19; 2.10; Heb. 10.10, 19; 1 Jn 1.7; Rev. 1.2, 9; 12.17; 14.12; 17.6; 19.10 [2×]; 20.4); Judas (Mt. 2.6; Heb. 8.8; Rev. 5.5); Isaac (Mt. 22.32; Mk 12.26; Acts 3.13); Israel (Mt. 15.31; Mk 15.32; Lk. 1.16; Acts 4.10; 5.21; 7.23, 37; 10.36; 13.24; Rom. 9.27; 2 Cor. 3.7, 13; Heb. 8.8, 10; 11.22; Rev. 2.14); John (Mt. 9.14; 11.12; 14.8; Mk 2.18 [2×]; 6.2, 25; Lk. 5.33; 7.24, 29; 20.4; Jn 1.42; 3.25; Acts 1.22; 12.2, 12; 18.5); Job (Jas 5.11); Jonah (Mt. 12.39, 41; 16.4; Lk. 11.29, 32); Joseph (Jn 6.42; Heb. 11.21); Caesar (Acts 17.7; 25.10); Caesarea (Mt. 16.13; Mk 8.27); Levi (Heb. 7.5); Lot (Lk. 17.28, 32; Heb. 8.8, 10; 11.22); Magadan (Mt. 15.39); Mary (Mt. 1.16; Jn 11.1); Melchizedek (Heb. 5.6, 10; 6.20; 7.11, 15, 17); Moses (Mk 12.26; Lk. 2.22; 24.44; Jn 7.23; Acts 15.5; 28.23; 2 Cor. 3.7; Rev. 15.3); Noah (Lk. 17.26); Paul (Acts 19.11; 23.16; 1 Cor. 1.13); Peter (Mt. 8.14); Sarah (Rom. 4.19); Simon (Mk 1.16, 29, 30; 14.3; Lk. 4.38; Jn 1.40; 6.8, 71); Zion (Mt. 21.5); Solomon (Mt. 12.42; Lk. 11.31; Acts 5.12); Stephen (1 Cor. 16.15, 17; Acts 22.20); Tiberius (Lk. 3.1); Timaeus

phrases with Χριστός,[109] and 6 are unexplained exceptions.[110] According to this pattern, proper nouns regularly follow a convention where the *nomen rectum* does not have the article while the *nomen regens* does. In the LXX, the translators treat κύριος as a proper noun when it translates יהוה, and so κυρίου is anarthrous following an articular *nomen regens*.[111] Out of 21 occurrences of this κύριος construction in the New Testament, 17 of these occur in Old Testament quotations, allusions, or Old Testament phrases.[112] Indeed, three of the four remaining occurrences may also have an Old Testament background.[113] There is one exception which demonstrates no possible Old Testament background, 1 Cor. 16.10. However, this one exception is probably due to grammatical necessity under the influence of the postpositive γάρ.[114] Therefore, when the

(Mk 10.46); Titus (2 Cor. 7.6, 13; 8.16); Tyrannus (Acts 19.9); Tyre (Mt. 15.21; Mk 7.24, 31; Lk. 6.17); Pharaoh (Acts 7.21); Philip (Mt. 14.3; Mk 6.17; Acts 21.8).

108. Mt. 1.24; 3.3; Mk 1.3; Lk. 1.38; 2.24, 26, 39; 3.4; Jn 1.23; 12.38; Acts 2.21; 5.9; Rom. 10.13; 16.25; 1 Cor. 16.10; 2 Cor. 3.17; 2 Tim. 2.19; Jas 5.4, 10, 11; 1 Pet. 1.25.

109. Phil. 2.30; 3.8.

110. Jude 15, πάντων τῶν ἔργων ἀσεβείας; 2 Cor. 10.13, ὁ θεὸς μέτρου; Heb. 9.13, τὸ αἷμα τράγων καὶ ταύρων; Acts 7.58, τοὺς πόδας νεανίου [the feet of *a* young man]; Rom. 2.13, αἱ ἀκρασταὶ νόμου, οἱ ποιήταὶ νόμου.

111. Gen. 12.8; 16.9, 10, 13; 18.19; 21.33; 26.25; Exod. 4.28; 9.20, 21; 12.41; 13.9; 16.7, 10; 24.4, 17; 34.5; Lev. 2.3, 10; 4.2, 13, 27, 35; 5.15, 17; 6.2, 17, 18, 7.25, 8.35; 9.23; 10.12; 16.4; 19.8; 21.6. 23.2, 38, 44; 24.16 [2×]; Num. 7.89; 8.11; 10.33 [2×]; 11.24, 29; 12.8; 14.10, 21, 41, 44; 15.31, 39; 16.3, 9, 19, 41, 42; 18.28; 19.13, 20; 20.4, 6; 22.18, 34; 24.13; 26.9; 27.7; 31.16 [2×]; 29, 30; 32.14; Deut. 1.43; 2.15; 4.2; 5.5; 8.6; 9.23; 10.8; 11.7; 18.5, 22; 23.8; 28.10; 31.9, 25; 32.3; 34.5.

112. Mt. 3.3, Mk 1.3, Lk. 3.4, Jn 1.23, Jn 12.38, Acts 2.21 and 1 Pet. 1.25 all occur in Old Testament quotations. Rom. 10.13; 2 Tim. 2.19; Jas. 5.4 and 5.11 are allusions to the Old Testament. Mt. 1.24, ὁ ἄγγελος κυρίου; Lk. 1.38, ὁ δοῦλος κυρίου; Lk. 2.24 and 39, ὁ νόμος κυρίου; Lk. 2.26, ὁ Χριστός κυρίου; and Jas 5.10, τὸ ὄνομα κυρίου occur in contexts which suggest an Old Testament background for the phrase.

113. The four remaining exceptions are Acts 5.9 and 2 Cor. 3.17, τὸ πνεῦμα κυρίου; 2 Cor. 3.18, τὴν δόξαν κυρίου; and 1 Cor. 16.10, τὸ ἔργον κυρίου.

114. I thank Dr Murray J. Harris for making this suggestion to me. Cf. J.A. Brooks and C.L. Winberry, *Syntax of New Testament Greek* (New York: University Press of America, 1979), p. 68; E. de Witt Burton, *A Critical and Exegetical Commentary on the Epistle to the Galatians* (ICC; Edinburgh: T. & T. Clark, 1921), p. 401; and B. Weiss, 'Der Gebrauch des Artikels bei den Gottesnamen. Exegetische Studie', *TSK* 84 (1911), p. 519. On a similar problem, see W.W. Graf von Baudissin, *Kyrios als Gottesname in Judentum und seine Stelle in der Religions-*

evangelists speak of τὴν ὁδὸν κυρίου they probably are using a convention which indicates that κύριος here is God's name.[115] Thus, to a Greek speaker it would be difficult to read τὴν ὁδὸν κυρίου without recognizing that κύριος functions as a proper noun. Since there is pre-45 CE evidence that κύριος was a translation surrogate for יהוה, and since the LXX translators apparently followed this convention in the LXX, the most likely proper noun for Jewish Greek speakers would be the translation surrogate of יהוה.[116] Thus, it is unlikely that these Greek-speaking Jews could read τὴν ὁδὸν κυρίου messianically. Furthermore, evidence of the closeness between the phrase τὴν ὁδὸν τοῦ κυρίου and τὴν ὁδὸν τοῦ θεοῦ exists in Acts 18.25 and 26.[117] Lk. 20.21, also,

---

geschichte (Giessen: Töpelmann, 1926–29), I, pp. 62-63, discussing Gen. 18.17; 28.13; Exod. 14.25; 16.29; 34.14; Num. 14.9; Deut. 2.7; 8.7; 10.17; and 17.16 and how the translators dealt with κύριος δέ or κύριος γάρ.

115.   Grammarians have noticed that κύριος functions as a proper name. See T.F. Middleton, *The Doctrine of the Article* (ed. H.J. Rose; no place: no publisher, no date given), p. 207, cited by Moule, *Idiom Book*, p. 115; F. Blass and A. Debrunner, *A Greek Grammar of the New Testament and Other Early Christian Literature* (trans. and ed. R.W. Funk; Chicago and London: University of Chicago Press, 1961), § 254; N. Turner, *Syntax*, vol. III, in J.H. Moulton, *A Grammar of New Testament Greek* (Edinburgh: T. & T. Clark, 1963), p. 174 n. 2, writes, 'This flatly contravenes the canon of Apollonius to the effect that an anarthrous noun may not be governed by a noun having the art.; but κύριος must be taken as a proper name = Yahweh'.

116.   For instance see the evidence in Philo cited by G. Howard, 'The Tetragram and the New Testament', *JBL* 96 (1977), p. 93, and A. Pietersma, 'Kyrios or Tetragram: A Renewed Quest for the Original Septuagint', in *De Septuaginta: Studies in Honour of John William Wevers on his 65th Birthday* (ed. A. Pietersma and C. Cox; Mississauga, Ontario: Benben, 1984), p. 93. Howard, 'Tetragram', p. 65; and H. Conzelmann, *An Outline of the Theology of the New Testament* (trans. J. Bowden; New York: Harper and Row, 1969), p. 84, both deny that the κύριος was the original reading of the LXX. See, however, Pietersma, 'Kyrios', pp. 85-101.

117.   𝔓[41], B, 614 and a few others omit τοῦ before κυρίου in v. 25. D and the thirteenth-century Latin MS Gigas omit τοῦ θεοῦ in v. 26. The Majority Text plus the Alexandrian Ψ reads τὴν τοῦ θεοῦ ὁδόν. A few unclassified minuscules read τὸν λόγον τοῦ κυρίου, 323, 945, 1891, along with the Western 1739. A few other MSS follow these in witnessing τὴν ὁδὸν τοῦ κυρίου, Western E and the SyrP, unclassified 36, and 2439. The reading of Nestle-Aland[26] has strong attestation in ℵ, A, B, 33, and 1175 in the Alexandrian and 614 in the Western. If the NA[26] reading were original there would be reason to change it to τοῦ κυρίου in assimilation to v. 25. If τοῦ κυρίου were original, there would be little reason to change it to τοῦ θεοῦ although the change could be unintentional due to a confusion of the *nomina sacra* which in this case would be KY versus ΘY.

speaks of τὴν ὁδὸν τοῦ θεοῦ. The two verses in Acts demonstrate that readers would initially read τὴν ὁδὸν κυρίου probably as a reference to the way of God not the way of the Lord (i.e. exclusively the messiah).[118]

In regard to the second major change, some scholars see the change of τοῦ θεοῦ ἡμῶν to αὐτοῦ as facilitating the application of the verse to Jesus.[119] One could indeed argue that the Synoptic writers made the second change in order to apply this text to Jesus without implying that Jesus could in some way be thought of as God. Several factors cast doubt on the idea of the evangelists deliberately changing the text to apply it to Jesus. First, it is possible that the evangelists followed a text which had already made the change.[120] Secondly, in the related text of Lk. 1.16-17, the evangelist implies that John will be the forerunner of the Lord God of Israel. Thus, it would be difficult to explain why Luke left κύριον τὸν θεόν αὐτῶν in 1.16 while he deliberately removed it in Lk. 3.4. Also, Mt. 1.23 interprets Jesus' name Emmanuel, as μεθ' ἡμῶν

118. See similarly Fitzmyer, *Luke*, I, p. 461, on the understanding of John's audience. Cf. R.L. Webb, '"In those days came John..."' The Ministry of John the Baptist within its Social, Cultural and Historic Context' (PhD thesis, University of Sheffield, 1990), pp. 231-330.

119. See Guelich, *Mark*, I, p. 11; E. Schweizer, *The Good News according to Mark* (trans. D.H. Madvig; Richmond: John Knox, 1970), p. 31; R. Pesch, *Das Markusevangelium* (Freiberg: Herder, 1984), I, p. 77; Kingsbury, *Mark's Gospel*, p. 59; Suhl, *Funktion*, p. 135 n. 218; U. Mauser, *Christ and the Wilderness* (London: SCM Press, 1963), p. 80; F. Hahn, *The Titles of Jesus in Christology: Their History in Early Christianity* (trans. H. Knight and G. Ogg; London: Lutterworth, 1969), p. 108; C.E.B. Cranfield, *The Gospel according to Saint Mark: An Introduction and Commentary* (Cambridge: Cambridge University Press, 1959), p. 39; E.P. Gould, *A Critical and Exegetical Commentary on the Gospel according to Mark* (ICC; Edinburgh: T. & T. Clark, 1901), p. 5; I.H. Marshall, *The Gospel of Luke: A Commentary on the Greek Text* (NIGTC; Exeter: Paternoster, 1978), p. 136; T. Holtz, *Untersuchungen über die alttestamentlichen Zitate bei Lukas* (TU, 104; Berlin: Akademie, 1968), p. 37; Davies and Allison, *Matthew*, p. 293; R.T. France, *The Gospel according to Matthew: An Introduction and Commentary* (TNTC; Leicester: Inter-Varsity Press; Grand Rapids: Eerdmans, 1985), p. 91; Stendahl, *Matthew*, p. 48; and Gundry, *Matthew* (1982), p. 45. The minor changes include the omission of πάντα in Lk. 3.4b and the change to a plural of τραχεῖα in Lk. 3.5d. Holtz, *Alttestamentliche*, p. 38, suggests that Luke is not dependent on the MT in omitting πάντα. He further notes that πεδίον may have a plural sense (p. 39).

120. Similarly see M. Black, *An Aramaic Approach to the Gospels and Acts* (Oxford: Clarendon Press, 3d edn, 1967), pp. 98-99; see too Davies and Allison, *Matthew*, p. 293; and Mauser, *Wilderness*, p. 80.

ὁ θεός, and while this text in and of itself may not call Jesus God,[121] Mt.
12.6; 18.20 and 28.20 perhaps tip the scales in so understanding the text
since it is possible that Matthew wants his readers to interpret 1.23 in
light of 28.20.[122] This possibility makes it unsafe to assume that Matthew
changed the text to avoid applying τοῦ θεοῦ αὐτῶν to Jesus in Mt. 3.3.

In regard to the other changes in Luke, some scholars suggest that
Luke preserves the Q text which Matthew abbreviated under the influence of Mark.[123] Other scholars see Luke as the source of the extension
due to his belief in universalism.[124] Luke also omits the phrase 'and the
glory of the Lord shall be revealed'.[125] Luke might have redacted this
verse out purposely to avoid any idea that Jesus is the glory of God, or
he may have changed the text accidentally.[126] Luke may have redacted
the text because Jesus' ministry did not represent the fulfilment of this
promise.[127] There is no other evidence that Luke had a polemic against
seeing Jesus as the glory of the Lord.[128] Luke's point is that 'all flesh'
will see the salvation of God, a point important to Luke's theme of a

121. See too M.J. Harris, *Jesus as God. The New Testament Use of* Theos *in
Reference to Jesus* (Grand Rapids: Baker, 1992), pp. 256-58, who does not think ὁ
θεός is here a title for Jesus.

122. G. Stanton, 'Matthew', in Carson and Williamson, *It is Written*, p. 216;
J.D. Kingsbury, 'The Composition of Mt. 28.16-20', *JBL* 93 (1974), pp. 578-79;
U. Luz, *Matthew 1–7: A Commentary* (trans. W.C. Linss; Edinburgh: T. & T. Clark,
1989), pp. 121-22; R.H. Smith, *Matthew* (ACNT; Minneapolis: Augsburg, 1989),
pp. 37-38; R.H. Mounce, *Matthew: A Good News Commentary on his Literary and
Theological Art* (Grand Rapids: Eerdmans, 1982); M. de Jonge, *Christology in
Context. The Earliest Response to Jesus* (Philadelphia: Westminster Press, 1988),
pp. 94. Cf. Davies and Allison, *Matthew*, I, p. 217.

123. See Davies and Allison, *Matthew*, p. 294; and Schürmann, *Lukasevangelium*,
I, p. 161 n. 105. Cf. M. Rese, *Alttestamentliche Motive in der Christologie des Lukas*
(SNT, 1; Gütersloh: Mohn 1969), p. 168.

124. See Nolland, *Luke*, I, p. 138; E. Schweizer, *The Good News according to
Luke* (trans. D.E. Green; Atlanta: John Knox, 1984), p. 68; Marshall, *Luke*, p. 137,
and Bock, *Proclamation*, p. 94.

125. Stendahl, *Matthew*, p. 49 n. 1, states that Luke agrees with the LXX in omitting the parallelism. However, the LXX has both sections and therefore does not agree
with Luke. Justin Martyr, *Dialogue* 50, quotes Isa. 40.5 following the LXX.

126. M.-J. Lagrange, *Evangile selon Saint Luc* (EB; Paris: Gabalda, 1921),
p. 105, hints at the first possibility when he says the phrase was not convenient to
Luke because of its Old Testament implications.

127. See Nolland, *Luke*, I, p. 144; and Marshall, *Luke*, p. 137 (Lk. 24.26; Acts
3.13). Cf. Rese, *Alttestamentliche*, p. 170 (Lk. 2.9; 9.26 and 32).

128. Similarly Bock, *Proclamation*, p. 94.

mission to the gentiles in Acts.[129] Also, Luke's phrase τὸ σωτήριον τοῦ θεοῦ' in 3.6 is one which he has already used in 2.30, τὸ σωτήριόν σου.[130] In 2.30, the phrase has clear reference to Jesus. Also, Acts 28.28 uses τὸ σωτήριον τοῦ θεοῦ, which God sends to the Gentiles.[131]

The Context of Exodus 23.20 and Malachi 3.1
The background to Exod. 23.20 is God's instruction to Moses that he was sending an angel of protection before Israel and that Israel must obey this angel. This angel was perhaps the angel 'in whom my name dwells.' In the context, 'you' singular refers perhaps to the nation of Israel as a whole rather than Moses (see v. 23). Thus, if the evangelist is thinking of that context, 'you' is the new Israel or its representative. If Malachi is the proper background 'you' (changed from 'me') is the Lord who will come to his temple (Mal. 3.1).

The combination of Exod. 23.20/Mal. 3.1 and Isa. 40.3 in Mark suggests an implicit midrash.[132] The text implies a certain amount of underlying exegesis has taken place prior to Mark's incorporation of this text into his Gospel.[133] The implied midrashist, be it Mark or his predecessor, may have taken the verbal similarities of the two texts to interpret each other on the principle of *Gezera Shawa*.[134] On this interpretation, the implied midrashist identified the 'you' of Exod. 23.20 or the 'you' changed from 'me' of Mal. 3.1 with the 'Lord' of Isa. 40.3.[135] The

129. Similarly Fitzmyer, *Luke*, I, p. 461.

130. So Nolland, *Luke*, I, p. 44.

131. σῴζειν is a favourite word for Luke–Acts. See Marshall, *Historian*, pp. 94-102.

132. For the traditional association of these two verses see Davies and Allison, *Matthew*, p. 294 n. 15, and Stendahl, *Matthew*, p. 50; cf. Pesch, *Markusevangelium*, p. 78 n. 16 (pre-Marcan redactor), and E.E. Ellis, 'Biblical Interpretation in the New Testament Church', in *Miqra: Text Translation and Interpretation of the Hebrew Bible in Ancient Judaism and Early Christianity* (ed. M.J. Mulder; CRINT, 2.1; Philadelphia: Fortress Press; Assen: Van Gorcum, 1989), p. 719 n. 155.

133. F.J. Matera, 'The Prologue as the Interpretative Key to Mark's Gospel', *JSNT* 34 (1988), p. 7, points out that Rabbinic exegesis joins Exod. 23.20 and Mal. 3.1 to identify Elijah as the messenger. So Mauser, *Wilderness*, p. 81.

134. So Stendahl, *Matthew*, pp. 51-52. For a summary of these hermeneutical rules formulated after the New Testament era, see D.J. Moo, *The Old Testament in the Gospel Passion Narratives* (Sheffield: Almond Press, 1983), pp. 27-30; and D.I. Brewer, *Techniques and Assumptions in Jewish Exegesis Before 70 CE* (TSAJ, 30; Tübingen: Mohr [Siebeck], 1992), pp. 17-18.

135. Guelich, *Mark*, p. 11, connects 'you' and 'the Lord' who is Jesus according

implied midrashist could have noticed that Exod. 23.20 and Isa. 40.3 both have to do with an exodus. He may have then used the idea of the angel of the LORD implied by Exod. 23.20 to interpret Mal. 3.1 which says 'before me'. In Mal. 3.1, the context deals with a theophany, yet the language strangely shifts from second person to third, as if God who was coming could speak of himself with a certain detachment. The implied midrashist may have interpreted this second figure as the angel in whom God's name dwells in Exod. 23.20. The difficulty with this view is 'the messenger' in Exod. 23.20 and Mal. 3.1 are different. One is 'the angel of the LORD' while the second is the coming Levite (Mal. 2.7).

Isaiah 40.3 in Matthew, Mark, Luke and John

This detailed look at Isa. 40.3 in the Gospels does not reveal why the Gospel writers applied this passage to Jesus. They indeed wanted Gospel readers to conclude that Jesus was sent by God as his special agent in the affairs of men (Mt. 21.9; 23.39; Lk. 13.35; 19. 38; Mk 11.9-10; Jn 12.13).[136] They indeed saw him as the messiah (Mt. 16.16; 26.63-64. Mk 8.29; 14.61-62; Lk. 9.20; 22.67-68). Moreover, all four Gospels and Acts agree that the one who comes after John is Jesus (Mt. 3.13-17; 27.42; Mk 1.9-11; 15.32; Lk. 3.21-22; 23.35; Jn 1.25-28, 29, 30-31, 45; 3.28; 6.14-15 [Deut. 18.18]; 11.27; Acts 13.24; 19.4). However, why does Jesus' coming become simply God's? It would have been natural to see Jesus, the messiah, as the new Moses leading the new people of God in a new exodus.[137] Did the evangelists mean only that Jesus was God's agent, or did they think of him in association with God's theophanic presence too?[138] One could argue that the reference to loosening or

to Mk 1.1-15. Pesch, *Markusevangelium*, p. 78, suggests that the combination of the two texts turns Mal. 3.1/Exod. 23.20 into an address of God to the messiah.

136. Webb, 'In those days', pp. 231-330. submits that, for the historical John the Baptist, Isa. 40.3 referred to Jesus on the basis of his being the agent of God because some texts assign God's activity to a second figure, because God acts through history and because there was an aversion to seeing God. See particularly pp. 272-74. Cf. Isa. 11.16 and Exod. 14.

137. See a similar comment in G.R. Beasley-Murray, *Jesus and the Kingdom of God* (Exeter: Paternoster, 1986), p. 261.

138. Some commentators dismiss the idea that the evangelists consider the Old Testament context of Isa. 40.3 (see Haenchen, *Markus*, p. 40 n. 5; and Davies and Allison, *Matthew*, pp. 293-94). Others see such application depending on a high Christology (see similarly Godet, *Luke*, p. 174; J. van Seters, 'Isaiah 40.1-11', *Int* 35 [1981], p. 404; Bonnard, *Isaïe*, pp. 87-88; and Alexander, *Isaiah*, p. 95). Other explanations for applying Isa. 40.3 to Jesus include the following. Pesch,

carrying the coming one's sandals implies that the coming one is strictly human not divine (Mt. 3.11; Mk 1.7; Lk. 3.16; Acts 13.25).[139] The problem with this argument is that the final redactor of John uses the same verse and probably did think of the coming one as divine (Jn 1.27 and 1.1). Moreover, this objection would also demand that because Abraham washed the feet of his visitors in Gen. 18.4 none of them was God's theophanic presence (cf. 18.1 [see above pp. 31-32]). John's statement only affirms the vast superiority of the coming one to himself. It should not function as a clear indication of the limit of that superiority. Some evidence points to the position that the evangelist classed Jesus as divine while maintaining monotheism (see below).[140]

In John's Gospel, Jesus is the Word made flesh (1.14) whom John interprets as 'pitching his tent' among humanity (ἐσκήνωσεν). This description likens him to God's Shekinah who radiates God the Father's glory (1.14).[141] The Word pre-exists John (1.15, 31) and functions as the theophanic presence of God in the past (12.41), who although distinct from God the Father in one respect is himself God (Jn 1.1b-c).[142] In the ministry of Jesus, men and women see the glory of God (Jn 11.40). Likewise, Mt. 18.20 applies an idea to Jesus which later Jewish writers

---

Markusevangelium, p. 78, considers the idea that the Christian understanding of Isa. 40.3 represents a second stage of the tradition which preserves a tradition of John which is changed in the Christian understanding. Mounce sees the straight paths as preparation for God to travel into men's hearts. D. Patte, *The Gospel according to Matthew: A Structural Commentary on Matthew's Faith* (Philadelphia: Fortress Press, 1987), p. 49, writes, 'In this context the quotation from Isa. 40.3 is to be read in a special way. It confirms that John is the forerunner of Jesus, the Lord. But it simultaneously means that John's ministry prepares the way of the Lord God. Making ready and making straight the way of the Lord is bringing people to have lives that befit repentance (3.8), that is, ways or paths (of life) that fulfill all righteousness and that befit submission to the Lord God.'

139.   So Dunn, *Christology*, p. xxxv n. 31.

140.   Some later Christian interpreters understood Christ's coming as a visit from God and not a visit of God's agent. See Apollinaris of Laodicea, *Fragment*, 70 (from R.A. Norris, *The Christological Controversy* [SECT; Philadelphia: Fortress Press, 1980], p. 109); Novatian, *Trinity* 12.714, connects God's coming in Isa. 35.3-6 with Christ's coming (see E. Burton, *Testimonies of the Ante-Nicene Fathers to the Doctrine of the Trinity and the Divinity of the Holy Ghost* [Oxford: Oxford University Press, 1831], pp. 116-18). Theodoret, *Commentary on Isaiah* 12.39-41.

141.   Cf. Josephus, *Ant.* 3.100-101, 203, for God himself inhabiting the tent in the wilderness.

142.   Notice the verbs γέγονεν and ἦν in Jn 1.15 are the same as those in 1.1-3.

applied to the Shekinah.[143] If one connects this verse with Mt. 1.23 and 28.20, Matthew presents a tradition which identifies Jesus as God's presence on earth.[144] Furthermore, Mt.11.27 identifies Jesus as the Son who reveals God the Father though personally distinct from him. This verse may equate him with Wisdom (Mt. 11.28-30);[145] Jesus moreover is greater than the place where men experience God's presence (Mt. 12.6; cf. 23.21). In addition, Jesus takes the function of sending prophets, wise men and teachers which further likens him to the 'Lord' of Mal. 3.1 and Exod. 23.20. In Lk. 1.16-17, John will be forerunner to the Lord God of Israel (see too Mal. 4.5-6 [3.23-24]; Lk. 1.68, 78; 7.16; 8.39).[146] The fulfilment of this passage is Lk. 19.44. Jerusalem's divine visitation (ἡ ἐπισκοπή) is Jesus' arrival in the temple.[147] Jesus, moreover, cleanses the temple which may indicate Luke's understanding of Mal. 3.1 where the Lord comes to his own temple for judgment (19.45-48).[148] According to Luke, Jesus sends messengers before him who prepare people for his coming (Lk. 9.52-54; 10.1). These texts even more clearly identify Jesus as the coming one, even as the coming Lord (see too Mt. 12.8; Mk 2.27; Lk. 6.5). Lk. 10.22 identifies the Son as revealing the Father though personally distinct from him. Moreover, Lk. 2.11 may suggest Jesus is the theophanic presence of God.[149] Mark's Gospel is the least clear how

143. J. Sievers, '"Where Two or Three...": The Rabbinic Concept of the Shekinah and Matthew 18.20', in *The Jewish Roots of Christian Liturgy* (ed. E.J. Fisher; New York: Paulist Press, 1990), p. 55.

144. Compare God's presence with Israel in the first exodus (e.g. Num. 11.20). See too n. 119 above.

145. See Witherington, *Christology*, p. 227; de Jonge, *Christology*, p. 93; see too Kingsbury, 'Composition', p. 581.

146. So Marshall, *Luke*, p. 59, and Hahn, *Titles*, p. 395 n. 111. Cf. Fitzmyer, *Luke*, I, p. 327; H. Sahlin, *Der Messias und Das Gottesvolk. Studien zur Protolukanischen Theologie* (ASNU, 12; Uppsala: Almquist & W. Ksells Boktryckeri, 1945), p. 79 n. 2; C.F. Evans, *Saint Luke* (TPI New Testament Commentaries; London: SCM Press; Philadelphia: Trinity Press International, 1990), p. 186.

147. So H.W. Beyer, 'ἐπισκοπή', in *TDNT*, II, p. 607; see too Marshall, *Luke*, p. 719; Fitzmyer, *Luke*, II, p. 1246; J. Reiling and J.L. Swellengrebel, *A Translator's Handbook on the Gospel of Luke* (HT, 10; Leiden: Brill, 1971), p. 635; Tiede, *Luke*, p. 331; L. Morris, *The Gospel according to St Luke: An Introduction and Commentary* (TNTC; London: Inter-Varsity Press, 1974), p. 281; Godet, *Luke*, p. 233; F.W. Danker, *Jesus and the New Age according to St Luke* (St Louis: Clayton, 1972), p. 315. See too the NIV and NRSV.

148. Cf. Godet, *Luke*, p. 233.

149. See I.H. Marshall, *Luke. Historian and Theologian* (Grand Rapids:

Jesus' coming relates to the coming of God though one recent inter-preter allows the possibility of connecting such a Christology and the new exodus theme.[150]

Moreover, the Gospel writers implicitly connect this theophanic presence of God with a new exodus which delivers the people of God from sin and God's wrath.[151] They also imply that, like the first exodus, the new one starts with the Passover since Jesus' crucifixion roughly corresponds to the Passover.[152] They may have seen the new exodus as a conquest of the world (Acts 1.8).[153]

There are other nuances of 'the way'. The Gospel writers understood the way of the Lord ethically (Mt. 21.32; 22.16; Mk 12.14; Lk. 1.79; 20.21; see too Heb. 12.13 and Deut. 5.33). The way of the Lord meant the way God has commanded one to live (see Deut. 5.33). Mt. 21.32 (way of righteousness); 22.16 (way of God), and 2 Pet. 2.15 (straight way) point in similar directions. In fact, 'the way' became a standard designation of Christianity (Acts 9.2; 19.23; 22.4; 24.14, 22). Luke may connect mountains becoming low with humble and haughty people (Lk. 1.52).[154] This is possible because of the ταπεινόω–ταπεινούς link between 3.5, 1.52, and 18.14.[155] Furthermore, σκολιά in Lk. 3.5 may have a link with the τῆς γενεᾶς τῆς σκολιᾶς of Acts 2.40;[156] Peter's rebuke of Simon's heart ἡ γὰρ καρδία σου οὐκ ἔστιν εὐθεῖα ἔναντι τοῦ θεοῦ (Acts 8.21) echoes Lk. 3.4, as does Paul's rebuke of

Zondervan, 1990), pp. 100-101, and the literature cited there.

150. R.E. Watts, 'The Influence of the Isaianic New Exodus on the Gospel of Mark' (PhD thesis, Cambridge University, 1990), p. 148.

151. Several New Testament writings include the idea of salvation from slavery to sin. See Jn 8.34; Rom. 6.16 and 20; and 2 Pet. 2.19. Mt. 1.21 includes the idea of Jesus saving his people from their sins. Luke includes the idea of Jesus bringing salvation in 2.30 and Acts 2.21. The idea of ransom also may bring up the idea of being sold in slavery (Mt. 20.28 and Mk 10.45).

152. Garret, 'Exodus', p. 669, also sees this parallel.

153. J. Mánek, 'The New Exodus in the Books of Luke', *NovT* 2 (1958), p. 19, suggests that Jesus' forty days after the resurrection parallel the 40 years in the wilderness. The implication is that the Ascension begins the new Israel's conquest of the land by means of the Spirit.

154. See R.C. Tannehill, *The Narrative Unity of Luke–Acts. A Literary Interpretation* (Philadelphia: Fortress Press, 1986), I, p. 48.

155. See Tannehill, *Narrative Unity*, I, p. 48; Schweizer, *Luke*, p. 70; and Marshall, *Luke*, p. 137.

156. So Schweizer, *Luke*, p. 70. Marshall, *Luke*, p. 137, adds Phil. 2.15 and 1 Pet. 2.18.

Elymas οὐ παύσῃ διαστρέφων τὰς ὁδοὺς τοῦ κυρίου τὰς εὐθείας (Acts 13.10 with Lk. 3.4; see further Mt. 21.32 and Acts 13.10).[157] Moreover, Luke could see this new exodus leading to the conquest of the nations as Christianity first spreads to Jerusalem and then Judea and then the uttermost parts of the world (Acts 1.8). All peoples in accepting Christ and his yoke become included in the people of God thus conquered (Acts 15.17 and Amos 9.12). If New Testament writers read Isa. 40.3 as relating to the Babylonian captivity, they nevertheless saw its ultimate fulfilment in the Christ-event.[158]

In regard to the chronology of the application of Isa. 40.3 to Jesus, the Gospels themselves provide the *terminus a quo* which is for Mark perhaps the late 60s.[159] Jn 1.23 suggests that John the Baptist applied the verse to himself and looked forward to the coming of Jesus as the one coming after him (3.28). Acts 19.4 provides a similar tradition that John was preparing the people for Jesus. It is possible that the usage of the passage does stem from the historical John though it is unclear how Jesus as the coming one related to the expectation of God's theophanic presence for the historical John.[160]

Conclusions

Evidence exists that just prior to the New Testament age some Jews read Isa. 40.3 to imply the coming of God. Moreover, the language of Isa. 40.3 suggests a similar idea. In post-Christian times writers took this verse to imply the visible coming of God's presence. In some texts, a second figure comes though the nature of this second figure is unclear. Given these points, the Gospels may create the expectation of God's coming or the coming of an undefined second figure. If one accepts the indications that the evangelists class Jesus as God's presence though dis-

---

157. So Tannehill, *Narrative Unity*, I, p. 48.

158. Similarly J. Calvin, *The Gospel according to St John 1–10* (trans. T.H.L. Parker; ed. D.W. Torrance and T. Torrance; Edinburgh: Oliver & Boyd, 1959), p. 28; E.E. Ellis, *The Gospel of Luke* (NCB; London: Oliphants, rev. edn, 1974), p. 89; France, *Matthew* (1985), p. 91; and Gundry, *Matthew* (1982), pp. 44-45. Martin Luther states that Jews of his day connected Isa. 40.3 with the expectation of God's Glory coming to Jerusalem when Jews retook their homeland (Martin Luther, 'Isaiah', in *Luther's Works* [ed. H.C. Oswald; St Louis: Concordia, 1972]), XVII, p. 10.

159. On the date of Mark, see W.G. Kümmel, *Introduction to the New Testament* (trans. H.C. Kee; Nashville: Abingdon Press, rev. edn, 1975), pp. 97-98 (c. 70).

160. See Webb, 'In those days', pp. 231-330.

tinct from God the Father, the expectation of God's coming finds fulfilment in the Jesus event. Matthew, Luke and John connect Jesus and God's presence and thus may well have applied the passage to Jesus on just such a basis. This possibility, however, is one among several, and one must look for other evidence. The date at which this application first occurred was at the latest around 70 CE and perhaps earlier depending on its place in the pre-Gospel tradition, but the data are unclear as to the christological implications in the pre-Marcan era. John's Gospel attributes its application to John the Baptist.

Chapter 4

JOEL 2.32[3.5]A IN THE NEW TESTAMENT*

New Testament writers found in the words, 'All who call on the name of the Lord will be saved', a promise which had much to do with the Christian message (Acts 2.21; Rom. 10.12-13). From the mid-50s, some Christians understood Jesus as the proper object of this invocation (1 Cor. 1.2; Rom. 10.13). Moreover, this invocation distinguished Christians from those outside God's plan (Rom. 10.12-13; 1 Cor. 1.2; Acts 2.21, 38; 9.14, 21; 22.16). Thus, the following questions pose the subject matter of this chapter: (1) What is the biblical background to this phrase? (2) Is there any pre-Christian evidence of application of this phrase to a figure other than God? (3) What pre-Christian or first-century evidence is there for the 'name of God' being a distinct or semi-distinct being apart from God? (4) What is the New Testament explanation, if any, of the application of this phrase to Jesus? And (5) what is the *terminus ad quem* and *terminus a quo* of the inception of such application to Jesus?

Background Information

קרא בשם יהוה

The phrase קרא בשם יהוה or its equivalent occurs at least 25 times in the MT.[1] Commentators and translators interpret this phrase in two basic ways.[2] One renders the words 'to call on the name of the

---

*   Joel 3.1-5[MT] is 2.28-32[EVV]. Joel 3.1-21[EVV] is 4.1-21[MT].

1.   See C.J. Labuschagne, 'קרא', in *THAT*, II, p. 673, and Gen. 4.26; 12.8; 13.4; 21.33; 26.25; Exod. 33.19; 34.5; 1 Kgs 18.24 (2×), 25, 26; 2 Kgs 5.11; Isa. 12.4; 64.6; Jer. 10.25; Joel 2.32[3.5]; Zeph. 3.9; Zech. 13.9; Ps. 79.6; 80.19; 105.1; 116.4, 13, 17; and 1 Chron. 16.8. For a discussion of Isa. 44.5, see n. 14.

2.   An interesting third way is reflected in the REB at Gen. 4.26, 'to invoke the LORD by name'. See similarly Exod. 31.2; 35.30; Isa. 40.26 and 43.1 where בשם means 'by name' when appearing with קרא.

LORD'[3] while the other translates them 'to proclaim the name of the
LORD'.[4] The majority of commentators translate קָרָא בְּשֵׁם יְהוָה as 'to
call on the name of the LORD' in the majority of cases. In Gen. 12.8;
13.4 and 26.25, the text associates 'calling on the name of the LORD'
with altar building. Thus, from the outset, the biblical narrative associates
this phrase with the heart of Israel's religion. Of the two remaining
examples in Genesis, Gen. 21.33 has to do with planting a tamarisk tree
at Beersheba,[5] while the other, Gen. 4.26, gives readers little indication
of the kind of activity involved.[6] The latter, however, signals a major
advance in the relationship of humanity to God since after all the blood-
shed (4.8) and threats (4.23-24) of fallen mankind, some people then
begin to tread a different path by 'calling on the name of the LORD'. In
Exod. 33.19 and 34.5, the words וַיִּקְרָא בְשֵׁם יהוה and וְקָרָאתִי בשם יהוה
occur with Yahweh probably as the subject in both cases. The majority
of commentators and translators sees these words expressing, 'I will
proclaim my name, Yahweh' and 'He proclaimed the name, Yahweh'.[7]

---

3.   Labuschagne, 'קרא', p. 670, translates the phrase 'den Namen Jahwes
anrufen' in the majority of cases. See too H.A. Brongers, 'Die Wendung בְּשֵׁם יְהוָה
im Alten Testament', *ZAW* 77 (1965), p. 12.

4.   BDB, p. 90 [III.3.4], take Exod. 33.19; 34.5; Isa. 44.5; and Ps. 49.12 as
cases where the phrase has the latter meaning based on context. Labuschagne, 'קרא',
p. 699, writes about such usage, 'The preposition בְּ has the same meaning here as it
does in connection with בְּ דְּבֶּר' (my translation). He cites Isa. 12.4; Ps. 105.1;
1 Chron. 16.8; Exod. 33.19 and 34.5. For דבר ב (see Deut. 6.7, 1 Sam. 19.3 and 4).
Brongers, 'Die Wendung', pp. 12-13, includes the idea of proclamation in the
phrase. For a discussion of בְּ see W. Gesenius, *Gesenius' Hebrew Grammar* (rev.
E. Kautzsch; trans. A.E. Cowley; Oxford: Clarendon, 2nd edn, 1985), pp. 379-80
(§119 K). H.W. Wolff, *Joel and Amos. A Commentary on the Books of Joel and
Amos* (trans. W. Janzen, S.D. McBride, Jr and C.A. Muenchow; ed. S.D. McBride,
Jr; Hermeneia; Philadelphia: Fortress Press, 1977), p. 56 n. y, writes, 'ב קרא does
not mean "to call with", but "to enter as one who calls into intensive contact with"'.

5.   Some writers see a sacred act in the planting of such trees (see S.R. Driver,
The Book of Genesis [London: Methuen, 3rd edn, 1904], p. 215; and J. Skinner, *A
Critical and Exegetical Commentary on Genesis* [ICC; Edinburgh: T. & T. Clark,
1912], p. 327). The suggestion of the religious significance of Beersheba finds
support in Gen. 21.14-27 where it is the site of an angelophany and 26.23 where it is
the site of the theophany to Isaac.

6.   Brongers, 'Die Wendung', p. 12, takes the phrase here as 'a technical term
for the legitimate Yahweh-cult' (my translation). See too Driver, *Genesis*, p. 71.

7.   See NIV, NASB (cf. 34.5), NRSV, RSV, NRSV, NJB, NEB, REB, Tanakh, Lamsa,
Luther (cf. 34.5), Onqelos, Origen (*Hexapla*, extant at 33.19), J.I. Durham, *Exodus*
(WBC; Waco, TX: Word Books, 1987), p. 445; B.S. Childs, *The Book of Exodus. A*

The opinion of these scholars has support from the LXX which does not translate this phrase with the usual ἐπικαλεῖσθαι τὸ ὄνομα κυρίου.[8] The difficulty involved in reading the phrase in its normal sense is that Yahweh would then be invoking his own name. It is possible that Yahweh himself performs this activity to demonstrate before Moses what it means to קרא בשם יהוה.[9] If so, קרא בשם יהוה in these verses includes a recitation of the LORD's qualities (34.6-7). If one takes 34.8 as the appropriate posture for humans when 'calling on the name of the LORD', worship accompanies this activity. In 1 Kgs 18.24-26, Elijah proposes that he 'call on the name of the LORD' while the prophets of Baal 'call on the name of their god'. The context is Elijah's challenge that the God who answers by fire from heaven is indeed the true God.[10] 1 Kgs 18.36 includes the words Elijah's says when he 'calls on the name of the LORD'. He says, '"O LORD, God of Abraham, Isaac, and Israel, let it be known this day that you are God in Israel, that I am your servant, and that I have done all these things at your bidding"'. When the prophets of Baal 'call on the name of Baal', they say, 'O Baal, answer us!' Similarly in 2 Kgs 5.11, Naaman expects Elisha to 'call on the name of the LORD' as a prelude to his being healed. In Isa. 12.4-6, 'calling on the name of Yahweh' accompanies giving thanks, making the LORD's deeds known to the nations, proclaiming his name as exalted, singing to the LORD, shouting and crying out in joy. In a similar way, Ps. 105.1 associates praise with 'calling on the name of the LORD'. Thus, Old Testament writers associate קרא בשם יהוה with religious activities and in particular such ones that occur during worship. Furthermore, Isa. 41.25 suggests that 'calling on the name of the LORD' came to be a

Critical, Theological Commentary (OTL; Philadelphia: Westminster Press, 1974), p. 583; U. Cassuto, *A Commentary on the Book of Exodus* (trans. I. Abrahams; Jerusalem: Magnes Press, 1967), p. 436 (33.19); and Labuschagne, 'קרא', p. 673. J.P. Hyatt, *Commentary on Exodus* (NCB; London: Oliphants, 1971), p. 322; NASB and Luther see the subject of 34.5 as Moses (cf. R.W.L. Moberly, *At the Mountain of God. Story and Theology in Exodus 32–34* [JSOTSup, 22; Sheffield: JSOT Press, 1983], p. 86).

8.   Exod. 33.19 reads καλέσω ἐπὶ τῷ ὀνόματί μου Κύριος. Exod. 34.5 reads ἐκάλεσεν τῷ ὀνόματι κυρίου.

9.   So Moberly, *Mountain*, p. 77. Along similar lines, see Cassuto, *Exodus*, p. 439. God speaks in the third person in this section which supports this thesis (see 34.7, ינקה).

10.   Josephus, *Ant.* 8.338-42, interprets the Old Testament here as an invocation of and prayer to God.

designation of those who worshipped God.[11] Similarly, Jer. 10.25 compares '...the nations who do not know you' (הגוים אשר לא ידעוך), to '...the tribes which do not call on your name' (משפחות אשר בשמך לא קראו). Ps. 79.6 also criticizes the 'kingdoms that do not call on your name'. Thus, these passages suggest that 'calling on the name of the LORD' was an activity indicative of one's inclusion in the people of God. Some passages associate 'calling on the name of the LORD' with a previous purification which perhaps suggests a cultic background (Zeph 3.9; Zech. 13.9 and Ps. 80.19). Ps. 116.4 associates 'calling on the name of the Lord' with an appeal for help. Verses 13 and 17 also associate 'calling on the name of the LORD' with cultic activities.[12] So far, 'calling on the name of...' referred to religious acts directed to the divine. However, Isa. 44.5 MT applies 'calling on the name of...' to Jacob. One can make a good case for either repointing the MT or reading the verb as reflexive.[13] Either of these options makes better sense in the context because 44.5a would then parallel 5c while 5b would parallel 5d.

In summary, 'calling on the name of the LORD' in the MT is a phrase which legitimately applies to the God of Israel and illegitimately to false gods. I saw one exception to this practice in Isa. 44.5 which a number of commentators and translators favour pointing differently from the MT. I furthermore saw that 'calling on the name of the LORD' was a religious act which characterised and even determined God's people.

ἐπικαλεῖσθαι τὸ ὄνομα κυρίου

The LXX frequently translates [יהוה] קרא בשם as ἐπικαλεῖσθαι τὸ ὄνομα [κυρίου].[14] The LXX translators usually read ב as marking the

---

11.   On this reading see NIV, NASB, Lamsa, and Luther. The NJB, and NRSV read a passive 'has been/was summoned by name' with a Qumran MS and the LXX (similarly REB). JB and NEB support 'summoned him.'

12.   Similarly in Josephus, *Ant.* 2.275, Moses learns God's name ἵνα θύων ἐξ ὀνόματος αὐτὸν παρεῖναι τοῖς ἱεροῖς παρακαλῇ 'so that, when sacrificing, he might invoke Him by name to be present at the sacred rites'.

13.   Isa. 44.5 (MT וְזֶה יִקְרָא בְשֵׁם־יַעֲקֹב) perhaps should be amended to יִקָּרֵא from קָרָא (so Symmachus and the editors of BHS, NRSV) or the verb is reflexive (so NEB, REB, NIV, NJB, JB, LXX, Tanakh, and Lamsa, cf. NASB 'call on the name of Jacob'; and Targum 'pray by the name of Jacob').

14.   Gen. 4.26; 13.4; 26.25; Jer. 10.25; Zeph. 3.9; Zech. 13.9; Ps. 78.6; 104.1; 114.4; 115.4; Joel 3.5. The following references deviate from the norm as indicated: Gen. 12.8 (ἐπι τῷ ὀνόματι κυρίου); 21.33 (τὸ ὄνομα κυρίου Θεὸς αἰώνιος); Exod. 33.19 (καλέσω ἐπὶ τῷ ὀνόματί μου Κύριος); 34.5 (ἐκάλεσεν τῷ ὀνόματι

object of the verb and used the translation surrogate κύριος as a translation replacement for יהוה.[15] Furthermore, they understood שם יהוה as having a genitival rather than an appositional relationship.[16] For קרא, the translators chose ἐπικαλεῖσθαι which could denote invocation either of gods or men.[17] The LXX shows a clear tendency toward using the middle for invoking God, and, according to my count, of the 114 occurrences of ἐπικαλέω in the middle voice all but 11[18] refer to invoking God or a god.[19] Thus, both the Hebrew and Greek phrases imply invocation.[20]

κυρίου); 3 Kgdms 18.24 (ἐν ὀνόματι κυρίου), (βοᾶτε ἐν ὀνόματι θεῶν ὑμῶν), 25 (ἐν ὀνόματι θεοῦ αὐτοῦ), 26 (ἐπεκαλοῦντο ἐν ὀνόματι τοῦ Βααλ); 4 Kgdms 5.11 (ἐν ὀνόματι θεοῦ αὐτοῦ); Isa. 12.4 (βοᾶτε τὸ ὄνομα αὐτοῦ); 41.25 (κληθήσονται τῷ ὀνόματί μου).

15. For a defence of κύριος as the original reading of the LXX for יהוה, see Albert Pietersma, 'κύριος or Tetragram: A Renewed Quest for the Original Septuagint', in *De Septuaginta: Studies in Honour of John William Wevers on His 65th Birthday* (ed. A. Pietersma and C. Cox; Mississauga, Ontario: Benben, 1984), pp. 85-101. Cf. G. Howard, 'The Tetragram and the New Testament', *JBL* 96 (1977), pp. 63-83. On κυρίου see Chapter 3, pp. 90-94.

16. See Gen. 21.33 where the Lord's name is the appellation 'God eternal'.

17. In the classical period, writers used ἐπικαλέω to denote summoning a god or goddess as early as the fifth century BCE (Herodotus, *Histories* 1.99; 2.39; 3.8, 65; Aristophanes, *Lysistrata* 1280). For use of the middle voice in summoning the gods see Xenophon, *Hellenica* 2.3.55. For invocation of men see Herodotus, *Histories* 8.64; 5.1, 63; Xenophon *Hellenica* 2.3.55; Thucydides 1.101; 3.59; Antiphon, 1.30; Plutarch, *Tiberius Gracchus* 16; *Marcellus* 2; and Homer, *Odyssey* 7.189.

18. 3 Kgdms 13.4 and 4 Kgdms 23.17 (2×) (ἐπὶ τὸ θυσιαστήριον Βαιθηλ); Jdt. 7.26 (the army of Holofernes); Job 17.14; Prov. 18.6 (death); Ps. 41.7 (abyss); Ps. 49.12 (names); Prov. 1.28; 2.3; 8.12; Wis. 7.7; 11.4 (wisdom/understanding); Hos. 7.11 (Egypt); Amos 4.5 (confessions); Jer. 4.20 (humility).

19. Gen. 4.26; 12.8; 13.4; 21.33; 26.25; Deut. 4.7; 33.19; 1 Kgdms 12.17, 18; 2 Kgdms 22.4, 7; 3 Kgdms 8.43, 52; 13.4; 17.21; 18.24, 25, 26, 27, 28; 4 Kgdms 5.11; 23.17; 1 Chron. 4.10; 16.8; 2 Chron. 6.33; Jdt. 3.8; 6.21; 8.17; 7.26; 9.4; 16.2; Est. 4.8; 5.1; Job 5.1, 8; 17.14; 21.10; Ps. 4.1; 13.4; 17.3, 6; 19.7, 9; 24.14; 30.17; 41.7; 48.12; 49.15; 52.4; 55.9; 74.1; 78.6; 79.18; 80.7; 85.5; 88.26; 90.15; 98.6. 101.2; 104.1; 114.2, 4; 115.4, 8; 117.5; 137.3; 144.18; 146.9; Prov. 1.28; 2.3; 8.12; 18.6; 21.13; Wis. 7.7; 11.4; 13.18, 19; Sir. 2.10; 46.5, 16; 47.5, 18; 48.20; 51.10; Hos. 7.7, 11; Amos 4.5, 12; 9.12; Joel 3.5; Jon. 1.6; Zeph. 3.9; Zech. 13.9; Mal. 1.4; Isa. 18.7; 55.5, 6; 64.7; Jer. 4.20; 10.25; 11.14; 20.8; Bar. 3.7; Lam. 3.55, 57; 2 Macc. 3.15, 22, 31; 7.37; 8.2; 12.6, 15, 28, 36; 13.10; 14.34, 46; 15.21, 22; *3 Macc.* 1.27; 5.7; 6.1; *4 Macc.* 12.18.

20. Philo, *Vit. Mos.* 2.203-204 and Josephus, *Ant.* 2.276 regard it as wrong to

Joel 2.32[3.5]a in the MT, LXX and Non-Canonical Jewish Literature
The book of Joel comes from an otherwise unknown prophet whose date
scholars debate with little consensus.[21] Furthermore, there is a question
over the book's unity.[22] These questions shall remain open for me since
I am studying the likely understanding of the verse which pre-Christian
or first-century Jews had. What is important is the text as it stood at that
time, thus I shall treat it as a unity. Joel 1.1-12 recounts the recent devastation of the land by locusts.[23] This devastation leads Joel to call for
repentance lest the 'day of the LORD' come immediately (1.15). 2.1-11
compares the coming day to the devastation which has just ravaged the
land. Verses 12-14 offer a way of escape for the inhabitants of Judah with
vv. 15-17 being the prophet's plea to the unrepentant people. 2.18 either
represents a promise of God's action (NIV) or the recounting of God's
action after a successful call to repentance (LXX, NJB, JB, REB, RSV).
God further promises restoration of the land in 2.19b-27 and that he will
pour out his Spirit on all flesh transcending age, sex and class distinctions
(2.28-29[3.1-2]). Joel 2.30-31[3.3-4] points to heavenly harbingers of
doom which will proceed the day of the LORD. Yet in the midst of these
portents, Joel promises that those who 'call on the name of the LORD'
will be saved. Joel 3.1-8[4.1-8] promises the restoration of Judah and
Jerusalem while 3.9-11a[4.9-11a] pledges judgment on Tyre and Sidon.

The differences between the LXX, Qumran and the MT in 3.1-5 are
not great (see my chart below).[24] The first is the addition of καί to 'I

speak God's name aloud, so invocation would not use God's sacred covenant name.

21.   Compare Wolff, *Joel*, pp. 4-5 (first half of the fourth century); L.C. Allen,
The Books of Joel, Obadiah, Jonah and Micah (NICOT; Grand Rapids: Eerdmans,
1976), p. 24 (favours 520–599); see too J.A. Soggin, *Introduction to the Old Testa-
ment from Its Origins to the Closing of the Alexandrian Canon* (trans. J. Bowden
(Philadelphia: Westminster, rev. edn, 1980), p. 352; T. Hiebert, 'Joel, Book of', in
ABD, III, pp. 878-79; H.G.M. Williamson, 'Joel', in *ISBE*, II, pp. 1077-79; and
P.C. Craigie, *The Old Testament. Its Background, Growth, and Content* (Nashville:
Abingdon, 1986), p. 178.

22.   Hiebert, 'Joel', pp. 873-74, supports a division between 1.1–2.27[1-2] and
2.28–3.21[3-4].

23.   See D.K. Stuart, *Hosea–Micah* (WBC; Waco, TX: Word Books, 1990),
pp. 232-34, who suggests that the locusts are figurative representatives of the
Babylonians.

24.   Joel 2.32[3.5] occurs in Qumran manuscript Mur 88 with no significant
changes from the MT. See P. Benoit, J.T. Milik, and R. de Vaux, *Les Grottes de
Marabba'ât* (DJD, 2; Oxford: Clarendon Press, 1961), p. 185.

will pour out' (אֶשְׁפּוֹך).[25] The next change is 'from my Spirit' (ἀπὸ τοῦ πνεύματός μου) which translates simply 'my spirit' (רוחי) in the MT. This change spells out that it is not the totality of God's Spirit which he outpours.[26] In v. 2, the LXX adds 'and' to 'your young men' (בחוריכם). Ἀμίδα 'vapour' translates 'columns' (תימרות). In v. 4, 'suddenly appearing' ἐμφανῆ replaces 'dreadful' (הנורא). ἀνασῳζόμενος in v. 5 translates the MT 'escaped remnant' (פליטה). If ἀνασῳζόμενος is middle, one could read the text, 'a deliverer', perhaps the messiah.[27] If passive, the meaning is 'delivered one' (reading פליט). Lastly, בשרידים 'among the remaining ones' in v. 5 becomes εὐαγγελιζόμενοι (reading בשרים).

In *Targum Jonathan*, one finds a few changes to the MT. The text is as follows:

> After that I will pour out my *Holy* Spirit on all flesh; and your sons and daughters shall prophesy; your old men shall dream dreams and your young men shall see visions. I will even pour out my *Holy* Spirit upon menservants and maidservants in those days. I will set signs in the heavens and on earth: blood and fire and columns of smoke. The sun shall be turned into darkness and the moon into blood before the coming of the great and terrible day *which will come from* the Lord. But everyone who *prays in* the name of the Lord shall be delivered, for there shall be *deliverance* on Mount Zion and in Jerusalem, as the Lord said. *They shall be delivered whom the Lord appoints.*[28]

'My Spirit' in the MT becomes 'the Spirit of my holiness' (i.e. my Holy Spirit) in vv. 1 and 2. In v. 4b, 'before the great and terrible day of the LORD comes' is 'before the great and terrible day which is destined to come from before the LORD.'[29] The phrase, 'among the remaining

---

25.   'And' here is the virtual equivalent of ו 'that' following היה in Hebrew.

26.   See too D.L. Bock, *Proclamation From Prophecy and Pattern: Lucan Old Testament Christology* (JSNTSup, 12; Sheffield: JSOT Press, 1987), p. 164; and D.L. Phelps, 'Implications of Lucan-Peter's Pentecost Homily for Christian Preaching of the Old Testament' (PhD dissertation, Southwestern Baptist Theological Seminary, 1990), p. 20.

27.   H. van de Sandt, 'The Fate of the Gentiles in Joel and Acts 2. An Intertextual Study', *ETL* 66 (1990), pp. 65-66 n. 36, recognizes the possibility of a middle but points to פליטה of Joel 2.3 which the translators render ἀνασῳζόμενος.

28.   The translation is that of K.J. Cathcart and R.P. Gordon, *The Targum of the Minor Prophets. Translated, with a Critical Introduction, Apparatus, and Notes* (ArB, 14; Wilmington, DE: Glazier, 1987), p. 71.

29.   The above is my translation of רבא ודחילא קדם מיתי יומא דעתיד למיתי מן קדם יוי. See Alexander Sperber, *The Bible in Aramaic* (Leiden: Brill, 1962), III, p. 414.

ones' becomes 'saved ones' in v. 5. The most significant Rabbinic text for my purposes is *y. Ber.* 9.13.[30] the text says,

> But in regard to God, it is not the same: if a calamity comes on a man, he should not invoke Michael or Gabriel but God who will hear it, as it is written, 'Everyone who calls upon the name of the Eternal one shall be saved'.[31]

This text states that men should not appeal to Michael or Gabriel but to God alone.[32] It underscores the idea that calling on the name of God was a Jew's right and did not imply the use of an intermediary. In the same work, R. Pineˢchas passes on a tradition where יקרא 'will call' in Joel 2.32[3.5]a becomes נקרא 'is called'. This modification is perhaps a limitation of the possibility that God's salvation was open to non-Jews.

The Name of the LORD as Distinct from God

Several scholars suggest that the name of the Lord has a certain distinction from God in the MT. For example, von Rad sees Israel's 'name of Yahweh' as 'a holy reality of a quite special kind (on occasion coming almost to the point of [their] understanding it in a material way)'.[33] Yet in a number of cases in the MT, the 'name of God' is a simple appellation (e.g. Gen. 16.13; Deut. 28.58; 32.3, and Josh. 9.9). This appellational usage is related to the Niphal of קרא + יהוה בשם denoting God's ownership.[34] Therefore, it is possible that 'calling on the name of the Lord' could refer to an appeal simply to God and not an appeal to 'the name' as somehow distinct from God.

In other verses, however, the 'name of the LORD' acquires a certain

---

30. H.L. Strack and P. Billerbeck, *Kommentar zum Neuen Testament aus Talmud und Midrasch* (Munich: Beck, 1924), II, pp. 615-17, provide several texts which use Joel 2.28-32[3.1-5] relating the passage to future times. P. Berakhoth also comes from Strack and Billerbeck.

31. The above is my translation of M. Schwab, *Le talmud de Jérusalem* (Paris: G.-P. Maisonneuve, 1960), I, p. 154.

32. P. Hayman, 'Monotheism—A Misused Word in Jewish Studies?', *JJS* 42 (1992), p. 10, notes several Talmudic texts which associate the name of angels and magical incantations.

33. G. von Rad, *Old Testament Theology* (trans. D.M.G. Stalker; London: SCM Press, 1975), I, p. 183. See similarly W. Eichrodt, *Theology of the Old Testament* (trans. J.A. Baker; London: SCM Press, 1967), II, pp. 41-42.

34. See Deut. 28.10; Isa. 63.19; Jer. 7.10, 11, 14, 30; 14.9; 15.16; 25.29; 32.34; 34.15; Amos 9.12; 1 Kgs 8.43; 1 Chron. 13.6; 2 Chron. 6.33; Dan. 9.19; and Brongers, 'Die Wendung', p. 13.

distinctiveness from God even if that distinctiveness is only linguistic. For instance, the Jerusalem temple is a house in which the 'name of the Lord' dwells.[35] Furthermore, the biblical writers begin to use language normally applied to individuals to the 'name of the Lord': one fears (Ps. 61.5[6]; 102.15[16], and Isa. 59.19), sings praises to (Ps. 7.17; 18.49[50], and 44.8[9]), gives thanks to (Ps. 44.8[9]; 122.4, and 1 Chron. 16.35), loves (Ps. 5.11[12]; 69.37[36], and Isa. 56.6), and finds protection in the 'name of the LORD' (Ps. 20.1[2]).[36] Moreover, Isa. 30.27-28, says,

> See, the name of the LORD comes from far away, burning with his anger, and in thick rising smoke; his lips are full of indignation, and his tongue is like a devouring fire; his breath is like an overflowing stream that reaches up to the neck—to sift the nations with the sieve of destruction, and to place on the jaws of the peoples a bridle that leads them astray.

Here, the connection with devouring fire may echo Deut. 4.11-12 and God's arrival at Sinai. Moreover in Exod. 23.21, God speaks of his angel in whom his name dwells.[37] There seems in this verse a distinction between God who will remain in heaven and his 'name' which, in the angel, will be with the Israelites on earth.

The question, however, remains whether in the MT the name of God is completely distinct or whether in some cases it was a way to speak of the immanence of God. The latter appears more probable to me since passages like 1 Kgs 8.13, 20, 27 and 29 seem to identify God and his name. Thus, the distinction between God and his name in the MT never succeeds in fully separating the two since frequently 'the name of the

35.   See Deut. 12.11; 14.23; 16.2, 6; 26.2; 1 Kgs 3.2; 5.3, 5; 8.17, 20, 44, 48; 9.7; 1 Chron. 22.7, 8, 10, 19; 28.3; 2 Chron. 2.1[1.18], 4[2.3]; 6.7, 9, 10, 38; 7.20 and 20.8.

36.   See Eichrodt, *Theology*, II, pp. 42-43.

37.   R.N. Longenecker, *The Christology of Early Jewish Christianity* (London: SCM Press, 1970), p. 42, calls this verse the classic one for seeing the name of God having a certain independence from God. The exact translation and meaning of this phrase is difficult to determine: see the NIV 'my Name is in him'; REB 'my authority rests in him'; NRSV 'my name is in him'; Durham, *Exodus*, p. 310, 'my Presence is with him'; Hyatt, *Exodus*, p. 251, 'my name is in him' (self-manifestation of the deity); Cassuto, *Exodus*, p. 306, (Yahweh's self-manifestation); and NJB 'for my name is in him' (note 'The name expresses and represents the person himself'). L.W. Hurtado, *One God, One Lord. Early Christian Devotion and Ancient Jewish Monotheism* (Philadelphia: Fortress Press, 1988), p. 160, questions Exod. 23.20-21 as a reference to the Angel of the LORD. Interestingly, Justin Martyr, *Dialogue* 75, equates the angel with Joshua and the LORD with Jesus.

LORD' appears in synonymous parallelism with 'God' or the 'LORD'.[38] The parallelism between κύριος and τὸ ὄνομα κυρίου in the LXX also makes it clear that 'the name of the Lord' is not a completely distinct being from God there (Ps. 68.31; 102.1; 114.4; Lev. 24.11, 15; 22.32).

However, once one turns outside the LXX and MT, one finds some evidence of 'the name of god X' in personal terms and distinct from that god. One example occurs in the Ugaritic literature dating from the fourteenth century BCE. In one place, the writer describes Ashtoreth as 'the name of Baal'.[39] Ashtoreth is a goddess like Baal's sister Anath.[40] In one story, Ashtoreth and Anath seize Baal's hands and keep him from killing god Yamm. Thus, the 'name of Baal' is somehow personally distinct from Baal.[41] Astarte in an Eshmuna inscription is also 'the name of Baal'.[42] In another inscription one finds, 'To the Lady, to Tanit "Face of Baal", and to the Lord, to Baal Hammon'.[43] Here 'the face of Baal' has a distinct name from Baal. However, a further inscription says, 'When God shines forth the mountains melt...Baal on the day of war...for the name of God on [the] day of War'.[44] The latter text compares Baal to the name of God. Closer to the first century CE, in Philo one finds,

---

38.   Ps. 99.6b; 30.4 [5]; 34.3[4]; 66.4; 69.30[31]; 148.5; Isa. 24.15; 50.10; 60.9, and 2 Sam. 22.50.

39.   *Poems of Baal and Anath*, III AB 8-9, 'May [Horon] break, [O Yamm, may Horon break] thy head, Ashtoreth [Name of Baal thy pate]'; *The Story of King Keret*, C VI 56-59, 'May Horon break, O my son, May Horon break thy head, Ashtoreth name of Baal thy pate' (in *ANET*, 130, 149).

40.   In *The Story of King Keret* A III 146-5, the writer says, '...whose fairness is like Anath's fairness, [whose] beau[ty] like Ashtoreth's beauty', thereby likening Ashtoreth to Anath (*ANET*, p. 144). See *Poems of Baal and Anath*, V AB D 85 for the identification of Anath as Baal's sister.

41.   Cf. A.A. Anderson, *The Book of the Psalms* (NCB; Greenwood, SC: Attic Press, 1972), I, p. 175, who sees Ashtoreth as a hypostasis of God.

42.   See Eichrodt, *Theology*, II, p. 44.

43.   M. Sznycer, 'Une inscription punique inédite de Carthage', *Semitica* 37 (1987), pp. 63-67, translated in abstract, Bernard F. Blatto, 'Abstract', *OTA* 12 (1989), 29.

44.   From M. Weinfeld, 'Kuntillet 'Ajrud Inscriptions and their Significance', *Studi Epigrafici e Linguistici* 1 (1984), pp. 121-30, 126, cited by R.S. Hess, 'Yahweh and His Asherah? Epigraphic Evidence for Religious Pluralism in Old Testament Times', in *One God, One Lord in a World of Religious Pluralism* (ed. A.D. Clarke and B.W. Winter; Cambridge: Tyndale House, 1991), p. 22.

But if there be any as yet unfit to be called a Son of God, let him press to take his place under God's First-born, the Word, who holds the eldership among the angels, their ruler as it were. And many names are his, for he is called, 'the Beginning', and *the Name of God*, and His Word, and the Man after His image, and 'he that sees', that is Israel (*Conf. Ling.*,146, my emphasis).

Philo, in this passage, identifies the 'Name of God' as the Logos. It is difficult to say what the Logos is for Philo, but in at least one passage, he seems to distinguish partially between the one transcendent God and the Logos:

Yet there can be no cowering fear for the man who relies on the hope of the divine comradeship, to whom are addressed the words, 'I am the God who appeared to thee in the place of God' (Gen. xxxi. 13). Surely a right and noble cause of vaunting it is for a soul, that God deigns to shew Himself to and converse with it. And do not fail to mark the language used, but carefully inquire whether there are two Gods; for we read 'I am the God that appeared to thee', not 'in my place' but 'in the place of God', as though it were another's. *What, then, are we to say? He that is truly God is One, but those that are improperly so called are more than one. Accordingly the holy word in the present instance has indicated Him Who is truly God by means of the articles saying 'I am the God', while it omits the article when mentioning him who is improperly so called, saying 'Who appeared to thee in the place' not 'of the God', but simply 'of God.'* Here it gives the title of 'God' to His chief Word, not from any superstitious nicety in applying names, but with one aim before him, to use words to express facts (Philo, *Som.* 1.227-30, emphasis mine).

Philo identifies the Logos as θεός improperly speaking but nevertheless sees the closest relationship between the two. D.T. Runia says, 'The Logos in Philo can be defined in the most general terms as that aspect or part of the divine that stands in relation to created reality'.[45] Philo could think of the Logos as the 'name of God' and thus could conceive of 'calling on the name of the Lord' as an invocation of the Logos though I underscore that he does not so apply that text to the Logos. Some further examples of the 'name' as a partially distinct being from God may occur in the post-New Testament times.[46]

45. D.T. Runia, *Philo of Alexandria and the* Timaeus *of Plato* (Philosophia Antiqua, 44; Leiden: Brill, 1986), p. 449.

46. See *The Gospel of Truth* 38; *Apoc. Abr.* 10.3-8; Longenecker, *Christology*, p. 42; and J. Fossum, *The Name of God and the Angel of the Lord. Samaritan and Jewish Concepts of Intermediation and the Origin of Gnosticism* (WUNT, 36; Tübingen: Mohr [Siebeck], 1985).

Thus, there is some evidence that 'the name of the Lord' was more than a appellation to some Jews. Furthermore, some evidence exists of a certain distinction between God and his name, but there is little evidence within the biblical narrative that 'the name of the Lord' was a completely distinct entity from God. In the literature outside the Old Testament, Philo offers some evidence that he understood the 'name of God' as a second figure though again the nature of that figure is unclear. Other Jews did not understand the name as a completely separate entity.[47]

'The Name of the Lord' as a Messianic Title

What evidence exists that a pre-Christian or first-century Jew could have understood 'the name of the LORD' as a messianic title? The earliest possible evidence I found depends on a close look at 1QIsaᵃ. John Chamberlain suggests that 'Torah' is a messianic title in 1QIsaᵃ 51.4. He also suggests that in several places 1QIsaᵃ has changed the pronominal suffixes in the Isaiah scroll so as to cause the texts to refer to the Messiah rather than particular aspects of God.[48] In ch. 51, one finds,

> (4) Attend to me, my people, and give ear to me, my nation, for Torah will go forth from me, and my judgment I will establish as a light for peoples. (5) Near is my righteousness; my deliverance has gone forth, and *his* arms will rule the peoples. In *him* the coastlands trust, and for *his* arm they wait.... (6) But my salvation shall be forever, and my justice will never be confounded... (8) But my justice shall be forever, and my salvation to the ages.

Thus, Chamberlain sees 'Torah' as a messianic title. The people will await 'Torah'. Chamberlain suggests that the messianic identification of 'Torah' explains some of the minor differences between 1QIsaᵃ and the MT. 'My arms', 'in me', and 'in my arm' become the third person singular 'his arms', 'in him', and 'in his arm'. If 'Torah' is a messianic title, there is evidence that 'the Name' was also a messianic title: 1QIsaᵃ 26.8 states, 'O LORD, we await your Name, and the desire of our soul is for your Torah'. That is, since Torah and Name are in parallelism, they may refer to the same thing, the messiah. If Chamberlain is right, it would be possible to read 'calling on the name of the LORD' as calling

---

47. E.g. Josephus, *Ant.* 6.186, connects 1 Sam. 17.45 with David coming with *God* as his armour. This passage makes me doubt whether Josephus understood the name as distinct from God although it could represent God's immanence.

48. J.V. Chamberlain, 'The Functions of God as Messianic Titles in the Complete Qumran Isaiah Scroll', *VT* 5 (1955), p. 369.

on the messiah though I underscore that 1QIsa[a] offers no further evidence that this possibility in fact happened.

The New Testament provides no clear evidence that writers identified the messiah as the name of God.[49] In the Gospels, some texts emphasize Jesus' name, but this is a long way from the idea of Jesus as 'the name' (Mk 9.38; 16.17; Lk. 9.49; 10.17; Mt. 7.22; 12.21 [cf. LXX Isa. 11.10 and Rom. 15.12]; Jas 5.14; see too 1 Cor. 6.11; 1 Jn 2.12; Heb. 13.15).[50] Jas 2.7 may imply that Jesus' name has been invoked over Christians.[51] This invocation is one in the Old Testament which denoted God's ownership.[52] But the text does not necessarily identify Jesus as God's Name. John's Gospel closely associates Jesus and the name: the Father will glorify his name by glorifying the Son (12.28; cf. 13.32). This is the closest example I found in the New Testament, but it does not clearly identify the Son as the Name (cf. 17.1, 5, 6, 11).

Other Data Regarding Invocation and the Name
Several extra-canonical texts allow a second figure to be the object of petition or invocation. In *1 En.* 90.37, the animals petition the snow-white cow whom some scholars identify as the messiah.[53] This petitioning is not necessarily the same as invocation since petitioning need not include an attitude of worship as does invocation in the Old Testament. In 90.30, all the animals petition the sheep (the true remnant of Israel) in the new temple and worship the sheep (compare Rev. 3.9). This 'worship' does not necessarily mean that the sheep replace the Lord as the object of cultic adoration (see *1 En.* 90.33, 34, 40).

49. On this question see A. Grillmeier, *Christ in Christian Tradition. From the Apostolic Age to Chalcedon (451)* (trans. J.S. Bowden; London: Mowbrays, 1965), pp. 46-47; J. Daniélou, *The Theology of Jewish Christianity* (trans. J.A. Baker; Chicago: Regnery, 1964), pp. 147-63; and Longenecker, *Christology*, p. 48.

50. J.A. Fitzmyer, 'κύριος', in *EWNT*, II, p. 815, takes Jas 5.10 as a reference to God. ἐν τῷ ὀνόματι κυρίου means while speaking the name of the Lord. If this refers to Christ, James would affirm that Old Testament prophets spoke in the name of Jesus. It may be the difference ἐν τῷ ὀνόματι τοῦ κυρίου and ἐν τῷ ὀνόματι κυρίου (see above pp. 94-97) is deliberate to draw a distinction between Jesus' name and God's name since Jas 5.14 seems clearly to refer to Jesus. However, some minuscules add τοῦ before κυρίου in Jas 5.10.

51. So Rudolf Bultmann, *Theology of the New Testament*, trans. Kendrick Grobel (New York: Scribner's, 1951-55), 1 pp. 125-26.

52. See above n. 34.

53. See G.R. Beasley-Murray, *Jesus and the Kingdom of God* (Grand Rapids: Eerdmans; Exeter: Paternoster, 1986), p. 57, and the literature cited there.

According to *T. Levi* 5.5, Levi wants to petition an angel on the day of tribulation. *T. Dan.* 5.10-11 associates Mal. 4.5-6[3.23-24] with the Lord's Salvation, the Leader of Judah, who will rescue those enslaved to Beliar (compare 11QMelchizedek). This one is the prophet, but it is unclear if it is he or the Lord on whom the delivered will call (cf. 5.13 which may suggest Christian interpolation). There may be a connection in *1 Enoch* 48 between the name and the Son of man (*1 En.* 48.7 and 50.3). Furthermore, it may have been possible that the angel in whom God's name dwells would have been the object of invocation as the Name or as housing the Name. Moreover, some texts use 'in the name of' formula for angels and God.[54] M. Werner submits that late Judaism invoked angels as 'lord'.[55] He implies that such was Paul's under-standing in so applying 'calling on' to Jesus. If 'calling on the name of' meant only invocation, one could indeed see the phrase as applied to Jesus as relatively meaningless.[56] However, the evidence for this position is lacking in pre-Christian Judaism, and the Old Testament background clearly points to prayerful even cultic activities associated with this phrase. Moreover, 'calling on the name of', unlike invocation in general, occurs, as far as I can find, only with the divine as the object in pre-Christian Judaism. Thus, it is possible that Jews distinguished between the invocation of angels and 'calling on the name of the LORD'.[57] The Old Testament prohibits invoking other gods (Exod. 23.13 by implica-tion; Josh. 23.7), although Prov. 1.28 allows that men may invoke Wisdom in terms that underline Wisdom as standing in the place of God (see Deut. 4.29). Josephus held that invoking God directly was possible and that Moses invoked God's name during sacrifices (*Ant.* 2.12.4; 2.16.1). Maccabean Martyrs made their last monotheistic confession by calling 'on the God of our ancestors' (*4 Macc.* 12.17).[58] These data make it likely that Jews distinguished invoking men and invoking God.

54.   See Hayman, 'Monotheism', p. 10, and the examples cited there.
55.   M. Werner, *The Formation of Christian Dogma. An Historical Study of Its Problem* (trans. and ed. S.G.F. Brandon; London: A. & C. Black, 1957), p. 123.
56.   Cf. Stephen in Acts 7.59 who calls on (ἐπικαλούμενον) Jesus the moment before his death which suggests ἐπικαλεῖσθαι when Jesus is its object is indeed a prayer (see too A.M. Hunter, *Paul and his Predecessors* [London: SCM Press, rev. edn, 1961], p. 84; cf. *Martyrdom of Polycarp* 14).
57.   At the end of the second century CE, Irenaeus, *Against Heresies*, 2.32.4, notes the distinction between the invocation of angels and 'calling on the name of the Lord Jesus'.
58.   In later times, the opponents of Christianity recognized that 'calling on the

Other Occurrences of 'Calling on the name of...'

'Calling on the name of...' occurs several times in pre-Christian and first-century Jewish Literature. Josephus, *War* 5.438, writes, 'and oft though their victims implored them, invoking the awful name of God...not a morsel was given them'.[59] Josephus understands 'calling on the name of God' as an action of the highest import for the Jews because his point in 5.438 is that the ruffians who stole food during the siege should have been ashamed to take such food when their victims 'called on the name of God' (see too 5.429).[60] Philo, *Det. Pot. Ins.* 138-40, also recognizes the importance of the phrase 'calling on the name of the LORD' when he states that this action greatly distinguishes Enos from the rest of humanity. Quoting Gen. 4.26 (LXX), Philo relates this action as seeking to obtain 'good things from the only bountiful God.' Philo, *Det. Pot. Ins.* 139, even connects this event with Gen. 5.1 and the 'nativity of men'. From the information in Philo and Josephus, I infer that 'calling on the name of the LORD' was an activity of the highest import for Jews. Both writers direct the phrase to the divine alone.

However, an interesting related datum occurs in Josephus, *War* 2.294. When Florus pillaged the Temple treasury, the Jews 'invoked the name of Caesar imploring him to liberate them from the tyranny of Florus'.[61] This passage is the closest example I found of a pre-Christian or first-century Jew applying 'calling on the name of...' to a non-divine second figure. However, one should notice that Josephus uses ἀνακαλέω not ἐπικαλέω. In a related text, Paul, according to Acts 25.11, 'called on Caesar' using ἐπικαλεῖσθαι but not ὄνομα καίσαρος. In *Roman History* 42.24.4, Dio Cassius (ca. 155–230 CE) relates a story of Caelius who 'invokes the name of Caesar' before Servilius to gain his request.[62] This evidence, though late for reference to New Testament data, when combined with Josephus, *War* 2.294 and Acts 25.11 at least makes possible that a non-Jew might read the phrase 'calling on the name

Most High' was central to Christianity (Origen, *Contra Celsum* 504-505). See J. Stevenson, *A New Eusebius. Documents Illustrative of the History of the Church to AD 337* (London: SPCK, 1968), pp. 69-70. The text adds, 'or whatever name you prefer' which could imply Jesus' name.

59. The relevant part is τὸ φρικτὸν ἐπικαλουμένων ὄνομα τοῦ θεοῦ.

60. In Josephus, *Ant.* 8.338-39, Josephus reads 'calling on the name of the their gods' as ἐπικαλέσασθαι τοὺς ἰδίους θεούς which he interprets as a prayer.

61. The Greek is καίσαρος ἀνεκάλουν ὄνομα καὶ τῆς Φλώρου τυραννίδος ἐλευθεροῦν σφᾶς ἱκέτευον.

62. The Greek is τό τε τοῦ Καίσαρος ὄνομα ἐπικαλούμενος.

of…' as invocation of a superior and not necessarily a deity.

In summary, the MT represents 'calling on the name of the LORD' as a particularly religious action to be directed exclusively to the divine. While several changes occur in the LXX and non-canonical Jewish literature, this 'calling on the name of the LORD' continued to refer to the divine in pre-Christian Jewish literature. Some evidence exists that 'the name of the LORD' was a way to describe the immanence of God, but evidence for the 'the name' being completely distinct in the MT and LXX is lacking. Josephus has a phrase very close to the biblical one which applies to Caesar, but among pre-Christian Jewish writers I found no example of the actual biblical phrase applied to anyone other than the LORD God of Israel.

'Calling on the Name of the LORD' in the New Testament

I shall now turn to the New Testament usage of 'calling on the name of the LORD.' These are Acts 2.21; 9.14, 21; 22.16; Rom. 10.13 and 1 Cor. 1.2. I shall examine the origin, date, and implications of this practice as applied to Jesus. First, I include a comparison of sources:

NT[63]	¹⁷καὶ ἔσται ἐν ταῖς ἐσχάταις ἡμέραις, λέγει ὁ θεός,	
LXX[64]	¹καὶ ἔσται μετὰ ταῦτα	καὶ
MT[65]	¹והיה אחר כן	
Qumran[66]		

NT	In the last days	it will be, God declares,
LXX	And after these things,	it will be that
MT	And afterward,	it will be
Qumran		

NT	ἐκχεῶ ἀπὸ τοῦ πνεύματός μου
LXX	ἐκχεῶ ἀπὸ τοῦ πνεύματός μου
MT	אשפוך את רוחי
Qumran	… א[שפוך את רוחי

NT	I will pour out from my Spirit
LXX	I will pour out from my Spirit
MT	I will pour out my Spirit
Qumran	I] will pour out my Spirit

---

63. Acts 2.17-21, 39.
64. Joel 3.1-5.
65. Joel 3.1-5.
66. Mur 88.

NT	ἐπὶ πᾶσαν σάρκα, καὶ προφητεύσουσιν
LXX	ἐπὶ πᾶσαν σάρκα, καὶ προφητεύσουσιν
MT	על כל בשר ונבאו
Qumran	על]

NT	on all flesh, and... will prophesy,
LXX	on all flesh, and... will prophesy,
MT	on all flesh, and... will prophesy,
Qumran	on]...

NT	οἱ υἱοὶ ὑμῶν καὶ αἱ θυγατέρες ὑμῶν
LXX	οἱ υἱοὶ ὑμῶν καὶ αἱ θυγατέρες ὑμῶν
MT	בניכם ובנותיכם
Qumran	

NT	...your sons and your daughters...
LXX	...your sons and your daughters...
MT	...your sons and your daughters...
Qumran	

NT	καὶ οἱ νεανίσκοι ὑμῶν ὁράσεις ὄψονται
LXX	
MT	
Qumran	

NT	and your young men shall see visions,
LXX	
MT	
Qumran	

NT	καὶ οἱ πρεσβύτεροι ὑμῶν ἐνυπνίοις ἐνυπνιασθήσονται·
LXX	καὶ οἱ πρεσβύτεροι ὑμῶν ἐνύπνια ἐνυπνιασθήσονται,
MT	זקניכם חלמות יחלמון
Qumran	יחל]מון

NT	and your old men shall dream dreams.
LXX	and your old men shall dream dreams,
MT	your old men shall dream dreams,
Qumran	

NT	
LXX	καὶ οἱ νεανίσκοι ὑμῶν ὁράσεις ὄψονται·
MT	בחוריכם חזינות יראו
Qumran	[ב]חוריכם [...] יראו[

NT			
LXX	and	your	young men shall see visions.
MT		your	young men shall see visions
Qumran		y]our	young men [shall see visio]ns

NT	[18]καί γε ἐπὶ τοὺς δούλους μου
LXX	[2] καὶ επὶ τοὺς δούλους
MT	2 וגם על העבדים
Qumran	וגם ע]ל

NT	And even	on my menservants
LXX	And	on my menservants
MT	And even	on my menservants
Qumran	And	o[n . . .

NT	καὶ ἐπὶ τὰς δούλας μου
LXX	καὶ ἐπὶ τὰς δούλας
MT	ועל השפחות
Qumran	

NT	and my maidservants
LXX	and my maidservants
MT	and my maidservants
Qumran	

NT	ἐν ταῖς ἡμέραις ἐκείναις ἐκχεῶ ἀπὸ τοῦ πνεύματός μου,
LXX	ἐν ταῖς ἡμέραις ἐκείναις ἐκχεῶ ἀπὸ τοῦ πνεύματός μου,
MT	בימים ההמה אשפוך את רוחי
Qumran	בימ]ים ההמה ̇ אשפוך את רוח]י

NT	in those days I will pour out from my Spirit;
LXX	in those days I will pour out from my Spirit.
MT	in those days I will pour out my Spirit
Qumran	in those days I will pour out [my] Spirit

NT	καὶ προφητεύσουσιν.
LXX	
MT	
Qumran	

NT	and they shall prophesy.
LXX	
MT	
Qumran	

NT	[19]καὶ δώσω τέρατα ἐν τῷ οὐρανῷ ἄνω καὶ σημεῖα ἐπὶ τῆς γῆς κάτω,
LXX	[3]καὶ δώσω τέρατα ἐν τῷ οὐρανῷ ἄνω καὶ σημεῖα ἐπὶ τῆς γῆς
MT	3ונתתי מופתים בשמים ובארץ
Qumran	ו]נתתי מופת]ים

NT	And I will show portents in heaven above and signs on the earth below,
LXX	And I will show portents in heaven and on the earth
MT	And I will show portents in heaven and on the earth
Qumran	A]nd I will show porten[ts . . .

NT	αἷμα καὶ πῦρ καὶ ἀτμίδα καπνοῦ.
LXX	αἷμα καὶ πῦρ καὶ ἀτμίδα καπνοῦ.
MT	דם ואש ותימרות עשן
Qumran	וא]ש ותימרות ע]שן

NT	blood, and fire, and smoky vapour
LXX	blood, and fire, and smoky vapour
MT	blood, and fire, and columns of smoke
Qumran	a]nd fire, and columns of smoke

NT	²⁰ὁ ἥλιος μεταστραφήσεται εἰς σκότος καὶ ἡ σελήνη εἰς αἷμα,
LXX	⁴ὁ ἥλιος μεταστραφήσεται εἰς σκότος καὶ ἡ σελήνη εἰς αἷμα,
MT	⁴השמש יהפך לחשך והירח לדם
Qumran	[לחשך והירח]

NT	The sun shall be turned to darkness and the moon to blood,
LXX	The sun shall be turned to darkness and the moon to blood,
MT	The sun shall be turned to darkness and the moon to blood,
Qumran	] to darkness and the moon [. . .

NT	πρὶν ἐλθεῖν ἡμέραν κυρίου τὴν μεγάλην καὶ ἐπιφανῆ.
LXX	πρὶν ἐλθεῖν ἡμέραν κυρίου τὴν μεγάλην καὶ ἐπιφανῆ.
MT	לפני בוא יום יהוה הגדול והנורא
Qumran	[יהוה הגדול והנו]רא

NT	before the coming of the Lord's great and glorious day.
LXX	before the coming of the Lord's great and glorious day.
MT	before the coming of the Lord's great and dreadful day
Qumran	]Lord's great and dreadfu[l day

NT	²¹καὶ ἔσται πᾶς ὃς ἂν ἐπικαλέσηται τὸ ὄνομα κυρίου σωθήσεται.
LXX	⁵καὶ ἔσται πᾶς ὃς ἂν ἐπικαλέσηται τὸ ὄνομα κυρίου σωθήσεται.
MT	⁵והיה כל אשר יקרא בשם יהוה ימלט
Qumran	[יקרא בשם]

NT	And it will be that everyone who calls on the name of the Lord shall be saved.
LXX	And it will be that everyone who calls on the name of the Lord shall be saved.
MT	And it will be that everyone who calls on the name of the Lord shall be saved
Qumran	] calls on the name [

NT
LXX   ὅτι ἐν τῷ ὄρει Σιων καὶ ἐν Ιερουσαλημ ἔσται ἀνασῳζόμενος,
MT   כי בהר ציון ובירושלם תהיה פליטה
Qumran צ[יון ובירושל[ם תה]יה פלי טה

NT
LXX   because on Mount Zion and in Jerusalem there will be a saved
       remnant.
MT   because on Mount Zion and in Jerusalem there will be a saved
       remnant
Qumran Zi]on and in Jerusale[m there will] be a saved remnant

NT
LXX   καθότι εἶπεν κύριος, καὶ εὐαγγελιζόμενοι,
MT   כאשר אמר   יהוה ובשרידים
Qumran כאשר אמר   יהו]ה ובשרי[דים

NT
LXX   just as the Lord   has said, and those proclaiming good news,
MT   just as the Lord   has said, and among the survivors
Qumran just as the Lo[rd] has said, [   ]s.

NT   ³⁹... ὅσους ἂν   προσκαλέσηται κύριος ὁ θεὸς ἡμῶν.
LXX   οὓς   κύριος   προσκέκληται.
MT   אשר יהוה קרא
Qumran א[שר יהו]ה קר]א[

NT   everyone whom   the Lord our God   calls.
LXX   whom   the Lord   has called.
MT   whom   the Lord   calls
Qumran   wh[om   the Lo]rd   cal[ls...

Numerous changes occur in the quotation, but none seem to be of any
christological import in regard to applying the passage to Jesus beyond
those I have already mentioned in my section on the LXX.

Acts 2.21 and Joel 2.32[3.5]a
Acts 2.17-21 cites Joel 2.28-32[3.5] as part of Peter's Pentecost sermon.
Initially Peter does not specifically refer Joel 2.32[3.5]a to Jesus and a
Jewish audience would expect that Joel's prophecy referred to 'calling
on the name of Yahweh'.[67] Elsewhere in Acts, however, Luke tells that
those who wish to be saved or are saved 'call on the name of Jesus'.

67.   See BAGD, p. 459; and Bock, *Proclamation*, p. 165. I am using 'Peter'
here only for convenience and will discuss the historicity of the passage below.

For instance, Acts 9.14 describes Christians as 'all those who call on your [i.e. Jesus'] name'.[68] Also, Acts 22.16 states, '...have your sins washed away calling on his (i.e. Jesus') name'.[69] The usage of Joel 2.28-32[3.1-5] in Peter's speech makes me expect a reference to 2.32[3.5] somewhere else, since Peter could prove his initial point by quotation of Joel 2.28-29[3.1-2]. In Acts 2.22 and 43, the τέρατα and σημεῖα echo those of v. 19 (Joel 2.30[3.3]). This echo suggests that Peter (v. 22) and Luke himself (v. 43) are making more points from Joel 2.28-32[3.1-5] than just the one established by Joel 2.28-29[3.1-2].[70] Also, in v. 39, Peter adds the phrase, 'as many as our Lord God may call', which echoes the 'whom the Lord has called' of Joel 2.32[3.5].[71] While Peter or Luke need not explain every part of the quotation, the placement of 2.32[3.5]a at the end of his quotation draws some attention to it.[72] In

---

68.   ὁ κύριος (vv. 10, 11 and 15) and κύριε (vv. 10 and 13) refer to Jesus because of the explicit reference in v. 17. ὁ κύριος ἀπέσταλκέν με, Ἰησοῦς ὁ ὀφθείς σοι ἐν τῇ ὁδῷ. The majority text and some manuscripts of the Sahidic Coptic omit Ἰησοῦς while the earliest and best Alexandrian manuscripts, ℵ, B and 33, include it. Even if omitted, 'Jesus' is the correct identification of ὁ κύριος because of the explicit identification of the Lord who appeared to Paul (Acts 9.5).

69.   αὐτοῦ grammatically refers to τὸν δίκαιον in v. 14 as does αὐτοῦ in the same verse. The second use of αὐτοῦ refers to Jesus because τοῦ στόματος αὐτοῦ refers to 22.7-8 which says, ἤκουσα φωνῆς... ἐγώ εἰμι Ἰησοῦς. Luke also puts great emphasis on the name of Jesus (see Acts 2.38; 3.6; 4.10, 18, 30; 5.40; 8.12, 16, 9.27; 10.48; 15.26; 16.18; 19.5, 13, 17; 21.13 and 26.9. See too 3.16 [2×]; 4.7, 12, 17; 5.28, 41; 9.14 , 15, 16, 28; 10.43; 22.16).

70.   Luke records in his Gospel at 23.44-45a the words, Καὶ ἦν ἤδη ὡσεὶ ὥρα ἕκτη καὶ σκότος ἐγένετο ἐφ' ὅλην τὴν γῆν ἕως ὥρας ἐνάτης τοῦ ἡλίου ἐκλιπόντος His statement may be the fulfilment of 2.20a (and the sun will be darkened). In the following sections there is an emphasis on the τέρατα and σημεῖα: Jesus (2.22 and 43), the Apostles (4.30 and 5.12), God (5.12), Stephen (6.8), and Paul with his companions (14.3 and 15.2) perform signs and wonders. Van de Sandt, 'Fate', p. 57, suggests Joel 2.28-32[3.1-5] 'is in fact significant for the whole of Acts'.

71.   C.H. Dodd, *According to the Scriptures: The Substructure of New Testament Theology* (London: Nisbet, 1953), pp. 47, 70-72, takes v. 39 as evidence Luke had the wider context of Joel 2.28-32[3.1-5] in mind. It was a common feature of the synagogue sermon to constantly refer back to the text according to J.W. Bowker, 'Speeches in Acts: A Study in Proem and Yelammedenu Form', *NTS* 14 (1967–68), pp. 96-111.

72.   So G. Schneider, 'Gott und Christus als κύριος nach Apostelgeschichte', in *Lukas, Theologe der Heilsgeschichte. Aufsätze zum lukanischen Doppelwerk*

addition, salvation is the goal of the crowd after being convinced that
they acted wrongly toward Jesus and would be numbered among the
enemies of the LORD'S Christ (vv. 35-37).

The net result is that a connection should exist between calling on the
name of Jesus and Acts 2.21.[73] Peter's speech furnishes this connection:
the converts of Peter's sermon are baptized ἐπὶ τῷ ὀνόματι Ἰησοῦ,
and this reference to τὸ ὄνομα in v. 38 is the only one in Peter's speech
other than 2.21.[74] Several scholars connect this phrase with 'calling on
the name of the Lord'.[75]

Peter immediately after his quotation of Joel 2.28-32[3.1-5]a begins an
explanation about Jesus (Acts 2.22-36). He first claims in v. 22 that Jesus
was a man proved to be true by God because of the miracles which God
did through him.[76] Peter's next point is that Jesus' execution was
according to God's will (v. 23), and he further claims that God loosed
him from the pangs of death because death had no hold over him
(v. 24).[77] Peter supports this last claim by using Ps. 16.8-11 and interprets Ps. 16.10 as David speaking in reference to the messiah (see too
v. 31).[78] In Acts 2.29, Peter proves that Psalm 16 does not refer to

(BBB, 59; Bonn: Peter Hanstein, 1985), pp. 219-20; and less explicitly Bock,
Proclamation, p. 167.

73.   Schneider, 'Gott', pp. 219-20; Bock, *Proclamation*, p. 165.

74.   In v. 38, D, E, 614, 945, 1739, 1891, r and p of the Old Latin, and the Syriac
(and apparently the Sahidic and Middle Egyptian Coptic) make this connection more
clear in adding τοῦ κυρίου after τῷ ὀνόματι in v. 38.

75.   See F.F. Bruce, *The Acts of the Apostles: The Greek Text with Introduction
and Commentary* (Grand Rapids: Eerdmans, 3rd edn, 1990), p. 129; BAGD, p. 288;
M.J. Harris, 'Prepositions', *NIDNTT*, III, p. 1210; Schneider, 'Gott', pp. 219-20;
and Wilhelm Heitmüller, *'Im Namen Jesu'. Eine sprach- und religionsgeschichtliche
Untersuchung zum Neuen Testament, speziell zur altchristlichen Taufe* (FRLANT, 2;
Göttingen: Vandenhoeck & Ruprecht, 1903), pp. 13-14, 88. See too 4.12 and
Longenecker, *Christology*, p. 44.

76.   The Greek is ἄνδρα ἀποδεδειγμένον ἀπὸ τοῦ θεοῦ. See E. Haenchen,
The Acts of the Apostles. A Commentary (trans. B. Noble and G. Shinn; rev. R.McL.
Wilson; Philadelphia: Westminster Press, 1971), p. 180 n. 2. John Chrysostom, *The
Homilies on the Acts of the Apostles* 6.1, takes this phrase as 'proved to be sent from
God'.

77.   On the underlying חבלי מות, see M. Wilcox, *The Semitisms of Acts* (Oxford:
Clarendon Press, 1965), pp. 46-48, 'having put an end to the pangs of death'.

78.   See Acts 2.25a. In the classical period the phrase λέγειν εἰς τινα would
refer 'to the persons to or before whom one speaks' (See LSJ, p. 491 [s.v. εἰς, I.3]).
Since classical times, however, εἰς may also have the meaning 'in reference to' which

David since he is buried and therefore has seen corruption. In v. 30, Peter assumes that since Ps. 16.10 cannot be literally true of David it must be true of someone, and thus Peter suggests that the proper referent of the verse is the messiah. According to v. 31, Peter sees the messiah's resurrection in v. 28. Peter then connects this promised resurrection in Psalm 16 with the one Jesus has experienced and thereby proves that Jesus is the Christ (v. 32). In v. 33, Peter connects Christ's resurrection with an exaltation to the right hand of God and with God giving Christ control over the distribution of the Holy Spirit. As a result Christ outpours the Spirit with the resulting fulfilment of Joel 2.28-29[3.1-2]. Verse 28 states that God has filled Jesus with joy with his presence which Peter takes as the Holy Spirit (see too Ps. 16.11b, unquoted in vv. 25-28). Thus, for Peter Psalm 16 is proof that God would give the messiah his Spirit. Peter then works back to Joel 2.28[3.1] which promised God would outpour his Spirit in the last days, and he uses the verb ἐξέχεεν (v. 33) which is the same one he used in his quotation of Joel 2.28[3.1] (ἐκχεῶ v. 17).[79] Thus, Peter is claiming that Jesus has been exalted by God to God's right hand and that Jesus is integrally involved in God's actions.[80] Some suggest Ps. 68.18 plays a part in this reinterpretation of Joel 2.28[3.1].[81] In v. 34, Peter adds additional evidence that David was not the subject of Ps. 16.10-11 in that David spoke of another at God's right hand (Ps. 110.1). In v. 36, Peter summarizes his argument by proclaiming that God has made Jesus both

many scholars take as the meaning in 2.25 (see 19.4; BAGD, p. 230; and Haenchen, *Acts*, p. 181). Thus, Jesus says first that he was keeping τὸν κύριον (Yahweh) ever before him. Either Jesus before his earthly life was constantly in Yahweh's presence, or he trusted in Yahweh during his entire life (see C.F.D. Moule, 'The Christology of Acts', in *Studies in Luke–Acts: Essays Presented in Honor of Paul Schubert, Buckingham Professor of New Testament Criticism and Interpretation at Yale University* [ed. L.E. Keck and J.L. Martyn; Nashville: Abingdon, 1966], pp. 178-79).

79.   Compare Acts 15.8 where it is God who gives his Spirit, and Acts 1.5 where 'baptized' is a possible divine passive, and Acts 10.45 (ἐκκέχυται).

80.   Other texts speak of God's Spirit poured out on someone (*1 En.* 62.1-2; Mt. 12.18; Lk. 4.18). An important point is Jesus' promise in Acts 1.5 where he says, 'For John baptized with water, but you will be baptized [divine passive?] with the Holy Spirit not many days from now'. Tit. 3.6 reflects the same understanding of Joel 3.1 as in Acts 2.

81.   See I.H. Marshall, *The Acts of the Apostles: An Introduction and Commentary* (TNTC; Grand Rapids: Eerdmans, 1980), pp. 78-79.

Lord and Christ (2.36).[82] Elsewhere Luke states that Jesus is Lord and Christ at birth (Lk. 1.43; 2.11; 9.20; see too 10.22; Mk 8.29; Mt. 16.16).[83] In Acts 1.21, Peter identifies Jesus as the Lord during his earthly ministry. He is already Christ according to Peter's confession at Caesarea Philippi. Thus, it is unlikely that Luke means to present Peter claiming that Jesus is only Lord and Christ after the resurrection. A better hypothesis is that God 'making' Jesus both Lord and Christ implies not installation to a completely new office, but rather a public exaltation to or installation in an office which he already possessed or a reaffirmation after that office has fallen into question (compare 1 Sam. 10.1, 24; 11.15; 16.13; 2 Sam. 2.4; 5.3; 19.1-43).[84] Christ's resurrection and exaltation is the denouement of something hidden though true of Christ all along. It is God's reversal of man's condemnation. Peter attempts to prove from Scripture that Christ's resurrection meant that God exalted him to his own right hand and has given him control over the distribution of the Holy Spirit. Moreover, God had given him the function of Lordship and as a result those who wanted to escape God's wrath and be included in the people of God must invoke his name. Thus, Peter's justification to the crowd is exegetical connection of Psalm 16 and Joel 2 and identification of the messiah as Lord based on his exaltation to God's right hand.

What does this pouring out of the Spirit and exaltation mean theologically to Luke and to the implied audience? What such a view meant to the possible historic audience at Pentecost is beyond my ability to determine, but there are several indications of what such a view might have meant to Luke. In Lk. 22.69-71, the high priest takes Jesus' statement of his future seat at God's right hand as blasphemy: Jesus' statement impinges upon God's unique glory by suggesting a certain equality

82.   It is not precisely clear what 'Lord' means here, but 'Lord' is a title for God elsewhere (e.g. Lk. 1.6, 9, 28, 46; Acts 10.33) approaching the point of being God's proper name (Lk. 1.16, 17, 25, 32, 38, 58, 68, 76).

83.   Haenchen, *Acts*, pp. 187-88, takes this passage as evidence of an earlier Christology than Luke's. But if such an early source contradicted his own Christology he surely could have changed it. G. Schneider, *Die Apostelgeschichte* (HTKNT; Freiberg: Heider, 1980), I, pp. 276-77; and Conzelmann, *Acts*, p. 21, reject the adoptionistic interpretation.

84.   Compare 2 Sam. 19.1-43 and Josephus, *Ant.* 7.266, 'Today I begin my reign after Absalom'.

between him and God (see too Mt. 26.64; Mk 14.62).[85] This same view of an exaltation occurs in Acts 7.55-56 where the Jewish leaders have Stephen stoned because he says Jesus is standing at God's right hand. There is a small amount of evidence that some later Jews so understood a literal 'sitting at the right hand'[86] although being seated at God's right hand could mean considerably less.[87] If Luke believed that such an exaltation implied a degree of equality with God, and that Jesus experienced such an exaltation, he was faced with a dilemma whose only real solution was to have rethought monotheism.[88] Any other explanation suggests the one true God shares his glory with another, and such a belief gainsays many parts of the Old Testament (e.g. Isa. 42.8; 46.9). The exaltation may have suggested an apotheosis of Jesus as a divine or semi-divine being, but this view runs into the difficulty of questioning monotheism (compare the idea of apotheosis with Jn 3.13; Philo, *Mut. Nom.* 181; *Omn. Prob. Lib.* 43).[89] Moreover, Jesus' possession of the Spirit was not possession out of need, but control in distribution[90] since

85.   So Joel Marcus, 'Mark 14.61: "Are You the Messiah-Son-of-God?"', *NovT* 31 (1989), pp. 139-40.

86.   For instance, a rabbinical source tells readers that later Rabbis debated the plurality of divine thrones in Dan. 7 and explained one as David's and one as God's. R. Yosi the Galilean rejected this explanation and posited rather one throne as Justice's and one as Mercy's which are God's two internal characteristics (see A.F. Segal, *Two Powers in Heaven. Early Rabbinic Reports about Christianity and Gnosticism* [SJLA, 25; Leiden: Brill, 1977], p. 47).

87.   See D.M. Hay, *Glory at the Right Hand. Psalm 110 in Early Christianity* (SBLMS, 18; Nashville: Abingdon Press, 1973), pp. 52-103.

88.   On a similar subject, see Longenecker, *Christology*, pp. 140-41; see too N.T. Wright, *The Climax of the Covenant. Christ and the Law in Pauline Theology* (Edinburgh: T. & T. Clark, 1991), p. 92.

89.   See C.E.B. Cranfield, 'Some Comments on Professor J.D.G. Dunn's *Christology in the Making* with Special Reference to the Evidence of the Epistle to the Romans', in *The Glory of Christ in the New Testament. Studies in Christology in Memory of George Bradford Caird* (ed. L.D. Hurst and N.T. Wright; Oxford: Clarendon Press, 1987), p. 275; A.E.J. Rawlinson, *The New Testament Doctrine of the Christ* (BL [1926]; London: Longmans, Green & Co., 1926), p. xii. For a different assessment of apotheosis in Judaism, see F. Young, 'Two Roots or a Tangled Mass', in *The Myth of God Incarnate* (ed. J. Hick; London: SCM Press, 1977), p. 106; Dunn, *Christology*, pp. xxi-ii. See too Josephus, *Ant.* 1.85; 3.96; and 4.326 (see J.D. Tabor, 'Returning to the Divinity': Josephus's Portrayal of the Disappearances of Enoch, Elijah, and Moses', *JBL* 108 [1989], pp. 225-38).

90.   So Haenchen, *Acts*, p. 183.

Luke could describe the Holy Spirit simply as the Spirit of Jesus.[91] There is, however, the possibility that Luke did not think through the implications of his ascription to Jesus.

In summary, Peter's implied changing of 'calling on the name of the LORD' to 'calling on the name of the Lord Jesus' depends on his view of the exaltation. Peter sees the exaltation of Ps. 16.11 and Ps. 110.1 as Christ's exaltation to God's right hand. For Peter, such an exaltation implies Christ's participation in the acts of God though the nature of that participation is unclear. Peter, also, with the help of Ps. 110.1, explains the exaltation in terms of God granting Jesus the function of Lordship as the one on whom those who wish to be saved must call. According to Luke, Peter applied this text to Jesus as a result of exegetical work on Joel 2, Psalm 16 and 110. Moreover, if one reads Luke–Acts as a whole, the evangelist implies that this hermeneutical perspective ultimately came from Jesus' post-resurrection instruction of his disciples (Lk. 24.13-48). It also suggests that 'calling on the name of the Lord Jesus' characterized the earliest Christian movement.

Acts 9.14, 21; 22.16 and 'Calling on the name of the LORD'
According to Acts 9.14, 'calling on the name of Jesus' characterized the Church at Damascus since Paul comes to arrest one group of people, those who call on the name of the Lord Jesus. Thus, in Luke's mind, their practice of 'calling on the name of the Lord Jesus' was the single most striking factor in describing this group. Moreover, Acts 9.21 implies that Jerusalem Christians 'called on the name of Jesus'. Luke presents the Jerusalem Christians as continuing the practice described in Acts 2.21 and 38. According to Acts 22.16, Paul himself, as a part of his conversion

---

91. In Acts 16.7, Luke relates that the Spirit of Jesus did not allow Paul and his companions to go into Bithynia. Acts 16.6 attributes a similar act to the Holy Spirit. Thus, the Spirit who exists in the Old Testament (Acts 28.25) and whom God gives believers (Acts 5.32) also is the Spirit of Jesus (see Haenchen, *Acts*, p. 484; Marshall, *Acts*, p. 263; Bruce, *Acts* (1988); p. 307, and G. Lüdemann, *Early Christianity according to the Traditions in Acts. A Commentary* (trans. J. Bowden; London: SCM Press, 1989); and F. Mußner, *Apostelgeschichte* (EcB; Würzburg: Echter-Verlag, 1984), p. 98. On the originality of Ἰησοῦ, see B.M. Metzger, *A Textual Commentary on the Greek New Testament* (London: United Bible Societies, 1975), p. 442. Cf. J.D.G. Dunn, *Jesus and the Spirit. A Study of the Religious and Charismatic Experience of Jesus and the First Christians as Reflected in the New Testament* (Philadelphia: Westminster Press, 1975), p. 180, who questions the identity of the Spirit of Jesus and the Holy Spirit.

experience 'called on the name of the Lord Jesus'. Furthermore 'calling on the name of the Lord Jesus' may have been part of the reason for Paul's persecution since, according to Ananias and the Jews of Damascus, Paul came to arrest those 'calling on the name of the Lord Jesus' (9.14, 21). It may have been that this practice was so different from the common practice of the Jews that Paul and his Jerusalem kinsmen felt justified to deprive Jewish Christians of all their rights and even their lives because of it (9.1-2).

The tie between Paul's conversion and early Jerusalem belief underscores Luke's purpose: his presentation shows that the conversion of Paul, though abnormal, included the same elements which the conversion of the early Christians included at Pentecost. These elements included those very ones for which he had previously persecuted the Church. This presentation underscores the unanimity which Luke emphasizes in first-century Christianity (Acts 2.42; 4.32). Moreover, by these data, Luke, in my view, is leading his reader to an ever clearer understanding of who Jesus is, and to this end he has left pointers along the way moving gradually his readers to see Jesus not just as God's messiah but as the Lord on whom all must call to be saved (see Lk. 1.68; 2.11; 7.16; 8.39; 19.44; 24.52[cf. 4.8]; Acts 9.20[cf. Lk. 22.69-71]; Acts 17.18).

Romans 10.13 and Joel 2.32[3.5]a
In Rom. 10.13, Paul quotes Joel 2.32[3.5]a in support of his statement, '...the same Lord is Lord of all and is generous to all who call on him'. In v. 13, some scholars debate whether κυρίου refers to God, as in the Old Testament, or to Jesus.[92] The telling feature pointing to a reference to Christ in τὸ ὄνομα κυρίου is v. 14 which asks, 'But how are they to call on one in whom they have not believed? And how are they to believe in one of whom they have never heard?' Since chs. 9–11 explain

---

92. The following scholars see a reference to Yahweh: B. Weiss, 'Der Gebrauch des Artikels bei den Gottesnamen. Exegetische Studie', *TSK* 84 (1911), p. 522; J.A. Fitzmyer, 'κύριος, ου, ὁ; κυριακός', in *EDNT*, 2 p. 330; On the other hand, L. Cerfaux, *Recueil Lucien Cerfaux. Études d'Exégèse et d'Histoire Religieuse* (Gembloux: Duculot, 1954), II, p. 179; W. Kramer, *Christ, Lord Son of God* (trans. B. Hardy; SBT, 50; London: SCM Press, 1966), p. 156 n. 570; Cranfield, *Romans*, II, p. 532; D.-A. Koch, *Die Schrift als Zeuge des Evangeliums. Untersuchungen zur Verwendung und zum Verständnis der Schrift bei Paulus* (BHT, 69; Tübingen: Mohr [Siebeck], 1986), pp. 87-88; and D.B. Capes, 'Paul's use of Old Testament Yahweh-texts and its implication for his Christology' (PhD dissertation, Southwestern Baptist Theological Seminary, 1990), pp. 204-207, see a reference to Jesus.

Israel's failure to attain a righteous standing before God, 'they' in 10.14 includes those Jews who have failed in God's plan (see too 10.12). The Jews had heard of Yahweh. Since 10.11 and 9.33 connect belief with Jesus, he is the one on whom the Jews have not believed and called. Also, Paul explicitly states that confession 'Jesus is Lord' is an essential element in one's salvation, and v. 12 further connects κύριος, belief, invocation, and calling on the name of the Lord.

However, the question still remains over the referent of κυρίου in v. 13; there are two ways of understanding the verse as an invocation of Jesus. The first is to understand τὸ ὄνομα as a reference to Jesus and κυρίου as a reference to God.[93] On this view, Jesus is 'the name' of God, and κυρίου is a possessive Genitive. The second is to understand the whole phrase τὸ ὄνομα κυρίου as a circumlocution for τὸν κύριον. Two factors tell against seeing the verse the former way. First, where Paul elsewhere uses the phrase, 'calling on the name of the Lord', he explains κυρίου with 'Ἰησοῦ' (1 Cor. 1.2). Secondly, there is little evidence that Paul understood τὸ ὄνομα as a separate christological title.[94]

Unlike Acts 2, Paul gives no supporting argument for the propriety of his application of this verse to Jesus. He simply assumes that the Roman church, which he did not establish, will not object to this application. This is a very telling assumption for it confirms the widespread usage of this verse for Jesus in the 50s. Moreover, he implies that both Jewish and Gentile Christians call on the Lord Jesus (Rom. 10.12).[95] Therefore, this practice must have been well established in Christianity before Paul uses it here.[96]

The broader context of Rom. 10.13 offers several clues as to how Paul was thinking of Jesus when he applied Joel 2.32[3.5]a to him. Jesus' function in Romans 10 is the one to whom all must call in order

93.   In a similar way, Longenecker, *Christology*, p. 128, writes, 'perhaps it would be truer to early Jewish Christian thought to say that since Jesus is the name of God, evidencing the presence and power of God, it is appropriate that the Old Testament title for God be his as well'. See too Daniélou, *Theology*, p. 157.

94.   See Phil. 2.9; See too Acts 15.14-19. Cf. Jn 17.1, 5, 6, 11; and Daniélou, *Theology*, pp. 149-50.

95.   So D. Guthrie, *New Testament Theology* (Leicester: Inter-Varsity Press, 1981), pp. 296-97.

96.   Also Bultmann, *Theology*, I, p. 125, takes 1 Cor. 1.2; 2 Tim. 2.22; Acts 9.14, 21; and 22.16 as clearly pointing to the pre-Pauline nature of this phenomenon. On the importance of Romans in the reconstruction of Paul's relationship to Jerusalem, see Hunter, *Paul*, pp. 13-14.

to have a righteous standing before God. In the context of Rom. 9.30–10.21, Paul faults unbelieving Jews for failing in God's plan because they pursued the law as if by works they could attain a righteous standing before God (9.31-32a).[97] Paul's point in Romans 9 and 10 is that only God can bring about a righteous standing for sinful people (10.3). The significant point then is that a righteous standing comes through invocation of Jesus. Moreover, Jesus as Lord is 'Lord of all' an idea which many Jews and pagans took as applicable only to God.[98]

1 Corinthians 1.2 and 'Calling on the name of the LORD'
In 1 Cor. 1.2, Paul addresses the church in Corinth together 'with all those, who in every place call on the name of our Lord Jesus Christ'. The phrase σὺν πᾶσιν τοῖς ἐπικαλουμένοις τὸ ὄνομα τοῦ κυρίου ἡμῶν Ἰησοῦ Χριστοῦ may not derive directly from Joel 2.32[3.5], but it is nevertheless illustrative of the New Testament usage of the biblical phrase therein contained.

There are four options for understanding this phrase. First, it could go with 'Paul...and Sosthenes' in v. 1. If this is the case, Paul is claiming that all other members of Christianity together with himself and Sosthenes share in sending this letter to the Corinthians. Two difficulties exist with this view: many words separate the subject and this prepositional phrase, and Paul's authority as an apostle did not depend on human agency but on Jesus Christ and God the Father (Gal. 1.1).[99] Secondly, the phrase could depend on τῇ ἐκκλησίᾳ or ἡγιασμένοις in v. 2. In this case, Paul assumes that his letter is authoritative for all Christianity. Two factors tell against this view: Paul's letter deals with the Corinthians' situation and not the universal situation of all Christians, and if Paul

---

97.   See B.L. Martin, *Christ and the Law in Paul* (SNT, 62; Leiden: Brill, 1989), p. 135; and F. Thielman, *From Plight to Solution. A Jewish Framework for Understanding Paul's View of the Law in Galatians and Romans* (SNT, 61; Leiden: Brill, 1989), pp. 111-13; Cf. E.P. Sanders, *Paul, the Law, and the Jewish People* (Philadelphia: Fortress Press, 1983), p. 150.

98.   See Acts 17.24; *Letter of Aristeas* 16, 195; Philo, *Quaest. in Gen.* 1.20. See too Bock, *Proclamation*, pp. 235-37. Godhood and Lordship are part of God's nature in Philo, *Dec.* 176; *Spec. Leg.* 30; and Josephus, *Ant.* 4.45. Josephus, *War* 118, states that God is lord of Jews in contrast to humans who would claim a similar title. See too Homer, *Odyssey* 20.102-20. Cf. Josephus, *Ant.* 7.151, where David is Lord of all tribes.

99.   See C.K. Barrett, *A Commentary on the First Epistle to the Corinthians* (BNTC; London: A. & C. Black, 2nd edn, 1971), p. 33.

wanted to construe this phrase with 'to the church', he could have done so unambiguously by moving the prepositional phrase nearer to the words on which it depends. Lightfoot points to the parallel in 2 Cor. 1.1 where a similar prepositional phrase goes with 'the church'.[100] However, this parallel is only apparent because in 2 Cor. 1.1 Paul refers to 'all those in Achaia' and puts the prepositional phrase immediately following 'the church'. In 1 Cor. 1.2, the phrase is not a geographical area closely situated to Corinth. Also, the phrase comes later in the sentence.[101] Thirdly, the phrase could depend on κλητοῖς with the meaning 'saints called together with...' In this case, Paul would be emphasizing the Corinthians' election by God. Yet elsewhere Paul uses the phrase κλητοὶ ἅγιοι meaning 'called to be saints' (Rom. 1.7).[102] Fourthly, the phrase could depend on κλητοῖς ἁγίοις as a whole. The meaning would then be 'called to be holy with all those who...' In other words, God calls the Corinthians to be holy just as he calls all Christians to be holy in Christ. This view has two features to commend it: it best explains why Paul put the phrase in its present place, i.e. to modify those words nearest it, and Paul's statement fits well with the context of 1 Corinthians which deals in many places with the holiness (or lack thereof) of the Corinthian Christians (see 1.10-16; 5.1-13; 6.19-20; 8.1–11.1). Thus, Paul, in the greeting, is beginning his admonition to holiness.[103]

Two points are significant for my work: first, Paul wrote this letter in the mid-50s,[104] and he implies that all Christians everywhere, Jewish and Gentile, call on the name of the Lord Jesus. This is perhaps the meaning of αὐτῶν καὶ ἡμῶν: Jesus is the Lord of not only the Christians in Corinth but of all other Christians too (1.2). Secondly, Paul simply assumes the propriety of 'calling on the name of the Lord Jesus' as a description of Christians everywhere. 1 Cor. 1.2 is evidence of the widespread nature of the application in the 50s. The Corinthian church had ties with Peter or his representatives (1 Cor. 1.12) and therefore also with the Jerusalem church. Such ties at least question whether Paul

100. See J.B. Lightfoot, *Notes on the Epistles of St Paul* (Grand Rapids: Zondervan, 1957), pp. 145-46.

101. See A. Robertson and A. Plummer, *A Critical and Exegetical Commentary of the First Epistle to the Corinthians* (ICC; Edinburgh: T. & T. Clark, 1911), pp. 2-3.

102. See Lightfoot, *Notes*, pp. 145-46.

103. So Robertson and Plummer, *First Corinthians*, p. 3.

104. Robertson and Plummer, *First Corinthians*, pp. xxvii-xxxi (early 55); G.D. Fee, *The First Epistle to the Corinthians* (NICNT; Grand Rapids: Eerdmans, 1987), p. 15 (53-55).

would have made this assumption had this practice been debatable. Paul elsewhere emphasized the unity of Jewish and Gentile believers (Gal. 3.28; Rom. 15.26-27). Such unity makes it unlikely Paul would assume the commonality of this practice if in fact it were an exclusively Gentile phenomenon. One possible objection to my view is the suggestion of Weiss who sees the prepositional phrase as an addition by a later redactor of Paul's letters in preparation for their publication.[105] However, Weiss's distinction between the action involved in Rom. 10.13; Acts 2.21; 22.16 and 1 Cor. 1.2 is not supported in the background material.[106] Moreover, if the action of Rom. 10.13 is 'der entscheidende grundsätzliche Akt der Anrufung bei der Bekehrung…der die Rettung verbürgt', it is unconvincing to object that 1 Cor. 1.2 is different because it is 'das dauernde und wiederholte "Anrufen" des Namens im Gebet'. There is nothing to suggest that such practice was a once only phenomenon. In addition, Rom. 10.12 τοὺς ἐπικαλουμένους τὸν κύριον is not a one time phenomenon but rather a continual practice of the Church. Moreover, the Old Testament background shows that this practice was one repeated over and over by God's people. Acts 9.14, 21; and 22.16 present the same picture as 1 Cor. 1.2, and Rom. 10.12-13. Furthermore, the highest suspicion must fall on those theories which have little or no textual support (as does this one).[107] Some interpreters question whether 'calling on the name of the Lord' was a prayer for Jesus.[108] The Old Testament background suggests so. Philo and Josephus suggest 'calling on the name of the Lord' was a prayer, thus the burden of proof lies on those who interpret 'calling on the name of the Lord Jesus' as something other than prayer.[109] One thus has evidence of widespread application of 'calling on the name of the Lord' referring to Jesus in the mid-50s. Moreover, Rom. 10.13 and 1 Cor. 1.2 imply the universality of that practice among Christians. Acts 2, here reflecting Luke's purpose, attributes such application to the leaders of the Christian community from the beginning.

105. J. Weiss, *Der erste Korintherbrief* (KEK; Göttingen: Vandenhoeck & Ruprecht, 1910), p. 4. See Barrett, *Corinthians*, p. 33; and Conzelmann, *Corinthians*, p. 23, who outline Weiss's view.

106. Cf. Weiss, *Korintherbrief*, p. 4.

107. This is the main objection I have with George Howard's thesis outlined in Chapter 1.

108. See Conzelmann, *Corinthians*, p. 23 n. 38.

109. For discussion of prayer to Jesus, see Heinrich Greeven, 'εὔχομαι', *TDNT*, II, pp. 805-806; and H. Schönweiss, 'Prayer', *NIDNTT*, II, p. 867.

Other Data

Several other passages are important for examination of 'calling on the name of the Lord.' One is 2 Tim. 2.22. This passage characterizes the Christian Church as τῶν ἐπικαλουμένων τὸν κύριον ἐκ καθαρᾶς καρδίας 'those who call on the Lord from a pure heart'. Earlier in my investigation, I noticed the connection between 'calling on the name of the Lord' and 'calling on the Lord' (see Rom. 10.12, 13 and 14). 'Calling on' could refer to calling on humans (Acts 25.11). However, the collocation of this verb with 'the Lord' has a degree of connection with the phrase 'calling on the name of the Lord' (see again Rom. 10.12-14). Thus, 2 Tim. 2.22 is evidence of the continued practice which I have outlined above.

Question of Chronology

The question I face is When did the early Church begin to apply Joel 2.32[3.5] to Jesus? Rom. 10.13 and 1 Cor. 1.2 show that the practice began sometime before the mid-50s. Acts 2.17-39 suggests that this practice began on the first Christian Pentecost. If Acts 2.17-39 is accurate at this point, it argues against those theories which suggest the practice was a later development from the Gentile part of the Church.[110] However, many scholars doubt the historicity of the Acts 2 account of Peter's Pentecost sermon.[111] The features which tell against historicity are the quotations from the LXX in particular κύριος as a translation of יהוה,[112] the difficulty of baptizing and preaching to 3000 people,[113] and the difficulty of so large an assembly going unchallenged by the Romans.[114] The quotations from the LXX are not telling against histori-

110.　See Chapter 1 n. 5 and pp. 14-21 above.

111.　Lüdemann, *Acts.*, p. 48. Lüdemann admits that Joel 2.32[3.5] 'was a proof text in early Christianity' (p. 49); Haenchen, *Acts*, p. 185; and R.F. Zehnle, *Peter's Pentecost Discourse. Tradition and Lukan Reinterpretation in Peter's Speeches of Acts 2 and 3* (SBLMS, 15; Nashville: Abingdon Press, 1971), pp. 111-12.

112.　Haenchen, *Acts*, p. 179 n. 5, writes, 'Since both the Hebrew and the Targum of the prophets read "Yahweh" here, it follows that it was only in Hellenistic Christianity that Joel 3.1ff. became available as a scriptural proof!' See too H. Conzelmann, *Acts of the Apostles. A Commentary on the Acts of the Apostles* (trans. J. Limburg, A.T. Kraabel, and D. Juel; ed. E.J. Epp with C.R. Matthews; Hermeneia; Philadelphia: Fortress Press, 1987), p. 19.

113.　See Haenchen, *Acts*, pp. 188-89 (preaching to 3000 people).

114.　Marshall, *Acts*, p. 82, notices that this has been a common objection to the historicity.

city since I do not know the extent of non-Aramaic speaking Jews at Pentecost. Luke states there were Hellenists (i.e. Greek speakers) who attended Synagogue in Jerusalem (Acts 9.29; see too 6.9; 2.9-11; and Jn 12.20).[115] If a large group of non-Aramaic speaking Jews were present at Peter's sermon (see Acts 2.5-13), reason would dictate use of the *Lingua Franca* of the day, which was Greek.[116] Moreover, even if Peter delivered the speech originally in Aramaic, nothing would prevent Luke from translating the text with the familiar translation of the LXX. Some would object that the replacement of יהוה by κυρίου precludes this possibility. This objection presupposes that κυρίου does not carry the sense of a designation of deity. Several observations are important here: (1) What would a Jew have said (this is a speech) when speaking the name יהוה? If 'Adonai' is the answer, the objection no longer holds since Luke would no longer have to depend on the LXX for his word κυρίου. (2) I have already demonstrated that translation of יהוה by κυρίου in the similar context does not remove the sense of the word as a designation of deity (pp. 90-93). I recall my discussion of the Canon of Apollonius. I pointed out the unlikelihood that a Greek speaker would read τὴν ὁδὸν κυρίου messianically since κυρίου functions as a proper name. I suggested that Jews of the day would understand it as the spoken replacement of God's proper name. The same argument holds true for τὸ ὄνομα κυρίου in Acts 2.21 and its usage of Joel 2.32[3.5]. Thus, it is not the case that Luke could only apply the LXX text to Jesus but not the underlying Hebrew phrase since even the LXX phrase implies it is a designation of deity. Therefore, Luke's point does not necessarily depend on the LXX.[117] Moreover, some scholars even suggest that Luke's text differs in some respects from the MT and LXX and possibly reflects traditional material.[118] The second difficulty is not weighty because the texts do not tell readers how this preaching to and baptism of 3000 people happened.[119] Peter may have preached to a

115. See T.W. Martin, 'Hellenists', *ABD*, III, pp. 135-36.

116. See J.N. Sevenster, *Do You Know Greek? How Much Greek Could the First Jewish Christians Have Known?* (SNT, 19; Leiden: Brill, 1968), pp. 176-91 and in particular pp. 131-34; J.A. Fitzmyer, 'The Languages of Palestine in the First Century AD', in *A Wandering Aramean. Collected Aramaic Essays* (SBLMS, 25; Chico, CA: Scholars Press, 1979), pp. 29-56, in particular p. 32.

117. See too Bock, *Proclamation*, pp. 165-66, 185-87, arguing from a different angle.

118. See Bock, *Proclamation*, pp. 161-64; Phelps, 'Implications', p. 66.

119. Zehnle, *Pentecost*, pp. 111-12, objects that such baptism by immersion in

smaller group who spread the contents of his speech to a larger one, or he may have had an exceptional voice (George Whitefield once preached to 20,000 at an outdoor meeting).[120] Concerning baptism, there may very well have been an adaptation in emergency. These Christians may have commandeered one of the many pools in and around Jerusalem (e.g. the Israel pool, Bethesda pool, Siloam pool).[121] In regard to the last objection, Marshall points out that the population during feasts was swollen and nothing prevented peaceful assembly.[122] Thus, I have shown the arguments against the historicity of Acts 2 are weak and do not move the question from the more rational *non liquet*. The historical value of Acts 2 must rest on other grounds.[123] One can observe, however, that if applying Old Testament passages about God to Jesus were a secondary intrusion from a group outside the leadership community, its early assumed validity is surprising.

Maranatha and 'Calling on the Name of the LORD'
Another bit of evidence to examine is 1 Cor. 16.22. This text is important for my discussion of 'calling on the name of the LORD' because one can read 1 Cor. 16.22 as an invocation of Jesus as Lord. Moreover, the preservation of 'Maranatha', which is transliterated Aramaic, could suggest some connection with the original Aramaic-speaking community.

However, there are questions over the division and meaning of Maranatha. The Greek transliteration may represent one of three or more

the height of the dry season would be improbable and that Pilate would have intervened in such a large crowd. He also notes that Acts 2 seems to contradict Jn 20.22 and that no early Christian celebration of Pentecost makes it unlikely that such a key event happened then. M. de Jonge, *Christology in Context: The Earliest Christian Response to Jesus* (Philadelphia: Westminster Press, 1988), p. 110, also doubts the historicity of the event.

120.   See A.S. Wood, 'Awakening', in *Eerdman's Handbook to the History of Christianity* (ed. T. Dowley; Grand Rapids: Eerdmans, 1977), p. 439. Marshall, *Acts*, p. 82, makes the same point. Haenchen, *Acts*, p. 188, takes this difficulty as clear evidence of the ahistorical nature of Acts 2.

121.   See R.P. Martin, *The Family and the Fellowship: New Testament Images of the Church* (Grand Rapids: Eerdmans, 1979), p. 127 n. 7 and his discussion of ritual immersion pools south of the temple mount.

122.   See Marshall, *Acts*, p. 82.

123.   On the historicity of Acts, see W. Gasque, *A History of the Criticism of the Acts of the Apostles* (BGBE, 17; Tübingen: Mohr [Siebeck], 1975).

Aramaic forms: מרנא תא אֱתָא מָרַן, or מָרַן אֱתָא.[124] In older Aramaic the first person plural nominal suffix is נַא.[125] However, in later Aramaic the unstressed א shortens leaving ן.[126] Thus, מָרַנָא or מָרַן could render the idea 'our Lord'. The second part of Maranatha comes from אתא 'to go, or come'. Either אֱתָא or תָא could represent the imperative.[127] אֱתָא represents the perfect. Thus, the first two options given above mean 'Our Lord, come!' while the last option is 'Our Lord has come'.[128] One could take the latter as a prophetic perfect meaning 'Our Lord will come'.[129] One might cite Phil. 4.5, 'The Lord is near', as conveying a similar idea as well as 1 Cor. 11.23-36.[130] These words might further connect with the idea of the Lord's presence in Church discipline (see 1 Cor. 16.22a; and Mt. 18.20); the meaning 'Our Lord has come', that is, is now present, may lie behind the perfect. One could take this idea as referring to Christ's incarnation or his presence in the believing community. Some early commentators on 1 Cor. 16.22 take the passage as past tense[131] The majority of modern commentators, however, see the phrase as an imperative rather than indicative. In support of this view, Rev. 22.20 presents a similar phrase in the words ἔρχου κύριε Ἰησοῦ 'Come, Lord Jesus!' *Did.* 10.6 preserves 'Maranatha' but does not help in deciding its meaning in 1 Cor. 16.22. If the imperative interpretation is right, there is still a question in 1 Cor. 16.22 over whether the words refer to a invocation of Christ (or God) to be present at the assembled community or whether the words are a prayer that the Lord

124. See K.G. Kuhn, 'μαραναθά', in *TDNT*, IV, p. 467. M. Wilcox, 'Maranatha', in *ABD*, IV, p. 514, allows that 'atha' may also represent an Aramaic participle.

125. See Kuhn, 'μαραναθά', p. 467.

126. See Kuhn, 'μαραναθά', p. 467.

127. See Kuhn, 'μαραναθά', p. 468.

128. See Kuhn, 'μαραναθά', p. 467.

129. Kuhn, 'μαραναθά', p. 469, states that he knows of no other example in all Aramaic of a prophetic perfect. Compare M. Black, 'The Maranatha Invocation and Jude 14, 15 (*1 Enoch* 1.9)', in Lindars and Smalley (eds.), *Christ and Spirit in the New Testament*, pp. 189-96.

130. I.H. Marshall, 'Jesus is Lord', in *The Origins of New Testament Christology* (ICT; Leicester: Inter-Varsity Press, 1976), p. 101, points out Phil. 4.5 'The Lord is at hand' which might support the prophetic perfect. Wilcox, 'Maranatha', p. 514, connects 1 Cor. 16.22 and 1 Cor. 11.23-26.

131. See Kuhn, 'μαραναθά', p. 469, and John Chrysostom, *Homilies on First Corinthians* 46.4; and Theodoret, *Interpretatio Epistolae ad Corinthios Secundae* 285 c.

come in his Parousia. Some scholars have taken this passage as directed to God the Father, but that position has not found widespread support.[132] If the text referred to God coming as Lord, this text would be out of step with the rest of Paul which looks forward to the coming Christ as well as with 1 Cor. 11.23-26. If the words point to the Parousia, these words could be a prayer for Jesus to come as Lord in terms of the coming of the Lord on the day of the Lord since elsewhere such is the association of Christ's Parousia.[133] On this interpretation, there would be a connection between מר 'Lord' and κύριος 'Lord' as titles for God. This connection would go back to an Aramaic-speaking community. However, there is a question over the origin of 'Maranatha'. Some suggest it developed in the bilingual Church or that מר and the confessional κύριος developed from two different sources.[134] But no one has given a convincing explanation of why in a bilingual community Christians would have taken over the Aramaic, which would not have been meaningful to Greek-speaking Christians rather than the Greek which would. The question then is, What does the title 'Lord' מר mean when applied to Jesus? Some have suggested that מר and the κύριος title of the Greek-speaking Church stem from two different sources.[135] On the other hand, I know that when Paul was writing 1 Corinthians he had already transferred day-of-the-LORD passages to Jesus, so it is possible that 'Lord' could carry those connotations. Widespread evidence that מר was the Aramaic equivalent of God's name is lacking although Joseph Fitzmyer has shown that such a connection is possible in the time frame in question.[136] If there is connection between מר and κύριος as God's name 'Lord', 1 Cor. 16.22 would suggest that the invocation

---

132. See W. Bousset, *Kyrios Christos: A History of the Belief in Christ from the Beginnings of Christianity to Irenaeus* (trans. J.E. Steely; Nashville & New York: Abingdon, 1970), p. 129 n. 36 rejects his earlier view that Maranatha refers to oath taking directed toward God. He favours instead the view that the words arose in the bilingual Church. Bultmann, *Theology*, I, p. 52, accepts Bousset's second view. Marshall, *Origins*, p. 101, states that this view no longer can claim serious support.

133. Marshall, *Jesus*, p. 202, takes this position based on Zech. 14.5 and its usage in *1 Enoch* and Jude 14.

134. See Marshall, *Christology*, pp. 104-106, who discusses this view as that of S. Schulz. I have not consulted Schulz's work first-hand.

135. Bousset, *Kyrios Christos*, pp. 126-29; Kramer, *Christ*, pp. 99-107.

136. See J.A. Fitzmyer, 'The Semitic Background of the New Testament *Kyrios*-Title', in *A Wandering Aramean. Collected Aramaic Essays* (SBLMS, 25; Missoula, MT: Scholars Press, 1979), pp. 116-27.

reflected in Joel 2.32[3.5] applied to Jesus did in fact go back to the Aramaic speaking community. However, while 1 Cor. 16.22 takes readers close to these conclusions, at the end of the day, the evidence in this text is not clear enough to change this possibility into a probability.

Conclusions and Implications

The Old Testament and intertestamental background of Joel 2.32[3.5] is one which suggests 'calling on the name of the LORD' was a cultic activity directed to Israel's God. In pre-Christian Judaism I found little evidence that this phrase applied to a non-divine figure. There were possible cases were a pre-Christian or first-century Jewish writer may have applied the passage to a second figure. This possibility is connected with these second figures being 'the name'. However, I found little New Testament evidence that New Testament writers followed this practice. In one place, a New Testament writer explains the New Testament application of the passage to Jesus (Acts 2). There, it deals with the exaltation and messianic exegesis of Psalms 16, 110 and Joel 2.28-32[3.1-5]. The writer associates Jesus with the actions of God and with Lordship. Non-Christian Jews regarded this exaltation as blasphemous. The *terminus ad quem* for the establishment of this practice was before Paul wrote 1 Corinthians. The *terminus a quo* is more difficult to determine. Luke dates it with the first disciples at Pentecost. This theory would well explain its implied universal, unimpeachable status in the 50s. I saw no further evidence which would confirm its historicity; therefore, the historicity of Luke's record stands or falls with the assessment of Luke as a historian in general.

'Calling on the name of the Lord Jesus' was an activity which meant inclusion or exclusion from God's people. Both Luke and Paul describe this practice as one fundamental in whether or not one is a Christian. In this aspect, Paul and Luke have converted a feature of the Old Testament background of the phrase in that it described one's inclusion in or exclusion from the people of God. But, in all my search of the New Testament data I saw little which clarified the implication which such a practice had for New Testament writers.

In the first four chapters of this work, I have suggested that parallels are ambiguous evidence both of the practice in general and of Isa. 40.3 and Joel 2.32[3.5] in particular. In general, such passages apply to agents of God and to the immanence of God. Joel 2.32[3.5] has no clear application to a non-divine intermediary, but there is always the possibility that a New Testament example is the first. Isa. 40.3 applied to several second figures though the nature of those figures is unclear. Thus, the search for parallels, while a necessary part of the investigation, in the end cannot decide the issue over the New Testament application of texts about the LORD to Jesus. Moreover, the evidence suggests slightly that such application was more prominent for figures such as the wisdom and glory of God. But, even though the evidence clearly points in that direction for Isa. 40.3, one is little better off since there is widespread and long-standing debate over the significance of these figures when used as christological terms. Furthermore, there is a problem in the question; for 'implications' imply certain attitudes held by certain people, and the possibility stands open that some Christians applied these texts to Jesus without reflection because Christian leaders introduced the practice as one fundamental to Christianity. What implications such application had in the first decades of the Christian movement, thus, is beyond the ability of the evidence to tell modern investigators. This inability is particularly true of the period 30–50 CE. Here, one may suggest that the historical Jesus research may shed light on the question, but again, even if one could prove that some texts indeed go back to Jesus, one has little information as to the clear implications which Jesus meant such application to evoke: Was he intending identification as God's final, fully authorized agent, or was he hinting at something far more? And again, there is the possibility that his disciples did not see these implications until after a period of reflection. The remaining question is, Are there any other early New Testament data which might further clarify the New Testament writers' attitude toward Jesus when applying Old Testament passages about God to him?

Chapter 5

OTHER IMPORTANT DATA

In surveying the data of Old Testament passages about God applied to a second figure I have suggested that the study of pre-Christian parallels in themselves cannot settle the issue of the significance to first-century Christians regarding their application of such passages to Jesus. Such Christians may have taken over a number of hermeneutical axioms in explaining their application of such passages to Jesus. Thus, the argument does not stand in and of itself that application of passages to a second figure is evidence of a view that the second figure was divine or of one that the second figure is strictly the agent of God. Thus, the question remains open what Christians between 50 and 90 CE thought when they applied such passages to Jesus. The issue is What were the Christologies of different groups between 50 and 90? If there were evidence that by a certain date some Christians worked with a redefined view of God so as to include Jesus, such evidence would swing probability away from the relative theological insignificance of such Old Testament passages when applied to Jesus to a view which took such application as an important theological consequence of the Christian view of God.

A full investigation of the chronology and development of the Christian view of God would require a full assessment of the Christology of each strand of christological tradition and the comparison of each strand for evidence of development or mutation.[1] Such an investigation would take me well beyond the limits of this book. However, more appropriate is to focus on the question of Christology in the 50s. It is to an examination of some important early christological data to which I now turn.

---

1. One such attempt is that of M. de Jonge, *Christology in Context: The Earliest Christian Response to Jesus* (Philadelphia: Westminster Press, 1988).

Possible Evidence of a Christian Redefinition of Monotheism

Paul Rainbow presents evidence that pre-Christian Jews did not apply monotheistic language to non-divine intermediaries.[2] Thus, one could take application of such passages to Jesus as favouring the possibility that New Testament writers in some undefined way included Jesus in their concept of the one God. An important passage in this regard is 1 Cor. 8.4-6.

1 Corinthians 8.4-6

Several exegetes take 1 Cor. 8.4-6 as evidence that Paul worked with a christological redefinition of monotheism whereby he was able to classify two figures as divine where monotheists would expect one deity. N.T. Wright avers,

> Here... we find a statement of the highest possible christology—that is, of Jesus placed within the very monotheistic confession itself—set within an argument which is itself precisely and profoundly monotheistic.[3]

Paul A. Rainbow in his examination of the passage comes to largely the same conclusions.[4] Larry Hurtado similarly writes,

> Our starting point is the fact that, although their devotion to Jesus may have caused other Jews to regard them as having violated the uniqueness of God, early Jewish Christians, like Paul after his Damascus road experience, apparently felt thoroughly justified in giving Jesus reverence in terms of divinity *and* at the same time thought of themselves as worshiping *one God*.[5]

His view is that 1 Cor. 8.5-6 represents a binitarian mutation of monotheism.[6]

---

2. P.A. Rainbow, 'Monotheism and Christology in I Corinthians 8.4-6' (DPhil thesis, Oxford University, 1987), p. 178.

3. N.T. Wright, 'Monotheism, Christology and Ethics: 1 Corinthians 8', in *The Climax of the Covenant: Christ and the Law in Pauline Theology* (Edinburgh: T. & T. Clark, 1991), p. 132.

4. Rainbow, 'Monotheism', pp. 106, 123, 127, and 178.

5. L.W. Hurtado, *One God, One Lord. Early Christian Devotion and Ancient Jewish Monotheism* (Philadelphia: Fortress Press, 1988), p. 2 (emphasis in the original), commenting on 1 Cor. 8.6.

6. Hurtado, *One God*, p. 128; *idem* 'The Binitarian Shape of Early Christian Devotion and Ancient Jewish Monotheism', in *Society of Biblical Literature 1985 Seminar Papers* (ed. K.H. Richards; Atlanta: Scholars Press, 1985), pp. 377-91.

Traugott Holtz comments,

> The uniqueness and unity of God, the real content of the confession which
> has come down to us, stand side by side on a par with the uniqueness and
> unity of the Kyrios. That at the same time the title κύριος is used, which
> in the Shema appears as the rendering of 'Yahweh', the 'name' of the one
> God, emphasises the boldness of such widening, which appears to divide
> the one God in two by means of the same 'one'-predication.[7]

Other interpreters, ancient and modern, take similar positions.[8] The
question is Does the text support these conclusions? If it does, this is an
important passage because it suggests that in the 50s at least some
Christians classed the Father and Jesus as divine in terms of the divinity
of the one God of monotheism. If Christians understood God in this
way, it swings probability to the view that such a developed understanding of God was responsible, at least for some, for the application of
texts about God to Jesus. 1 Cor. 8.4-6 is also apropos for the question of
Old Testament passages about God applied to Christ since several
scholars suggest these verses develop Deut. 6.4 included in the *Shema*
which has as its subject the one LORD God of Israel.[9] But does the text
support these conclusions?

1 Cor. 8.1–11.1 is Paul's treatment of the problem of meat sacrificed

7.   T. Holtz, 'Theo-logie und Christologie bei Paulus', in E. Grässer and
O. Merk (eds.), *Glaube und Eschatologie. Festschrift für Werner Georg Kümmel
zum 80. Geburtstag* (Tübingen: Mohr [Siebeck], 1985), pp. 107-108 (my translation).
Holtz sees an early Christian formula behind 1 Cor. 8.6.

8.   Some commentators point out the connection of εἷς θεός and εἷς κύριος to
the εἷς in v. 4 (see John Chrysostom, *The Homilies of Saint John Chrysostom
Archbishop of Constantinople on the Epistles of Paul to the Corinthians* [trans. and
ed. T.W. Chambers], *NPNF*, 12 p. 113 [section 20.7]; Theodoret, *Interpretatio
Epistulae I ad Corinthios*, 214-15, in *PG* 82, p. 287; Theophylact, *Expositio in
Epistula I ad Corinthios*, 167 c, in *PG* 124, p. 655; K.H. Schelkle, *Theology of the
New Testament* (trans. W.A. Jurgens; Collegeville, MN: Liturgical Press, 1978), II,
p. 298; B.B. Warfield, *The Lord of Glory: A Study of the Designations of our Lord
in the New Testament, with Especial Reference to his Deity* (New York: American
Tract Society, 1907), pp. 228-29, 234 n. 17; and J.M. Robinson, 'The Witness of
Paul: Christ, The Lord', in *Who say Ye That I Am? Six Theses on the Deity of Christ*
(ed. W.C. Robinson; Grand Rapids: Eerdmans, 1949), pp. 131-45; D.R. de Lacey,
' "One Lord" in Pauline Christology', in *Christ the Lord. Studies Presented to
Donald Guthrie* (ed. H.H. Rowdon; Leicester: Inter-Varsity Press, 1982), p. 202.

9.   See J.D.G. Dunn, *Christology in the Making. A New Testament Inquiry into
the Origins of the Doctrine of the Incarnation* (London: SCM Press, 2nd. edn, 1989),
p. 180; and Wright, *Climax*, p. 127.

to idols. 1 Cor. 8.4-6 appears at the beginning of Paul's response to the Corinthian question concerning the propriety of Christians eating such meat. In 1 Cor. 8.1, Paul uses περὶ δέ which indicates this section concerns a topic about which the Corinthian church had written Paul (see too 7.1, 25; 12.1; 16.1 and 12). According to the Corinthian position, all Christians possess knowledge that idols do not represent divine realities,[10] and therefore Christians could eat such meat because such objects had no power to affect the meat in any way.[11] Paul criticizes their argument by affirming that knowledge causes its possessor to become exalted in his opinion of himself, and Paul chides that such knowledge does not replace God's love which is of first importance for Christians (vv. 1-3). Paul returns to the question of eating meat sacrificed to idols by quoting the Corinthian letter, '[W]e know that "no idol in the world really exists," and that "there is no God but one"'(v. 4).[12] Here Paul indicates the content of this Corinthian knowledge and their argument: there is only one God, therefore, idols cannot be truly divine for that would compromise monotheism. These Corinthian Christians held the belief in one God as the common property of all Christians, and they used monotheism as a primary resource in their own determination of their personal conduct in the world. Verses 5-6 are probably Paul's expansion

10. For exegetes who take 8.1 as a quotation of the Corinthian position see A. Robertson and A. Plummer, *A Critical and Exegetical Commentary on the First Epistle of St. Paul to the Corinthians* (ICC; Edinburgh: T. and T. Clark, 1914), p. 166; E.-B. Allo, *Première épître aux Corinthiens* (EB; Paris: Gabalda, 1934), p. 196; C.K. Barrett, *A Commentary on the First Epistle to the Corinthians* (BNTC; London: A. & C. Black, 1968), p. 191; and J. Calvin, *The First Epistle of Paul the Apostle to the Corinthians* (trans. J.W. Fraser; ed. D.W. Torrance and T.F. Torrance; Edinburgh: Oliver & Boyd, 1960 [translated from 1546 original edition]), p. 173. Cf. W.F. Orr and J.A. Walther, *I Corinthians* (AB; Garden City, NY: Doubleday, 1976), p. 231.

11. Similarly H. Conzelmann, *1 Corinthians. A Commentary of the First Epistle to the Corinthians* (trans. J.W. Leitch; ed. G.W. MacRae; Hermeneia; Philadelphia: Fortress Press, 1979), p. 142.

12. See J.C. Hurd, Jr, *The Origin of 1 Corinthians* (Macon, GA: Mercer University Press, 1983), pp. 120-23, for a defence of the view that this verse contains a quotation from the Corinthian letter. The rendering of the NRSV suggests that Paul is quoting from the Corinthians' letter. See too Chrysostom, *Corinthians* 20.4; Theodoret, *Interpretatio* 214; Conzelmann, *Corinthians*, p. 142. If the two clauses are parallel, οὐδέν is attributive rather than predicative. So Robertson and Plummer, *First Corinthians*, p. 166. Cf. Vulgate, Calvin, *Corinthians*, p. 173, Luther, Lamsa, and Allo, *Corinthiens*, p. 199.

of the Corinthian argument though they may in fact be a continuation of the Corinthian position.[13] If the verses belong to Paul, he, after the initial correction of the Corinthians (vv. 1-3) and statement of their position (v. 4), adds his own support of their argument: yes, you are right, idols may fill every street corner, but we Christians do not accept that sort of world-view. If the verses belong to the Corinthian Church's letter, it is their own further development of their position in v. 4. Either way the verses apparently agree with Paul's basic position since he does not correct this part of the expansion as he does in 8.1-3. In 8.7 and following, Paul persuades the Corinthians that such knowledge and argumentation should not be the determining factor in the issue. For, although the Corinthian position is correct in one sense, weaker Christians may not share wholeheartedly in this knowledge, and their consciences being bolstered by other mature Christians' actions would entice them to do what they thought was wrong and thus defile their consciences before God. Paul furthermore argues that love of one's fellow Christian should be the chief rule in determining conduct. Moreover, Paul goes on to develop the idea that demonic realities, though not divine, lie behind idols and therefore Christians should avoid them (10.14).

All of this is relatively clear, but the christological implications of the passage and areas of real debate lie in vv. 5-6. If, following the majority, I take vv. 5-6 as Paul's expansion of the Corinthian argument, Paul identifies idols of v. 4 as 'so-called gods' (λεγόμενοι θεοί) and creates an implicit comparison: 'If [for the world] there are... [v. 6] yet for us there is...' Paul's argument is: yes, idols are only so-called gods for us, because we have the Father and Jesus. Areas of uncertainty arise when one questions the nature of Paul's expansion of the idea of so-called gods into a heavenly and an earthly class. Paul also speaks of many gods and lords.[14] These θεοὶ πολλοί and κύριοι πολλοί either correspond

13. Some take vv. 5-6 as a continuation of the Corinthian letter (see literature cited in Robertson and Plummer, *First Corinthians*, p. 168 n. 2; and Allo, *Corinthiens*, pp. 200-201). Theodoret, *Interpretatio* 214, takes vv. 5-6 as Paul's restatement of the Corinthian argument of v. 4.

14. Scholars, both ancient and modern, have disagreed over the identification of these gods and lords. The following is a representative sample of views. Chrysostom, *Corinthians* 20.5, sees the first group as the sun, moon and stars, and the second as demons and those whom men have made gods (see similarly Theophylact, *Corinthios* 165 A; and Calvin, *Corinthians*, p. 174). Theodoret, *Interpretatio* 215, sees the heavenly gods as Zeus, Apollo, Hera and Athena, while the earthly ones are Streams, Rivers, so-called Nymphs, Heracles, Dionysus, Asclepius and 'countless others'.

to ἐν οὐρανῷ and ἐπὶ γῆς respectively or to the λεγόμενοι θεοί. The exact nature of the κύριοι πολλοί is unclear. Yet based on Paul's classification whatever they are, they belong to that class of beings which non-Christians would regard as divine. Whether that divinity was in terms of the divine emperor or a lord like Serapis or Isis is impossible to tell given only the information in v. 5. There is little evidence when 'gods' and 'lords' appear together describing divine beings that 'lords' describes a lower class.[15] So one would be going beyond Paul and doing injustice to the grammar if he or she took the κύριοι πολλοί as not belonging to that class of beings which the world would class as divine.[16] Thus, Paul has expanded the Corinthian argument that idols, which represent what for Christians are falsely divine realities, indeed are quite numerous and of diverse names. But the second part of Paul's expan-

Robertson and Plummer, *First Corinthians*, p. 167, suggest the prepositional phrases describe the two main divisions of the cosmos. They quote Atto (tenth century) who sees the so-called gods in heaven as the sun, moon and stars, while those on earth are the images of Jupiter, Mercury and Hercules. Allo, *Corinthiens*, p. 200, suggests the heavenly are the Olympians while the earthly are deified humans. Barrett, *First Epistle*, p. 192, sees a distinction between the natural and part time abode of the so-called gods. Allo, *Corinthiens*, p. 200, sees the κύριοι as Semitic deities.

15. Cf. J. Weiss, *Der erste Korintherbrief* (KEK; Göttingen: Vandenhoeck & Ruprecht, 2nd edn, 1925), p. 222. Weiss's reasoning is circular: since Paul does not call Jesus God, he argues, there must be some distinction between the two words. See too W. Bousset, *Kyrios Christos: A History of the Belief in Christ from the Beginnings of Christianity to Irenaeus* (trans. J.E. Steely; Nashville and New York: Abingdon, 1970), pp. 147 n. 103, and 205-206. Cf. Philo, *Virt.* 179, who sets the monotheistic creed against 'a multiplicity of sovereigns.' See too Justin Martyr, *Dialogue* 55, 'For such expressions are used, not as if they really were gods, but because the Scripture is teaching us that the true God, who made all things, is Lord alone of those who are reputed gods and lords' (trans. from A. Roberts and J. Donaldson, *The Ante-Nicene Fathers Translations of the Writings of the Fathers down to AD 325* [rev. A.C. Coxe; Grand Rapids: Eerdmans, n.d.], I, p. 220).

16. So Rainbow, 'Monotheism', p. 161; Theodoret, *Interpretatio* 214-15; Warfield, 'God our Father', p. 18; Conzelmann, *1 Corinthians*, p. 143; and L. Morris, *The First Epistle of Paul to the Corinthians. An Introduction and Commentary* (TNTC; Grand Rapids: Eerdmans; Leicester: Inter-Varsity Press, 1958), p. 126. Philo, *Spec. Leg.* 1.331, similarly chides those who introduce a numerous company (πλῆθος) of deities (θεῶν) which Philo then calls a multiplicity of sovereigns (πολυαρχίας). Furthermore, if the Old Testament is the background of Paul's thought here, he might have remembered a verse like Deut. 10.17, 'For the LORD your God is God of gods and Lord of lords' (see too Deut. 4.39; and Josephus, *Ant.* 13.68; 20.90; Cf. Weiss, *Korintherbrief*, p. 221.

sion in v. 6 has important implications christologically. For v. 6 contrasts the εἰς θεός with the θεοὶ πολλοί and the εἰς κύριος with the κύριοι πολλοί.[17] That is, the one God and one Lord (v. 6) on one side oppose the many gods and many lords on the other.[18] Paul is restating the Corinthian argument: even if all the world regards heavenly and earthly beings of diverse name as truly divine, yet for us there is still one God and one Lord. However, the christological implications become evident when one traces the logic of Paul's expansion: if the many gods and many lords explain more fully the so-called gods, Paul implicitly contrasts the one God and one Lord of v. 6 to these so-called gods of v. 5.[19] What the world regards as divine, Christians reject because they hold only one God and only one Lord. Yet if this implicit comparison is true, the one God and one Lord also implicitly contrast the idol and no God of v. 4. But the telling point, if one looks closely at v. 4, is that the εἰς of v. 4 stands on the side of the equation which Christians hold as truly divine. That is, in v. 6 Paul here replaces the εἰς of v. 4 with the εἰς θεός *and* εἰς κύριος of v. 6. At least in Paul's mind, Jesus stands on that side of the equation which represents truly divine realities when Paul has already agreed it is the one God who contrasts all that is falsely divine. The argument shifts, without support or explanation, from the 'one' in v. 4 to 'one God and one Lord' of v. 6. Parallelism between the two distinct references of θεοί in v. 5 may suggest two distinct referents of the implied εἰς θεός of v. 4 and the explicit εἰς θεός in v. 6. That is, θεοὶ πολλοί is but a partial subset of λεγόμενοι θεοί in v. 5. Thus, εἰς [θεός] in vv. 4 and 6 may appear with a broader and narrower meaning.

What is more amazing is that Paul ascribes all things as being through Jesus. The question is All what things? The context is suggestive here. 'All things' appears twice in v. 6 in each case contrasting ἡμεῖς. The second element in each of these sections attributed to the one God and one Lord deals with the Christian community: God the Father is the goal of the Christian community while Jesus Christ is its sustainer. The contrast with 'all' versus 'we' thus further contrasts the world as opposed to Christians. But if this is the case, all things suggests creation. This

17. So Chrysostom, *Homilies*, 20.7; Schelkle, *Theology*, 2 p. 213; and Rainbow, 'Monotheism', p. 161.

18. So Rainbow, 'Monotheism', p. 178; and Orr and Walther, *Corinthians*, pp. 233-34.

19. So Rainbow, 'Monotheism', pp. 161, 178.

suggestion finds confirmation elsewhere.[20] Thus, God the Father is the
source of creation and Jesus Christ is the mediator of creation.[21]
Elsewhere, Paul makes clear that he believed that Jesus had a human
aspect which descended from David (Rom. 1.3 and 9.5). However, Paul
gives the name Jesus Christ to the mediator of creation. That is, he
retrojects the personhood of Jesus Christ and his distinctiveness from
God the Father back into the creation of the world.[22] One explanation of
this phenomenon is that Paul believed Jesus Christ while being a man
nevertheless was not simply the offspring of David: rather Paul recognizes a continuity in personhood between Jesus Christ, a man who lived,
died and rose again, and the one who carried out the will of God the
Father in the creation of the world. Furthermore, δι' οὗ is interesting
because of where it appears elsewhere in Paul. In Rom. 11.36, Paul
writes, ὅτι ἐξ αὐτοῦ καὶ δι' αὐτοῦ καὶ εἰς αὐτόν τὰ πάντα. Paul
here writes about God and uses what many regard as a formula from
the secular world.[23] He reinterprets its parts to apply it to the Christian
God. Interestingly, Rom. 11.36 and 1 Cor. 8.4-6 have four points of
similarity.[24] In Romans, Paul uses this formula to stress the uniqueness

---

20. See Jn 1.3; Rom. 11.36; Eph. 3.9; Col. 1.16-17; Rev. 4.11; Heb. 1.1-3. See in
the Old Testament, Eccl. 11.5; Isa. 44.24; Jer. 10.16; 51.19. See too Philo, *Quaest. in
Gen.* 1.4; and Augustine, *Trinity* 1.12.

21. Compare Philo, *Quaest. in Gen.* 1.57, where Wisdom manages the universe.

22. Cf. Dunn, *Christology*, p. 182, who writes, 'That is to say, since presumably
for Paul too Wisdom was not a being distinct from God, but was 'the wisdom of
God' (I Cor. 1.24), God acting wisely, then *8.6b is not in fact a departure from
Jewish monotheism*, but asserts simply that Christ is the action of God' (emphasis in
the original). Similarly Dunn, 'Monotheistic', pp. 330-31, holds that the impersonal
Logos first became personal in Jesus.

23. Ed. Norden, *Agnostos Theos: Untersuchungen zur Formengeschichte
religiöser Rede* (Stuttgart: Teubner, 1956), pp. 250-60, suggests a Stoic Pantheistic
background to the formula. See too R.A. Horsley, 'The Background of the Confessional Formula in 1 Kor 8,6', *ZNW* 69 (1978), pp. 130-35, who takes the background
as 'an adaptation of a Platonic philosophical formula concerning the primal principles
of the universe' (p. 135). Holtz, 'Theo-logie', p. 107, discusses the Hellenistic Jewish
modification of this formula. See too C.E.B. Cranfield, *A Critical and Exegetical
Commentary on the Epistle to the Romans* (Edinburgh: T. & T. Clark, 1979), II,
pp. 591-92. See too Heb. 2.10.

24. See ἐξ οὗ / ἐξ αὐτοῦ; δι' [2×] / δι' αὐτοῦ; εἰς αὐτόν / εἰς αὐτόν; τὰ
πάντα [2×] / τὰ πάντα. Augustine, *Trinity* 1.12, also recognizes the similarity of
Rom. 11.36 and 1 Cor. 8.6.

of God; he makes the same point in 1 Cor. 8.6 when applying one element of the formula to Jesus.[25]

Also interesting is the idea that Paul developed this formula as a modification of the Jewish monotheistic creed. Though the punctuation and exact interpretation of this creed is the subject of dispute, it is possible that Paul saw a way to find two figures in this confession and apply the κύριος side of the confession to Jesus and the θεός part to the Father all the while distributing the εἰς to both sections and thereby affirming monotheism and the distinctiveness of the Father and Son. Such is a possibility.

The most difficult idea to integrate with Paul's idea here is his affirmation of subordination of Jesus to the Father. 1 Cor. 15.28 is one example of this subordination.[26] The question is Could Paul hold both that Jesus Christ was subordinate to God the Father and that Jesus and the Father were divine in terms of the one God of monotheism? Such might be the case since one can interpret many passages as suggesting the Son took a position of subordination when he chose to redeem fallen humanity. The Son though being rich became poor (2 Cor. 8.9). He emptied and humbled himself (Phil. 2.6-8). Another possibility is that Paul perhaps thought of some unexplained subordination within God (compare 1 Cor. 2.10-11, 12).[27] This possibility would explain the Son's

25. See too Augustine, *Trinity* 1.12.

26. Arians found in this verse support for their thesis of the inferiority of the Son. For a history of interpretation of this verse see A. Grillmeier, *Christ in Christian Tradition. From the Apostolic Age to Chalcedon (451)* (trans. J.S. Bowden; London: Mowbrays, 1965), pp. 311-12; and J.F. Bethune-Baker, *An Introduction to the Early History of Christian Doctrine to the Time of the Council of Chalcedon* (London: Methuen, 1903), p. 191. O. Cullmann, *The Christology of the New Testament* (trans. S.C. Guthrie and C.A.M. Hall; Philadelphia: Westminster Press, rev. edn, 1963), p. 248, comes very near Tertullian, Novatian, Marcellus, Evangrius, and the Origenists in seeing the verse as 'a complete eschatological absorption of the Son in the Father'. Cf. Hilary, *Trinity* 11.39-40, 49; and 9.6.

27. I see all the subordination passages as pointing to a functional not ontological subordination. Compare too 1 Cor. 2.10-11 and Philo, *Praem. Poen.* 40, where God alone apprehends God. See too Jn 3.34-35; and Mt. 12.18. See too the explanations Wright, *Climax*, p. 30; G.E. Ladd, *A Theology of the New Testament* (Grand Rapids: Eerdmans, 1974), p. 421; F. Prat, *The Theology of Saint Paul* (trans. J.L. Stoddard; London/Dublin: Burns, Oates and Washbourne, 1957), II, pp. 123-24. Luke held that Jesus was subordinate to his parents (2.51) yet the Lord (2.11). Furthermore, the final redactor of John was able to hold both that Jesus the incarnate Word was subordinate to God the Father (14.28), while at the same time maintaining that the Word incarnate

subordination not only in the period of redemption but also in the coming age (1 Cor. 15.28).[28]

A question then is Does the New Testament offer any other early evidence that some Christians worked with a christological redefinition of monotheism? Such might be the case in Philippians 2. In Phil. 2.10-11, Paul applies what many recognize as an allusion to Isa. 45.23.[29] Twelve times in the context of this Old Testament verse, God affirms his uniqueness, his sole right to universal homage, or his jealousy over his own glory (Isa. 42.8; 43.10-11; 44.6, 8; 45.5, 6, 14, 18, 21, 22; 46.9; 48.11). Paul uses Isa. 45.23 also in Rom. 14.11 and applies it to God.[30] Jesus as the object of this monotheistic universal homage in no way diminishes the Father's glory. It could be that this is the case because both share in that exclusive glory which is God's alone. That 'to the Father's glory' is a way to exclude Jesus from Paul's concept of the one God appears unlikely to me.[31] For then Paul should not have applied such a monotheistic passage to Jesus at all. Such explanation also impugns the truthfulness of God since on that view the God who swore that he would not share his glory (42.8 and 48.11) or by implication the universal homage due him alone (45.23) in fact did the very thing he swore not to do in allowing Jesus a share in his universal homage. Phil. 2.10-11 is less clear support than 1 Cor. 8.4-6 that Paul had redefined his view of the one God so as to include Christ since it is possible that the author of the Philippian hymn may not have taken Isa. 45.23 in its context.

One is able to note similar monotheistic language applied to Jesus in

was equal to God, even God (Jn 1.1, 14, 18; 5.23; 8.58; 10.30; 12.41, 45; 17.4, 11, 12; 20.28). In Philo, *Vit. Mos.* 2.252, 254, God sends an 'invincible help', i.e. a subordinate, which is nevertheless 'self-sent' and contains a 'vision of the Godhead'.

28. Some however see the Son included in ὁ θεός of 1 Cor. 15.28 (see the end of n. 26 above).

29. See R.P. Martin, *Carmen Christi. Philippians 2.5-11 in Recent Interpretation and in the Setting of Early Christian Worship* (Grand Rapids: Eerdmans, rev. edn, 1983), pp. 255-57; Wright, *Climax*, p. 93; and Dunn, *Christology*, p. 118.

30. T. Nagata, 'Philippians 2.5-11. A Case Study in Contextual Shaping of Early Christian Christology' (PhD dissertation, Princeton University, 1981), p. 283, suggests the Greek text of Isa. 45.23 allowed a midrashist to see two individuals therein. See too Casey, *Jewish Prophet*, p. 114. While this observation may be correct, I would add that in so doing such a reader would not have given up the overriding principle that there is only one God because the entire tenor of the passage points in that direction.

31. Cf. Casey, *Jewish Prophet*, p. 114.

later New Testament books.[32] A related idea concerns the worship of Jesus in the light of prohibitions to worship the one God alone[33] since Judaism in general understood that worship should be God's alone.[34] The key point is that within that very context of prohibition of worship of all but the one God, Christians freely worshipped Jesus.[35] One could consider a whole range of cultic activities which suggest that Jesus was the object of worship.[36]

Epistolary Data

Some other evidence which supports my position in 1 Cor. 8.4-6 occurs in some of the epistolary blessings and prayers in Paul. Some ancient documents include prayers and blessings similar to those which occur in the Pauline corpus. In these salutations, it is customary to direct this prayer to a god, gods, or God,[37] yet Paul directs this wish-prayer

32. Eph. 4.5; Rev. 1.8; 2.8; 21.6; 22.13.

33. See Mt. 4.10; Lk. 4.7, 8; 24.52; Acts 7.43; 8.7; 10.25-26; 14.8-18; 24.11; Heb. 1.5-7; Rev. 19.10; 22.9.

34. Josephus, *Ant.* 3.91, summarizes the first commandment as teaching the unity of God and his right to exclusive worship.

35. Hurtado, *One God*, II, pp. 125-28, takes this worship as the decisive factor in the binitarian mutation of monotheism. Horbury in his address at the 1990 British New Testament Conference suggested that worship of David provided an analogy to the worship of the Davidic messiah. D. Steenburg, 'The Worship of Adam and Christ as the Image of God', *JSNT* 39 (1990), pp. 95-109, suggests that speculation on Adam and Wisdom led by analogy to the worship of the second Adam and Wisdom of God, Jesus. In my opinion Hurtado is right because the worship of Jesus occurs in implicitly monotheistic contexts. See too L.W. Hurtado, 'Revelation 4-5 in the Light of Jewish Apocalyptic Analogies', *JSNT* 25 (1985), p. 116; R. Bauckham, 'The Worship of Jesus in Apocalyptic Christianity', *NTS* 27 (1981), pp. 322, 330-31.

36. See R.T. France, 'The Worship of Jesus—A Neglected Factor in Christological Debate?', *Vox Evangelica* 12 (1981), pp. 19-33, particularly 23-32.

37. A number of documents have statements at the beginning which speak of a prayer for health. See A.S. Hunt and C.C. Edgar, *Select Papyri*. I. *Non-Literary Papyri Private Affairs with an English Translation* (LCL; London: Heinemann; Cambridge, MA: Harvard University Press, 1932), §§111, 112, 113, 115, 117, 120, 121, 124, 126, 128, 133, 134, 136, 137, 148, 149, 150, 153, 155, 156, 157, 161, 163, and 164 from the second, third and fourth centuries CE. The following state that this prayer is directed to the gods or God: §§ (2nd) 111, 120, 121, 125 (3rd) 133, 134, 137, 155 (3rd or 4th) 153, and (4th) 163. A. Cowley, *Aramaic Papyri of the Fifth Century BC. Edited, with Translation and Notes* (Oxford: Clarendon Press, 1923), includes the following letters which have prayers to God or the gods for health or favour §§ 21, 30, 31, 37, 38, 39, 40, and 41. D. Pardee, *Handbook of Ancient Hebrew*

explicitly to God the Father *and* the Lord Jesus Christ.[38] Similarly,
1 Thess. 3.11 and 2 Thess. 2.16 are wish-prayers for God and Jesus to
do something.[39] 1 Thess. 3.11 and 2 Thess. 2.16 reverse the order of

Letters. A Study Edition (SBLSBS, 15; Chico, CA: Scholars Press, 1982) (with a
chapter on Tannaitic letter fragments by S. David Sperling, with the collaboration of
J.D. Whitehead and P.E. Dion), lists the following letters which have prayers to
Yahweh for good things: §§18, 24, 25, 26, 27, 28, 29, 30. C.K. Barrett, *The New
Testament Background: Selected Documents* (London: SPCK, 1961) §20, lists a
letter from 168 BCE which also includes a prayer to the gods for someone's well
being. H.L. Ginsberg, 'Aramaic Letters', in *ANET*, pp. 491-92, lists a number of
letters from Elephantine which contain a blessing from the gods, or from God. See
'Passover Papyrus', 'Greeting from a Pagan to a Jew', 'Letter from one Jew to
another of Superior Station', and 'Petition for Authorization to Rebuild the Temple
of Yaho'. J.L. White, *Light From Ancient Letters* (Philadelphia: Fortress Press,
1986), lists the following letters with prayers or thanksgivings with the gods being the
source of blessings: §26 (260–50 BCE); and § 34 (168 BCE). Others include a prayer
for health: §64 (28 BCE); § 103 Letter A (second century CE); Letter B; § 104 Letter
A (Second century CE); Letter B; § 105 (107 CE); §108 (second century CE); §109
(second century CE); §111 (second century); §112 (second century CE); §113
(second century CE); §114 (second century CE); §115 (second century CE); Letter B.
Some blessings occur in non-epistolary literature where God or a god is the sole
source of blessing (1QS 2; Homer, *Odyssey* 7.347-49; Deut. 1.11; Num. 28.16;
Josephus, *Ant.* 6.289).

38. See 2 Thess. 1.2; Gal. 1.3; 1 Cor. 1.3; Rom. 1.7; Phil. 1.2; and if Pauline,
Eph. 1.2; 1 Tim. 1.2; 2 Tim. 1.2; Tit. 1.4. See too Jn 3; Rev. 1.4; 2 Cor. 13.13; and
Eph. 6.23. On the relationship of this wish-prayer to the opening, see W.G. Doty,
Letters in Primitive Christianity (Philadelphia: Fortress Press, 1973), pp. 29-31.
Some examples of wish-prayers which do not occur in the beginnings or endings of
letters include, Josephus, *War*,1.584, 595, and 670, and *2 Bar.* 49.1. See K. Berger,
'Apostelbrief und apostolische Rede/Zum Formular frühchristlicher Briefe', *ZNW* 65
(1974), pp. 190-207.

39. So France, 'Worship', p. 29. There is some question over the precise nature
of the grammar of these verses. Warfield suggests that αὐτός in 1 Thess. 3.11 and
2 Thess. 2.16 binds the two subjects together the rubric of one αὐτός (so
B.B. Warfield, 'God our Father and the Lord Jesus Christ', *PTR* 15 [1917], p. 7; J.E.
Frame, *A Critical and Exegetical Commentary on the Epistles of St. Paul to the
Thessalonians* [ICC; Edinburgh: T. & T. Clark, 1912], pp. 136-37; E. Best, *A
Commentary of the First and Second Epistles to the Thessalonians* [BNTC; London:
A. & C. Black, 1972], p. 147; W. Marxsen, *Der erste Brief an die Thessalonicher*
[Zürich: Theologischer Verlag, 1979], p. 56; I.H. Marshall, *1 and 2 Thessalonians*
[NCB; Grand Rapids: Eerdmans; London: Marshall Morgan & Scott, 1983], p. 100).
Others see αὐτός as governing only ὁ θεός (So C. Masson, *Les deux épitres de
Saint Paul aux thessaloniciens* [CNT; Paris: Delachaux & Niestlé, 1957], p. 42).

subjects in this wish-prayer. Jesus equally with the Father is the source of this divine blessing.[40] The significant point is that Paul regards the Father and Jesus as together clearing a way for Paul; that is, the Father and Jesus share, as F.F. Bruce writes, 'the divine prerogative of directing the ways of men and women'.[41] Bruce also aptly points to Old Testament passages where the prerogative to direct man's ways belongs to God (Ps. 32.8; 37.23; Prov. 3.6b and 16.9). Again whether by accident or intent, Paul switches God in 1 Thess. 5.23 with the Lord in 2 Thess. 3.16 and the latter may refer to Jesus.[42] To my knowledge, there are no examples of such binitarian prayer within pre-Christian monotheism.[43]

Some scholars see the singular verb as significant (so Frame, *Thessalonians*, p. 136; W. Neil, *The Epistle of Paul to the Thessalonians* [London: Hodder and Stoughton, 1950], p. 71; L. Morris, *The Epistle of Paul to the Thessalonians: An Introduction and Commentary* [Grand Rapids: Eerdmans, 1957], p. 69; Marxsen, *Thessalonicher*, p. 56; Marshall, *Thessalonians*, p. 100; T. Holtz, *Der erste Brief an die Thessalonicher* [EKK; Neukirchen–Vluyn: Neukirchener Verlag, 1986], p. 44; Athanasius, *Orations* 3.12). Others see the singular verb as agreeing with the nearer of the two nouns (F.F. Bruce, *1 & 2 Thessalonians* [WBC; Waco, TX: Word Books, 1982], p. 71).

40. The above statement rests on the observation that Paul makes both Jesus and the Father the subject of this action. Paul does not state that Jesus is only the instrument of the Father's action. See Athanasius, *Orations* 3.11-12; and Bruce, *1 & 2 Thessalonians*, p. 195.

41. Bruce, *1 & 2 Thessalonians*, p. 71.

42. BAGD, p. 460, lists 2 Thess. 3.16 as one of the ambiguous passages as to whether κύριος refers to Christ or God. Bruce, *1 & 2 Thessalonians*, p. 213, sees it as a reference to Christ. Paul's usual method is to refer κύριος to Christ unless the passage is clearly an Old Testament citation or allusion. However, see Num. 6.26 LXX which may suggest an Old Testament background. 2 Thess. 2.16 in my opinion sways the evidence toward a reference to Jesus. See too 1 Thess. 4.16.

43. There are examples where a writer joins God and a second figure without implying equality; see Josephus, *Ant.* 3.52; 6.24; 1 Chron. 29.20 (Yahweh and the King as objects of worship [cf. Josephus, *Ant.* 7.381, who reads this as a case of zeugma]); Josephus, *Ant.* 6.24 (God and Samuel as the source of salvation); Luke 2.52 (God and men); Acts 24.16 (God and men); 1QM 19 (the Lord and Israel); Lk. 3.16 (Holy Spirit and fire); See too *Sib. Or.* 3.47-49, 611-17; Mt. 25.3 (Son and angels); Lk. 9.26 (Son, Father and Angels); Rev. 3.5 (the Father and Angels); cf. Homer, *Odyssey* 20.40-68 (Zeus's grace and yours [Athena's]). On the ancient assessment of this practice see E. Burton, *Testimonies of the Ante-Nicene Fathers to the Doctrine of the Trinity and the Divinity of the Holy Ghost* (Oxford: Oxford University Press, 1831), p. 14; Athanasius, *Orations* 11.41; and Basil, *On the Holy Spirit*, p. 17.

Paul's practice here may be because he classed Jesus as divine while pre-serving monotheism: the Father and Jesus are the same divine source from which grace and peace have always sprung. They jointly or individually are the object of prayer. Moreover, such a suggestion is one reason for the omission of Jesus' name in Col. 1.2. Colossians did not share a proper view of Jesus, so Paul, if Colossians is Pauline, does not presume they do until he sets them straight (Col. 1.15-20). The evidence from 1 and 2 Thessalonians, if both are genuinely Pauline, is early. Many scholars agree that placing Jesus together with the Father as the source of blessings implies the divinity of Jesus.[44] Other examples occur whereby an author joins Jesus and God the Father.[45]

Conclusion

I have suggested in this chapter that some evidence exists which favours the view that Paul classes Jesus and the Father as divine in terms of the exclusive divinity of the one God of monotheism. Given the parallels which I outlined in Chapter 2, the evidence slightly favours the view that

44. See R.P. Martin, *2 Corinthians* (WBC, 40; Waco, TX: Word Books, 1986), p. 4; M.J. Harris, *Colossians & Philemon* (EGGNT; Grand Rapids: Eerdmans, 1991), p. 247; C. E. B. Cranfield, *A Critical and Exegetical Commentary on the Epistle to the Romans* (ICC; Edinburgh: T. & T. Clark, 1975), p. 72, sees this phe-nomenon as a pointer that Paul believed Christ to be divine. Conzelmann, *Corinthians*, p. 24, sees the formula suggesting, 'the two are a unity from the stand-point of salvation and faith; hence they can be coordinated by the simple word "and" (cf. also 8.6)'. F. Lang, *Die Briefe an die Korinther* (NTD; Göttingen: Vandenhoeck & Ruprecht, 1986), p. 17, writes, 'Gott und Christus sind als Personen unterschieden, aber in ihrem Heilswirken als Einheit verstanden'. A. Plummer, *A Critical and Exegetical Commentary on the Second Epistle of St Paul to the Corinthians* (ICC; Edinburgh: T. & T. Clark, 1915), pp. 4-5, sees this practice showing an equality between the Father and Jesus. C.K. Barrett, *A Commentary on the Second Epistle to the Corinthians* (HNTC; New York: Harper & Row, 1973), p. 56, makes similar observations. France, 'Worship', p. 29, sees the practice as evidence that the early Church worshipped Jesus and hence held him as divine.

45. See 1 Thess. 1.1; 2 Thess. 1.1; Gal. 1.1; 2 Tim. 4.1; cf. Rev. 3.5, but see 1 Tim. 5.21; Rev. 14.14 (Lev. 23.9-14); 20.6; 21.22; 22.1, 3. Jesus and the Father are a different category from all else: they share a joint throne (Rev. 22.1, 3); they are a joint temple (Rev. 21.22); they have joint priests (Rev. 20.6); they jointly receive the first fruits (Rev. 14.4); they have a joint kingdom (Eph. 5.5; Rev. 11.15); they are joint salvation (Rev. 7.10); they are the joint source of love (Jude 1). See too 1 Jn 2.22; 2 Jn 9; 1 Jn 1.3; 2 Pet. 1.2; Jas 1.1; 1 Tim. 6.13; 2 Tim. 4.1; 1 Tim. 1.1.

at least Paul applied passages about the divine to Christ because his redefinition of monotheism allowed for this practice. The question is Does this theory explain anything? It is to this question that I now turn.

Chapter 6

SALVATION HISTORY, INVOCATION AND REVELATION OF GOD,
AND CONNECTIONS BETWEEN JOEL 2.32[3.5]A AND ISAIAH 40.3

If some New Testament writers worked with a christological redefinition
of monotheism, would such a view add anything to one's understanding
of Old Testament passages about the divine applied to Christ? One such
element which such a view of God might explain is New Testament
writers' belief in a continuity between the Old Testament and the New.
In this chapter, without endorsing the later philosophical ideas implied in
Heilsgeschichte, I seek to show that the New Testament writers shared
that aspect of Salvation History which stressed continuity with the Old
Testament and that with such a perspective they raise important implications for the idea of the continuity in God's revelation and God as the
object of invocation.[1] I shall also draw some parallels between Joel
2.32[3.5] and Isa. 40.3.

Salvation History

The New Testament betokens a modified continuity with the Old
Testament at nearly every turn. The New Testament writers looked at
their own times as the fulfilment of the Old Testament.[2] Moreover, the

---

1. On Salvation History, see O. Cullmann, *Christ and Time. The Primitive
Conception of Time and History* (trans. F.V. Filson; London: SCM Press, rev. edn,
1962), p. 27. For the recent discussion of Salvation History see J. Goldingay,
'Salvation History', in *DBI*, pp. 606-607; and J.C. O'Neill, 'Heilsgeschichte', in
NDCT, p. 248.

2. Mt. 1.22-23[Isa. 7.14]; 2.15[Hos.11.1]; 2.17-18[Jer. 31.15]; 4.14[Isa. 8.23–
9.1]; 5.17[the Law and the Prophets]; 8.17[Isa. 53.4]; 12.17[Isa. 42.1-4];
Mt. 13.35[Ps. 78.2]; 21.4[Zech. 9.9]; Mt. 26.54, 56[the Scriptures]; Mt. 27.9[Zech.
11.13]; Mk 14.49[the Scriptures]; Lk. 4.21[Isa. 61.1]; 24.44[the Law, Prophets and
the Psalms]; Jn 12.38[Isa. 53.1]; 13.18[Ps. 41.10]; 15.25[Ps. 35.19]; 17.12[?];
19.24[Ps. 22.9]; 19.36[Exod. 12.46]; Acts 1.16[Ps. 41.9{10}]; 3.18[the Prophets];

New Testament provides numerous allusions to not only key Old Testament events but also relatively obscure happenings and laws (e.g. 1 Cor. 9.8-10 [Deut. 25.4]; Mt. 2.15 [Hos. 11.1]). Writers exhibit this phenomenon while underlining the authoritative nature of the Old Testament.[3] This continuity with the Old Testament is particularly true in regard to the Christians' view of Jesus who is the antitype of Adam, Melchizedek, Moses, Elijah, Elisha, David, Solomon, Jonah and Ezekiel.[4] He is the promised Mosaic prophet (Deut. 18.15-19; Acts 7.37; by implication John 1.21; Exod. 1.22; Mt. 2.16), the new Passover lamb (1 Cor. 5.7; Jn 1.29; 18.28; 19.14), and the new brazen serpent (Jn 3.14). Not only does this continuity exist in regard to Jesus, but it also exists in regard to Christianity in general. Jesus's twelve disciples parallel the twelve tribes of Israel (Mt. 19.28; Lk. 22.30).[5] Jesus' demands on his disciples in one respect parallel the demands of God on Nazirites (compare Num. 6.6-7 to Mt. 8.21-22 and Lk. 9.59-60). His rest and conquest surpass Joshua's (Heb. 4.7-8 by implication). Old Testament institutions point to New Testament greater realities (Heb. 10.19-20; 1 Cor. 10.11). Jesus' Last Supper changes the meaning of the Passover meal (Mk 14.22-25; Mt. 26.26-29; Lk. 22.15-20; 1 Cor. 11.23-26; 10.16-17). Christian baptism parallels salvation through the flood (1 Pet. 3.21) and redemption at the Red Sea (1 Cor. 10.1-6). Indeed, Christianity experiences a new Red Sea (1 Cor. 10.1, 6), manna (1 Cor. 10.3, 6; Jn 6.31-35), and Sinai (Heb. 12.18-29). The new exodus event replaces the first exodus as

13.27[the Prophets]; Jas 2.23[Gen. 15.6].

3. See 'It is written' in Mt. 2.5; 4.4, 7, 10; 11.10; 21.13; 26.31; Mk 1.2; 7.6; 9.12, 13; 11.17; 14.21, 27; Lk. 2.23; 3.4; 4.4, 8, 17; 7.27; 10.26; 18.31; 19.46. 20.17; 21.22, 37; 24.44, 46; Jn 2.17; 6.31, 45; 8.17; 10.34; 12.14, 16; 15.25; Acts 1.20; 7.42; 13.29, 33; 15.15; 23.5; 24.14; Rom. 1.17; 2.24; 3.4, 10; 4.17; 8.36; 9.13, 33; 10.15; 11.8, 26; 12.19; 14.11;15.3, 9, 21; 1 Cor. 1.19, 31; 2.9; 3.19; 9.9; 10.7; 14.21; 15.45, 54; 2 Cor. 4.13; 8.15; 9.9; Gal. 3.10, 13; 4.22, 27; 1 Pet. 1.16.

4. He is the new Adam (Rom. 5.14). He is the new Melchizedek (Heb. 5.6; 7.1-3). He surpasses Moses (Heb. 12.22-24 and Jn 1.17). He is the new Elijah (Mk 5.41-42; Mt. 9.18; Lk. 7.14 [cf. 1 Kgs 17.17-24]; Lk. 8.54-55; Jn 11.43). He is the new Elisha (Mt. 14.16-21; Jn 6.1-13; Mk 6.37 and Lk. 9.13 [cf. 2 Kgs 4.44] and Lk. 9.61-62 [1 Kgs 19.19-21]). He surpasses David in Mt. 22.44; Mk 12.36; Lk. 20.42-3; and Acts 2.34-5. He surpasses Solomon according to Mt. 12.42 and Lk. 11.31. He is the new Jonah according to Mt. 12.39-41 and Lk. 11.29-32.

5. See J.H. Charlesworth, *Jesus within Judaism: New Light from Exciting Archaeological Discoveries* (ABRL; New York: Doubleday, 1988), p. 138.

God's chief redemptive event.[6] Christians saw the Old Testament as pointing to New Testament times which formed the initial stage of its ultimate fulfilment, and they understood Jesus' movement as in step with the prophets (Mt. 5.12 and Lk. 6.23).[7] Christians perhaps saw many more correspondences.[8] This typology and correspondence played an important part in how Christianity understood itself.[9] Christians sought to clarify their experiences on the basis of what had previously happened in Israel's history.

These Christians saw the Jesus event as the initial step in the culmination of history.[10] All that remained was Jesus' final coming which would fulfil the day-of-the-LORD expectations.[11] But one element which needs explaining is the idea of God's visible earthly presence: How is God's earthly self-revelation in the New Testament congruous with that of the

6. See S.R. Garrett, 'Exodus from Bondage: Luke 9.31 and Acts 12.1-24', *CBQ* 52 (1990), pp. 656-80.

7. On the New Testament as the initial step in the fulfilment of the Old Testament, see Lk. 24.24-27; Jn 4.34; Acts 2.17; 1 Cor. 9.9-11, 2 Cor. 1.20; Eph. 1.10; 1 Tim. 3.16; Heb. 1.2; 1 Peter 1.12. See too Rom. 15.4 and 1 Cor. 10.11 (R.B. Hays, *Echoes of Scripture in the Letters of Paul* [New Haven: Yale University Press, 1989], p. 123).

8. They perhaps saw the new Temple prophecy (Ezek. 40-48) as fulfilled in their own times (Jn 2.20; Rev. 21.22; by implication Mk 14.5, 8; 15.29; Mt. 12.6).

9. See L. Goppelt, *Typos. The Typological Interpretation of the Old Testament in the New* (trans. D. Madvig; Grand Rapids: Eerdmans, 1932). Many writers recognize the Salvation Historical perspective of the New Testament (Irenaeus, *Epistle to the Ephesians* 1.10 and 3.11 [see A. Grillmeier, *Christ in Christian Tradition: From the Apostolic Age to Chalcedon (451)* (trans. J.S. Bowden; London: Mowbrays, 1965), pp. 114-16]; J.F. Bethune-Baker, *An Introduction to the Early History of Christian Doctrine to the Time of the Council of Chalcedon* [London: Methuen, 1903], p. 132). See too E.E. Ellis, *The Old Testament in Early Christianity: Canon and Interpretation in the Light of Modern Research* (WUNT, 54; Tübingen: Mohr [Siebeck, 1991], pp. 46-47; Cullmann, *Christ*, pp. 22, 24, 32. M. Casey, *From Jewish Prophet to Gentile God* (Cambridge: James Clarke, 1991), p. 80, recognizes that Jesus has a fundamental role in Salvation History.

10. Grillmeier, *Christ*, p. 13, writes, 'The background of the synoptic christology is the history of God's doings with men... But Jesus goes on to show that in these historical acts of God he himself has a special, indeed, the one decisive, place.'

11. 1 Cor. 1.8; 3.13 (Mal. 4.1[3.19]); 4.5; 5.5; 2 Cor. 1.14; 1 Thess. 1.13; 4.15[!]-17; 5.2; 2 Thess. 1.7; 1.8 (Isa. 66.15); 1.9 (Isa. 2.10, 19, 21); 1.10 (Ps. 88.8 LXX and 67.36 LXX both about ὁ θεός); 2.2. See too Mt. 24.30-31, 43-44; Mk 13.26-27, 35; Lk. 12.40; 21.27-28; Jn 14.3; Acts 2.20; 2 Cor. 15.23; Phil. 1.6, 10; 2.16; 4.5; Col. 3.4; 1 Thess. 4.15, 17; 2 Thess. 2.8; 1 Tim. 6.14; 2 Tim. 4.1, 8; 2 Pet. 3.10-12; Rev. 3.3; 16.15-16.

Old Testament? How is Jesus as the object of invocation congruous with God as the object of this invocation in the Old Testament? I shall turn to the first question first. In the Old Testament, God revealed himself many times, and there is little linguistic evidence that the authors meant to deny that what appeared was in some sense 'God'.[12] God's theophany was prominent during the exodus when God's presence visibly delivered Israel (Exod. 14.14-25).[13] God promised an eschatological coming in which he would again reveal himself (Mal. 3.1; Isa. 40.3-5; 60.1-2), and with some modification, many Jews continued to expect the visible intervention of God (see note 10).[14] Yet in the Gospels, Jesus is the high point of God's earthly revelation.

In regard to the second question, God was the universal object of invocation from Gen. 4.26, through Abraham (Gen. 21.33), Isaac (Gen. 26.25), Elijah (1 Kgs 18.24), Elisha (2 Kgs 5.11 by implication), the Psalmist (Pss. 17.6; 116.4, 13, 17), Isaiah (Isa. 12.4; 55.6; 62.6), Jeremiah (Jer. 10.25); Jonah (Jon. 1.6 by implication), Zechariah (Zech. 13.9), and Zephaniah (Zeph. 3.9). In fact, all God's redeemed would one day call on his name (Joel 2.32[3.5]; Zeph. 3.9). And the phrase 'calling on the name of the LORD' distinguished God's people from those outside the fold (Pss. 14.4; 53.4; 79.6; Jer. 10.25). Pre-Christian Jews called on God directly without going through a non-divine intermediary (see chapter three). The author of 1 Pet. 1.17 calls on the Father directly, and Jesus

12. Gen. 12.7; 17.1; 18.1; 26.2; 26.24; 28.13; 32.30; 35.7; 35.9; 46.2; 48.3; Exod. 3.4, 16; 4.24; 6.3; 17.6; 24.10; 33.23; Lev. 9.4; 16.2; Num. 12.8; Deut. 31.15; Judg. 13.22; 1 Sam. 3.21; 1 Kgs 3.5; 9.2; 11.9; 2 Chron. 1.7; Pss. 17.15; 63.2; 77.16; 84.7; Zech. 9.14. This idea of God's theophany continues in the Apocrypha (Wis. 1.2; 2 Macc. 3.30 [cf. 26!]; and *2 Esdras* 9.29), Pseudepigrapha (*1 En.* 14.20; *2 En.* 20.3; 39.5 [A]; *Jub.* 1.28; *LAE* [Vita] 25.3; *Mart. and Asc. Isa.* 3.10; *Pseud. Philo* 8.3; 11.15; *T. Isaac* 6.27; *T. Jac.* 2.14-15; 3.5; 7.8; *T. Job* 42.1), and Qumran (CD 8.25). God appeared sometimes as Elohim and then to Moses as the LORD (Exod. 6.3). Cf. the definition of theophany and epiphany in A.H.W. Curtis, 'Theophany', *DBI*, pp. 694-95. See too W. Eichrodt, *Theology of the Old Testament* (trans. J.A. Baker; London: SCM Press, 1967), II, pp. 16-27; G.R. Beasley-Murray, *Jesus and the Kingdom of God* (Grand Rapids: Eerdmans; Exeter: Paternoster, 1986), pp. 3-25, who suggests the messiah is God's representative, even his manifesting presence; and S. Kim, *The Origin of Paul's Gospel* (WUNT, 4; Tübingen: Mohr [Siebeck], 1981; Grand Rapids: Eerdmans, 1982), pp. 208-209, 246.

13. Garrett, 'Exodus', pp. 656-80, notes that the exodus event is paradigmatic for all future redemption.

14. See O. Betz, 'The Eschatological Interpretation of the Sinai-Tradition in Qumran and the New Testament', *RevQ* 6 (1967), pp. 89-107, especially 92-93.

himself using a different word also speaks of summoning God's help (Mt. 26.53). Yet Jesus, for Christians, is the object of invocation.

To be sure, the idea of God's theophany carried with it the idea of God's partial revelation (Exod. 33.20-33; Deut. 4.12; 1 Kgs 8.12-13, 27); but these safeguards of God's partial transcendence are by no means proof that Old Testament writers believed in God's absolute transcendence. The same could be said of pre-Christian and first-century Jews. In Philo, for example, revelation of God is a function of the Logos related to God in an undefined way.[15] For Josephus, the possibility of seeing God as he truly is, is non existent (*Apion* 2.167, 191). However, Josephus, *Ant.* 3.208, speaks of God's presence in a dark cloud coming to the Tabernacle, and according to *Ant.* 3.188, God appeared to Moses (see too 2.275; 6.38).[16] Thus, the evidence does not support the view that Jews around the time of Jesus believed in the absolute transcendence of God to the exclusion of the idea of his manifestation. Moreover, pre-Christian and first-century Jews developed ways to speak about God which while not denying the reality of his presence did not suggest God's total immanence.[17] Intermediaries such as wisdom, glory and logos were God as he was available to human perception. One must distinguish between these divine and the other non-divine intermediaries (angels, kings, prophets, priests and other men). The latter group are creatures and excluded from the Jewish concept of the one God.[18] However, the glory, wisdom and logos are necessary to God's existence; without them God would not be the same.[19]

Casey uses both these groups as support for his theory.[20] Yet the first group is divine in that they are attributes of God. But Casey equivocates

15. See Chapter 2, pp. 53-55.
16. God is also manifest in events (Josephus, *Ant.* 9.60).
17. See Josephus, *Ant.* 8.107-109.
18. Cf. A.R. Johnson, *The One and the Many in the Israelite Conception of God* (Cardiff: University of Wales, 2nd edn, 1961).
19. See Philo, *Spec. Leg.* 1.209. Dionysius of Rome, *Against the Sabellians*, in Stevenson, *New Eusebius*, p. 269, made a similar argument that the Son could not have come into being since then God would have existed without his attributes which is absurd. The same argument appears in Augustine, *Trinity* 6.
20. See M. Casey, *From Jewish Prophet to Gentile God: The Origins and Development of New Testament Christology* (Cambridge: Clarke, 1991), pp. 79-85, 147, 159; and M. Casey, 'Chronology and the Development of Pauline Christology', in *Paul and Paulinism. Essays in Honour of C. K. Barrett* (ed. M.D. Hooker and S.G. Wilson; London: SPCK, 1982), pp. 124-34.

on the term 'divine' by using a definition of divinity which only is applicable to an independent second divine figure.[21] However, such is not what modern exegetes mean when calling Jesus divine.[22] Therefore, Casey's argument misses the point. Rather, it is a shared divinity between Jesus and the Father resulting from a redefinition of monotheism. It is not the addition of a Gentile god to the Jewish God of monotheism. I would agree that the New Testament writers do not regard Jesus as 'divine' in Casey's sense for they would be polytheists.

Does a redefinition of monotheism explain how the writers might have looked at the idea of continuity between the Old Testament and Christian practice? To answer this question, I shall look at the New Testament idea of theophany and invocation of God. John affirms that no one has ever seen God (1.18; 5.37. 6.46; 1 Jn 4.21), as do the writers of Colossians, 1 Timothy and Hebrews (Col. 1.5; 1 Tim. 1.17; Heb. 11.27). Yet in the New Testament itself, evidence exists of a belief in God's theophany (Acts 7.2, 30-32; Rev. 15.8). Moreover, precisely those places in the New Testament which speak of the invisibility of God also identify Jesus as God's image, radiance of his glory, means by which God reveals himself to the world, or his glory (Mt. 11.27; Lk. 10.22; Col. 1.15; Heb. 1.3; Jn 1.18; 6.46; 14.9).

Mt. 11.27 and Lk. 10.22 include a saying in which Jesus makes an absolute claim to reveal the Father and implies that such is a benefit not a deficit to believers.[23] This passage claims a mysterious knowledge

21. E.g. Casey, *Prophet*, p. 114.

22. See for example N.T. Wright, *The Climax of the Covenant: Christ and the Law in Pauline Theology* (Edinburgh: T. & T. Clark, 1991), pp. 94, 129.

23. There is a question whether the ὁ υἱός in Q or Jesus' original words refers to Jesus specifically or rather is a proverbial saying: 'No one knows a father but a son' (see the discussion on this point in I.H. Marshall, *Jesus the Saviour: Studies in New Testament Theology* [London: SPCK, 1990], pp. 137-38). Cf. R. Bauckham, 'The Sonship of the Historical Jesus in Christology', *SJT* 31 (1978), p. 251, who supports the generic use of the article. In the Lucan and Matthean contexts, reference to Jesus is clear (Lk. 1.35; Mt. 3.17; Lk. 3.22). Once the Gospels identify Jesus as the Son of God, it becomes almost impossible to take Mt. 11.27 and Lk. 10.22 to refer to anyone else (see Marshall, *Jesus*, pp. 137-38, and B. Witherington, III, *The Christology of Jesus* [Minneapolis: Fortress, 1990], p. 221). In the Gospel context, Jesus takes over a function of Wisdom in the exclusivity of mutual knowledge (Job 28.1-27; Prov. 8.12; Sir. 1.6, 8; Bar. 3.15-32; Wis. 7.25-26; 8.3-8; 9.4, 9, 11). See Witherington, *Christology*, p. 227. M. de Jonge, *Christology in Context: The Earliest Response to Jesus* (Philadelphia: Westminster Press, 1988), p. 93, sees Jesus implicitly identified with Wisdom.

between the Father and the Son which none may enter except those whom the Son allows. If one placed this framework on the Old Testament, the Son would function in those places where God revealed himself in theophany, angelophany and wisdom traditions.[24] This interpretation of the data would support the above explained hypothesis on the preservation of the continuity between the Old Testament and the New Testament. That is, if this revelation is the result of a redefinition of monotheism, there is continuity in the God who revealed himself in the Old Testament and Jesus revealing the Father in the New Testament; if there is no redefinition, the New Testament is out of step with the Old Testament at this point. A further important question is What is the date of this tradition? If one accepts the two document hypothesis (the priority of Mark and Q), this passage is part of Q, and as such it would date to the formulation of Q.[25] Some scholars see Mt. 11.27 and Lk. 10.22 as an authentic word of Jesus which would push the inception of the above idea back into Jesus' lifetime.[26] Moreover, some scholars argue that since Q dates from a period in which many of Jesus disciples were still alive, the burden of proof lies on those who claim Q Christology differs from that of the early Church.[27] The difficulty lies however in the exact implications in the Q passage which may be different from the implications of the passage as it now stands.[28] In the passage as it stands in the Gospels, however, it is clear that Jesus occupies a position similar to that of God's theophanic presence in the Old Testament.

Other data which may liken Jesus to God's theophanic presence are Paul's ideas of Christ as the image and glory of God.[29] Some scholars suggest that εἰκών used in a certain sense suggested participation with

---

24. See Justin Martyr, *First Apology* 63, for his connection between Old Testament theophany and Mt. 11.27 and Lk. 10.22. Compare these verses to Philo, *Abr.* 75-80, 'For it were impossible that anyone should by himself apprehend the truly Existent, did not He reveal and manifest himself' (80).

25. The redactional changes between Mt. 11.25a-27 and Lk. 10.21b-22 are stylistic.

26. See the discussions of Marshall, *Jesus*, pp. 137-42; and Witherington, *Christology*, pp. 221-28. Cf. Bousset, *Kyrios Christos*, pp. 83-84.

27. See Witherington, *Christology*, p. 224.

28. It is possible that Jesus is the messenger of Wisdom in Q (see the discussion of E. Schweizer, 'What Q Could Have Learned from Reginald Fuller', *ATR* Supplement 11 [1990]: pp. 65-66, and the literature cited there).

29. See Rom. 8.29; 1 Cor. 15.49; 2 Cor. 3.18; 4.4; if Pauline Col. 1.15; and 3.10 for the idea of Christ as the image of God.

the object it represents.[30] Some passages in the New Testament support the idea that εἰκών does not carry the idea of inferior copy.[31] It may be that a similar idea lies behind the idea of Jesus as the image of God. Paul also speaks of Christ as the glory of God (2 Cor. 4.4-6)[32] though here too debate exists over the exact implications of this ascription.[33] Carey Newman makes the point that in Rom. 9.4 and 2 Cor. 3.8-9, Paul refers to past theophanies as δόξα and in each case Jesus now supersedes the old (Rom. 9.5; 2 Cor. 4.4).[34]

Heb. 1.3 identifies Jesus as the ἀπαύγασμα τῆς δόξης καὶ

30. See Hermann Kleinknecht, 'εἰκών', in *TDNT*, II, p. 389; R.P. Martin, *Carmen Christi. Philippians 2.5-11 in Recent Interpretation and in the Setting of Early Christian Worship* (Grand Rapids: Eerdmans, rev. edn, 1983), p. 113, and the literature cited there. The chief difficulty with this suggestion is that one could argue it proves too much in that Adam is also the image of God (1 Cor. 11.7; cf. 1 Cor. 15.22, 45; Rom. 5.14). However, Christ may be 'image' in a different sense than Adam. In Col. 1.15, the writer places the Son of God outside created order which owes its creation, continued existence and ultimate allegiance to Christ (1.16). When one takes such an interpretative framework to Gen. 1, the writer of Colossians sees the Son of God as the model to which the earthly man belongs (Gen. 1.26-27). Paul may class Jesus as the image of God in one place concerned with theophany (2 Cor. 3.18; 4.4). J.D.G. Dunn, *Christology in the Making: A New Testament Inquiry into the Origins of the Doctrine of the Incarnation*,(London: SCM Press, 2nd edn, 1989), p. 119, has raised the objection that Paul could hardly have called Jesus the second Adam if in reality the Son of God pre-existed Adam. But the question is one of perspective. Adam is the 'first' Adam for humanity because he is the one to whom humanity is most closely related. Jesus is the one in whose image God presently is remaking (Rom. 8.29 and 2 Cor. 3.18) and ultimately conforming believers (1 Cor. 15.49; Col. 3.10) and therefore one step removed. Philo gives evidence that such a view was possible in the time under consideration (see *Leg. All.* 1.31, 53-54; *Op. Mund.* 134; *Conf.* 41, 62-63, 146-47; and *Quaest. in Gen.* 1.4 [cf. Dunn, *Christology*, p. 100]).

31. See Rom. 1.23 and the phrase ἐν ὁμοιώματι εἰκόνος which shows that 'image' may refer to the visible portion of the reality it represents. Heb. 10.1 likewise contrast 'the shadow of the good things to come' with 'the image itself'. The idea of 'image' is a complex one and one which I have not been able to investigate adequately given the space and time restrictions of this exercise. I look forward to further future work on this subject.

32. For a recent review of Christ as 'glory' see, C.C. Newman, *Paul's Glory Christology: Tradition and Rhetoric* (SNT, 69; Leiden: Brill, 1992).

33. This is particularly true because of 1 Cor. 11.7 where man is the δόξα θεοῦ. One could argue that since man is the glory of God, Jesus as the δόξα or as sharing the δόξα need mean little more.

34. Newman, *Christology*, pp. 217-18.

χαρακτὴρ τῆς ὑποστάσεως αὐτοῦ. That is, what can be seen of the Father's glory is the 'radiance' which is the Son.[35] This description makes the Son of God the visible means by which the Father acts (1.2) and by which the invisible God becomes visible (compare 11.27 and 1.3). This same book seems to attribute creation to the Son (1.2 and 1.10-12 citing Ps. 101.26-28 LXX).[36] Thus, Hebrews suggests personal distinction between the Father and Son yet continuity in revelation and action. A redefinition of monotheism would adequately explain this phenomenon as well as the book's Salvation Historical perspective.

John's Gospel alludes to portions of Scripture dealing with theophany (see Jn 1.51 and Gen. 28.12; Jn 12.41 and Isa. 6.1).[37] Moreover, 1.18 suggests that for John the Logos participated in revelation of God. This belief is why Jesus can be the new Bethel (by implication 1.51)[38] and why Isaiah could have seen Jesus' glory (12.41 by implication with Isa. 6.1).[39] Moreover, the Logos participates in revelation without compromising the transcendence which God the Father enjoys (1.18) or the distinctiveness of the Father and the Logos (1.1). This suggestion also begins to explain how Jesus, the Word incarnate (1.14), could claim that those who have seen him have seen the Father (14.7, 9, and 10). The same idea of Jesus as the culmination of revelation exists in Rev. 21.22 which identifies the new Temple as the Lord God *and* the Lamb. Since the Temple and Tabernacle in the Old Testament were the places where God's particularized earthly presence existed (e.g. Exod. 25.8; Isa. 8.18), to include the Lamb together with the Lord God as the Temple means that the ultimate presence of God must include at least two distinct

35. Cf. NRSV 'reflection'.

36. See Cullmann, *Christ*, pp. 25-26. T.F. Glasson, ' "Plurality of Divine Persons" and the Quotations in Hebrews 1.6ff.', *NTS* 12 (1965–66), pp. 270-73, suggests that the writer of Hebrews develops the same theme which Church fathers developed when justifying the Son's activity in the Old Testament.

37. I here use the name 'John' for the person responsible for the final product of the Gospel. I do not wish here to enter the debate on hypothetical sources in the composition of the Gospel. W. Loader, *The Christology of the Fourth Gospel* (New York: Peter Lang, 1989), p. 23, recognizes that the only Christology to which one has access is the one in the text. He assumes that it reflects the Christology of the author.

38. A.T. Hanson, *The Prophetic Gospel: A Study of John and the Old Testament* (Edinburgh: T. & T. Clark, 1991), p. 37, sees Jesus corresponding to the LORD of Jacob's vision at Bethel.

39. See C. Rowland, 'John 1.51, Jewish Apocalyptic and Targumic Tradition', *NTS* 30 (1984), p. 499.

figures. A similar idea may lie behind the Synoptic tradition of Jesus and the new Temple of God.[40] A redefinition of monotheism would also explain these data as well as the above books' Salvation Historical perspective.

Apart from Jesus, the idea of God's theophany in history has all but disappeared in the New Testament.[41] It is no longer God's parousia but Christ's.[42] God did not reveal himself visibly in the new exodus, only Christ. Nor did God the Father reveal himself visibly to any human during Jesus' lifetime.[43] This absence of theophany in the New Testament is more striking since pre-Christian and first-century Judaism allowed for

40. See Mt. 12.6 [compare with 23.21]; Mt. 26.61; 27.40, 51; Mk 14.58; 15.38; Jn 2.19; Acts 6.14. See Athanasius, *On the Incarnation* 39, commenting on Dan. 9.24-25; Hanson, *Prophetic*, pp. 72, 43-44; L. Hartman, 'He Spoke of the Temple of His Body', *SEÅ* 54 (1989), pp. 70-72. Cf. H. Anderson, *The Gospel of Mark* (NCB; London: Oliphants, 1976), pp. 329-30; and D. Juel, *Messiah and Temple: The Trial of Jesus in the Gospel of Mark* (SBLDS, 31; Missoula, MT: Scholars Press, 1977). It is possible that 'Temple' means considerably less; see Philo, *Praem. Poen.* 108-109 (mind as temple); *Epistle of Barnabas* 16 (individual as temple); 1 Cor. 3.17; 2 Cor. 6.16; Eph. 2.22. On the possible historicity of the Synoptic Gospel's account see C.E.B. Cranfield, *The Gospel according to Saint Mark: An Introduction and Commentary* (Cambridge: Cambridge University Press, 1963), p. 441.

41. One could point to Lk. 9.26 which speaks of the Son of Man coming in his own glory and that of the Father and the holy angels. The 'glory of God' appeared in Lk. 2.9. Jn 14.23 speaks of the Father and Jesus coming and making their abode with the one who loves Jesus. In neither of these cases however does the Father come alone. It is unlikely that these writers believed that Jesus would come only in preparation of a final more glorious coming of God. For a discussion of the Parousia replacing Old Testament theophany see T.F. Glasson, *The Second Advent: The Origin of New Testament Doctrine* (London: Epworth, 3rd edn, 1963), pp. 167-71. Another possibility is Acts 7.55 (cf. Martin, *Carmen*, p. 312).

42. For example Isa. 60.2 and Zech. 14.5. Cf. Lk. 1.78 (an allusion to Isa. 60.2?); Mt. 25.31 and 1 Thess. 3.13 (allusions to Zech. 14.5?). Furthermore, there is little hope that God would ever come to Israel apart from Jesus. Notable exceptions to God's revelation in the New Testament are the transfiguration (Mt. 17.5; Mk 9.7 and Lk. 9.34). However, in this pericope, the visible figure is Jesus not God (cf. Moses seeing a figure on Sinai in Exod. 33.23). Also, the appearance of the cloud is secondary in the transfiguration (i.e. Jesus transfigures before the cloud comes). Another reference to the appearance of God is Acts 7.55. There however, attention is on Jesus. Rev. 4.2-3 is the revelation of God in heaven which in ch. 5 includes the Lamb.

43. Cf. Mt. 17.1-8; Mk 9.2-8; Lk. 9.28-36; Mt. 3.16; Mk 1.10; Lk. 3.22; and Mt. 5.8.

the addition of second figures in the end time (*T. Mos.* 10.1-10 and perhaps 1QS 3.24; 8-9). Christian writers could have followed their contemporaries and simply made Jesus' coming an intermediate action before God's final intervention. Moreover, in post-New Testament times, Jews continued in their expectation of God's coming theophany (e.g. *Lev. R.* 1.15 and the Isaiah Targum 40–66]).

The idea of invocation is a little less clear. Appeal to God for justification is an appeal to Christ (Acts 2.21, 38; 22.16; Rom. 10.12-14). But in the Old Testament, such appeal was made directly to God. Jesus taught his disciples to pray to the Father (Mt. 6.9-13; Mk 11.25 by implication; Lk. 11.2-4; 12.29-30). At the same time, he is the mediator through whom all must go to know the Father (Mt. 11.27; Lk. 10.22; Jn 14.6; Rom. 5.2; Eph. 2.18; 3.12; Heb. 4.16; 6.19; 10.20; 1 Pet. 3.18). Another standing in God's place in theophany would be little more than idolatry. Another standing in God's place as the object of invocation makes a verse like Deut. 4.7 terribly hollow.

If writers had redefined monotheism, there is ample continuity: Christians call upon Jesus because he shares the divinity of the one God on whom God's faithful have always called. Jesus is the high point of God's earthly self-revelation because he shares in the divinity of the one God who revealed himself in the past and will yet again reveal himself in the future. This new self-revelation of God in some respects even surpasses that of the old: God's glory is no longer hidden in pillars of cloud and fire but manifest in Jesus Christ (2 Cor. 4.4). Where before God's theophanic presence was available to a few, in Jesus' ministry it was available to many. What was temporary (God on Sinai or at the Tabernacle door) is more permanent in the earthly revelation of Jesus. Jesus like God's presence in the pillar of Cloud saves God's people from their enemies (Rom. 1.18; Col. 1.13; Exod. 15.1-3; 14.25). Jesus reverses the departure of the Glory of the Lord in Ezek. 11.23 by coming from the Mount of Olives to the Temple (Mt. 21.1-12; Mk 11.1-11; Lk. 19.28-45).[44] Jesus in a few places may even explicitly take the position of God in theophany (Jn 12.41; 2 Cor. 4.4-6; perhaps 1 Cor. 10.9; 2 Cor. 3.16-18 and Jude 5). One could submit that the New Testament writers

---

44. God may 'come' in historical events other than theophanies (cf. Aristobulus, *Fragments* 2.15; Origen, *Against Celsus* 8.69). But other texts give all indications that what appeared was God. One could argue that the Jesus event is another case of God coming in a historical event. But the problem is that first-century Christian perspective saw Jesus as uniquely the pinnacle of God's action.

understood the manifestations of God in the Old Testament as the second person of the Godhead[45] or as the whole Godhead manifesting itself by taking temporary forms.[46] In either case, the Salvation Historical perspective has adequate explanation. But, *if Jesus is less than Old Testament theophanies, the earthly revelation of God in the New Testament pales in comparison to his Old Testament revelation*; and therefore it is inconsistent with the general Salvation Historical tenor of the New Testament. *If Jesus is less than the object of invocation in the Old Testament, in this activity the closeness of the people of God to their God in the New Testament pales in comparison to the closeness of the people of God to God in the Old Testament.*[47]

Objections

Monotheism

A key objection to this theory of a redefinition of monotheism is the difficulty of a view of monotheism which allows for personal realities *within* the unity of God. Several observations are important here. First, it is clear that early Christians held firmly to monotheism (1 Cor. 8.4; Jas 2.19; Mk 12.29; 1 Tim. 2.5; by implication Lk. 4.8 and Mt. 4.10; perhaps Gal. 3.20).[48] To class Christ as divine in that context could mean one of three things: (1) the early Christians had a lack of theological understanding as to the implication of their belief in regard to monotheism; (2) they believed the divinity of Jesus was impersonal, or (3) they refined monotheism so as to see an undefined plurality within the basic unity of God.[49] Option one is an option of last resort, since any reader must give

45. See Irenaeus, *Demonstratio* 45; Novatian, *Trinity* 17-18 (see M.F. Wiles, 'Some Reflections on the Origin of the Doctrine of the Trinity', *JTS* 8 [1957], pp. 92-93); Cullmann, *Christ*, p. 24. Cf. W. MacDonald, 'Christology and 'The Angel of the Lord', in *Current Issues in Biblical and Patristic Interpretation. Studies in Honor of Merrill C. Tenney Presented by his Former Students* (ed. G.F. Hawthorne; Grand Rapids: Eerdmans, 1975), pp. 324-35.

46. Augustine, *Trinity* 2.12-34; 3.4-27.

47. See too D.R. de Lacey, 'Jesus as Mediator', *JSNT* 29 (1987), pp. 102-103; and Deut. 4.7.

48. For further evidence of the strength of monotheism during pre-Christian and Christian times see P.A. Rainbow, 'Jewish Monotheism as the Matrix for New Testament Christology: A Review Article', *NovT* 33 (1991), pp. 81-83; see too Josephus, *Ant.* 4.201.

49. The phrase 'plurality within a basic unity' comes from R.N. Longenecker,

his author the benefit of the doubt that his presentation forms a coherent whole until there is overwhelming evidence to the contrary. Moreover, I have presented evidence that Paul had worked out the implications of his belief and monotheism (1 Cor. 8.4-6). If the writers held to impersonal divinity, one would wonder at Mt. 11.27; Lk. 10.22 and 1 Cor. 8.6 because Matthew and Luke preserve the personhood of Christ as the revealer and because 1 Cor. 8.6 retrojects that personhood back into creation. So the third option is promising. I regard the pre-Christian parallels as building material for this redefinition of monotheism. That is, Christians did not take over their view from any existing parallel but exploited the material in a way so as to favour their understanding. Philo, for example, holds that within the being of God there are a plurality of attributes, one of which he calls 'God' and the other 'Lord'.[50] Later Rabbis held a similar view about God's character.[51] If one supposed for a moment that Philo had lived long enough to encounter Paul's teaching in 1 Cor. 8.4-6, no doubt Philo's own system of understanding of monotheism would differ from Paul's, but the initial idea of plurality within unity would be similar. Paul saw this plurality of figures as having personal distinction while Philo did not. Casey attributes Philo's whole system to a Hellenization of pure Judaism and implies that thereby Philo weakened his commitment to monotheism. But many experts doubt that Philo would have been anything other than a devout Jew.[52]

The Christology of Early Jewish Christianity (London: SCM Press, 1970), p. 141; and D.A. Hagner, 'Paul's Christology and Jewish Monotheism', in *Perspectives on Christology. Essays in Honor of Paul K. Jewett* (ed. M. Shuster and R. Muller; Grand Rapids: Zondervan, 1991), pp. 34-35. Philo, *Leg. Gai.* 118, writes, 'sooner could God change into a man than a man into God'. This statement makes it unlikely that apotheosis was an option. On the possible options of 'divinity of Jesus' within monotheism, see Wright, *Climax*, p. 94.

50. See Philo, *Abr.* 121-22; *Quaest. in Gen.* 2.53; and R. Williamson, *Jews in the Hellenistic World: Philo* (CCWJCW, 1.2; Cambridge: Cambridge University Press, 1989), p. 51.

51. See G.F. Moore, *Judaism in the First Centuries of the Christian Era. The Age of the Tannaim* (Cambridge, MA: Harvard University Press, 1927), I, pp. 386-88.

52. See Philo, *Spec. Leg.* 1.209; Williamson, *Jews*, p. 5; R. Beckwith, 'Intertestamental Judaism, Its Literature and Its Significance', *Themelios* 15 (1990), p. 78; B.D. Chilton, 'Commenting on the Old Testament', in *It is Written: Scripture Citing Scripture, Essays in Honour of Barnabas Lindars, SSF* (ed. D.A. Carson and H.G.M. Williamson; Cambridge: Cambridge University Press, 1988), p. 133; I.H. Marshall, 'Palestinian and Hellenistic Christianity: Some Critical Comments', *NTS* 19 (1972–73), p. 274 n. 5.

Thus, a gifted Jewish teacher could exploit ambiguities and difficulties in the Old Testament presentation of God to the point that these difficulties could begin to point to more than one figure bearing the name God and Lord in the Old Testament.[53] While holding firmly to monotheism on the one hand, on the other one could reinterpret that one God so as to introduce a plurality of figures within that concept. One could argue that the first words of the Old Testament, ברשׁית ברא אלהים show a plurality within the unity of God in that ברא indicates that the subject of the sentence must be singular, yet אלהים is plural.[54] It is possible that Jn 1.1-3 is developing just such an idea.[55] Thus, early Christians could have argued that Old Testament data prepare the way for this New Testament view of God.[56]

The unstated assumption in many recent New Testament Christologies is that any view of the one God of monotheism wherein one was able to see a plurality of figures, would be too polytheistic, or too polytheistic sounding to have been the view of the early Jewish-Christian community.[57] For instance Maurice Casey writes in regard to Col. 1.15-20 and Phil. 2.6-11,

> The christology of this piece is in no way less developed than that of Paul. As at Philippians 2.6-11, Jesus is on the verge of deity. We may not infer that Jesus was perceived as fully God, because monotheism was such a significant identity factor of the Jewish and early Christian communities that any perceived alteration could only be made deliberately.[58]

---

53. I wonder if just such a debate was the object of contention between Paul and the Jews of the Corinthian Synagogue (see particularly Acts 18.15 where Gallio suggests the debate is about names).

54. Philo, *Quaest. in Gen.* 1.54, questions the 'one of *us*' from Gen. 3.22. See too G.A.F. Knight, *A Biblical Approach to the Doctrine of the Trinity* (Edinburgh: Oliver & Boyd, 1953), pp. 19-20.

55. ὁ θεός and ὁ λόγος in Jn 1.1 are an explanation of the אלהים while Jn 1.2-3 is an explanation of ברא...השׁמים והארץ. For a further discussion of the Logos in John see T.H. Tobin, 'Logos', *ABD*, IV, pp. 352-55.

56. Similar ideas appear in Athanasius, *Orations Against the Arians* 3.29; H.P. Liddon, *The Divinity of Our Lord and Saviour Jesus Christ. Eight Lectures Preached before the University of Oxford* (BL [1866]; London: Rivingtons, 1875), pp. 44-96; and K.H. Schelkle, *Theology of the New Testament* (trans. W.A. Jurgens; Collegeville, MN: Liturgical Press, 1973), II, pp. 296-97.

57. Wright, *Climax*, p. 16, notices this unstated assumption too.

58. Casey, *Jewish Prophet*, p. 116. This passage is one of many similar ones.

It will help to spell out the implications of Casey's passage: (1) the one
God of monotheism for Paul is exclusively the Father, (2) Jesus cannot
be deity or God (i.e. a second God beside the one God of monotheism)
without abandoning monotheism, (3) for Jesus to be divine, Paul would
have explicitly to renounce monotheism, (4) Paul did not renounce
monotheism, therefore, Jesus is not divine. But here Casey has set up a
false dichotomy: it is not divine (i.e. a second God) or non-divine (i.e.
creature) but a third way (i.e. a redefinition of monotheism). This false
dichotomy exists because Casey is using 'divine' and 'God' in a peculiar
sense. A Gentile god in addition to the God of Israel would be polytheistic and contrary to the teaching of Mark (Mk 12.29-30) Paul (1 Cor.
8.4-6), Q (Mt. 4.10; Lk. 4.8), Matthew, Luke, and James (2.19). It is not
that Jesus is a second God *beside* the one God of monotheism but rather
a reinterpretation of that one God so as to include one God, the Father
and one Lord, Jesus Christ. Talk of endangering monotheism misses the
point.[59] Others make arguments similar to Casey's.[60] A key argument in
Casey's position is that pre-Christian Jewish monotheism was a unity
which disallowed any plurality within that concept. Yet a number of
scholars have questioned that assumption.[61]

Moreover, a recent view is that early Judaism was the mother from
which sprang Rabbinic Judaism, Christianity and Gnosticism.[62] On this
view, the orthodoxy of later Rabbinic Judaism did not hold absolute

59. See too J.D.G. Dunn, *Romans* (WBC; Waco, TX: Word Books, 1988), II,
pp. 535-36.

60. A.E. Harvey, *Jesus and the Constraints of History* (BL [1980]; London:
Duckworth, 1982), pp. 154-73.

61. For instance, R. Fuller holds that Hellenistic Judaism before Paul's time held
to a view of Wisdom as in some way separate from God yet existing within him
('The Theology of Jesus or Christology? An Evaluation of the Recent Discussion',
Semeia 30 [1984], p. 109; 'Lower and Higher Christology in the Fourth Gospel', in
The Conversation Continues: Studies in Paul & John in Honor of J. Louis Martyn
[ed. R.T. Fortna and B.R. Gaventa; Nashville: Abingdon Press, 1990], p. 363). See
too P.A. Rainbow, 'Monotheism and Christology in I Corinthians 8.4-6' (DPhil
thesis, Oxford University, 1987), p. 98; and P. Hayman, 'Monotheism—A Misused
Word in Jewish Studies?', *JJS* 42 (1991), pp. 1-15.

62. See J. Fossum, 'The New Religionsgeschichtliche Schule: The Quest for
Jewish Christology', in *SBL 1991 Seminar Papers* (ed. E.H. Lovering, Jr; Atlanta:
Scholars Press, 1991), pp. 638-31; and A.F. Segal, *Rebecca's Children: Judaism and
Christianity in the Roman World* (Cambridge, MA: Harvard University Press, 1986).
There are other views of Judaism, and this area is one which requires further study on
my part.

sway and allowed for differing interpretations of the data. This view explains how different Jewish interpreters came to radically differing conclusions in regard to the second figures which I have been discussing, in the short space of a century or two. What to one Jew was a personification, to another was an entity which had personal existence apart from God, and to another was a personal entity within God. Moreover, even if every pre-Christian Jew regarded Wisdom as a 'personification', when Christians regarded Jesus, the human being, as Wisdom and retrojected that personhood into his preincarnate existence, the boundary stones had moved. The whole question then is could the early Palestinian Church have exploited such ambiguity in their understanding of Jesus? To begin with the *a priori* assumption that they could not begs the question.

Other Passages
A second major objection is the number of passages which seem to deny that the New Testament writers classed Jesus as divine. Scholars who support the evolutionary model explain these texts by seeing them as evidence that the Church did not hold a view of Jesus as divine, or when such difficult texts occur in later documents, they take these texts as artefacts from an earlier period. Indeed, many texts are difficult to explain for one who holds that some New Testament writers held to a redefinition of monotheism.[63] 1 Cor. 15.28 seems to distinguish Jesus from God who is all in all. Other texts are those which speak of God as the Father and God of Jesus Christ (Jn 20.17; Mk 15.34; Mt. 27.46; 2 Cor. 1.3; 1 Pet. 1.3, Eph. 1.3, and 17). And other texts still are those which identify the God of Old Testament as the Father (Heb. 1.2; Rev. 21.22). Moreover, the word 'God' in the New Testament usually signifies the Father apart from a few debated occurrences where it perhaps refers to Jesus (Jn 1.1, 18; 20.28; Rom. 9.5; Tit. 2.13; Heb. 1.8-9; 2 Pet. 1.1).[64] Jn 17.3 identifies the Father as the only true God. Similarly 1 Cor. 8.6 (though compare above), Eph. 4.4-6 and 1 Tim. 2.5 seem to distinguish between the one God, the Father, and Jesus. Later Christian formulae continued to distinguish God and Jesus.[65] Other texts point to God's power in the resurrection, and thus seem to point to a lower level of dignity for the person of Christ than that of God the Father (Acts 2.36;

63. See R.E. Brown, *Jesus: God and Man. Modern Biblical Reflections* (New York: MacMillan; London: Collier MacMillan, 1967), pp. 7-10.

64. See now M.J. Harris, *Jesus as God. The New Testament Use of* Theos *in Reference to Jesus* (Grand Rapids: Baker, 1992).

65. See Brown, *Jesus*, p. 8 n. 14.

5.31; Phil. 2.9; Heb. 2.10; 1 Pet. 1.21). God the Father raised Jesus from
the dead (Acts 2.24, 32; 3.15; 4.10; 5.30; 10.40; 13.30, 34, 37; 17.31;
Rom. 4.24, 25; 6; 8.11; 10.9; 1 Cor. 6.14; 15.15; 2 Cor. 4.14; Gal. 1.1;
Eph. 1.20; Col. 2.12; 1 Thess. 1.10; and 1 Pet. 1.21). Jesus himself says,
'The Father is greater than I' (Jn 14.28), and seems to exclude his own
goodness (Mk 10.18; Mt. 19.17 and Lk. 18.19). Other texts distinguish
between the absolute knowledge of God the Father versus the limited
knowledge of the Son (Mk 13.32; Mt. 24.36; perhaps Acts 1.7; cf. Zech.
14.7).

In my opinion, the data are much more complex than that interpretation. Although Dunn has argued in detail that Paul did not hold a belief
in the incarnation,[66] Dunn's view has not won unanimous support.[67]
Thus, the older view is still possible that Paul held a three stage Christology rather than a two stage one. Thus, the person Jesus has two aspects,
a human one (Rom. 9.5; 1.3) and a divine (Rom. 9.5; perhaps 1.4).[68] If
Paul held to a three stage Christology and considered Christ from two
viewpoints, it is possible that Christ's subordination to the Father has to
do with his becoming poor (2 Cor. 8.9) or his humbling himself (Phil.
2.6-7).[69] There are other interpretations of subordination.[70] Those passages which identify God as the Father do not do so to exclude the Son.[71]
'God' does not mean 'God to the exclusion of Jesus' just as 'Lord'
even 'one Lord', itself a monotheistic catch phrase, does not exclude the
Father from lordship. The same linguistic difficulty exists in Philo between
'God' as the transcendent one and 'God' as one of his attributes.
Moreover, the pericope in which Jesus attributes goodness to God alone
has another good explanation.[72]

---

66. See Dunn, *Christology*.

67. See e.g. Wright, *Climax*, pp. 91-95.

68. On Rom. 9.5, see Harris, *Jesus*, pp. 143-72, who writes, 'It is...highly
probable that the term θεός is applied to ὁ Χριστός' (p. 172). On Rom. 1.3, see
Marshall, *Jesus*, p. 58; Ignatius, *Ephesians* 7.2, may allude to Rom. 1.3-4 making a
similar point (see Grillmeier, *Christ*, p. 105).

69. Augustine, *Trinity* 1.14, makes a similar argument.

70. See Chapter 5, pp. 149-50. The Spirit is subordinate to the Father in that the
Father 'sends' the Spirit (Jn 3.34; 14.16, 26; Acts. 2.17, 18, 33, 38; by implication
Rom. 5.5; 2 Cor. 1.22; 5.5; Gal. 3.4; 1 Thess. 4.8; cf. Ezek. 36.27; 37.14; 1 Pet. 1.12;
1 Jn 3.24; 4.13).

71. There is, moreover, a linguistic difficulty inherent in the data. Augustine, *Trinity*
5.12, similarly notes the difficulty of God in his entirety being called Holy Spirit.

72. Jesus understands the man to assume other men can be good before God (so

A Methodological Difference

Both Casey and Dunn share the explicit methodological starting point that New Testament writers would have had to make explicit a redefinition of monotheism if such had been the belief of the Church. Dunn writes,

> Had Paul indeed taught a doctrine of incarnation (the pre-existence of the Son of God, the man Christ Jesus)[73] in his mission it would inevitably have been open to misunderstanding and abuse—the sort of misunderstanding and abuse which followed his teaching on the resurrection and Lordship of Christ at Corinth (see particularly I Cor. 1-4; 15; II Cor. 10-13)—so that a greater clarification and fuller exposition of it would almost certainly have appeared elsewhere in his writings. It does not seem a very sound basis for an exegesis of Gal. 4.4 to argue both that Paul had already taught an explicit doctrine of incarnation, and also that such a novel teaching caused scarcely a ripple in the often troubled waters of the Pauline mission.[74]

Casey holds a similar view:

> On a strict definition of 'incarnation',[75] Philippians 2.6-11 does not qualify because Jesus was not fully divine, in the view of the original author. As we have seen, 'form' overlaps too much with 'image', 'equality with God' is too close to 'like God', and 'highly exalted' throws into relief the final status of Jesus as still below that of God the Father even when he was more exalted than when he was pre-existent. Not only that —monotheism was an identity marker of the Jewish community. Consequently, an author could breach it, in his own view, only deliberately, not by mistake. If an author so imbued with Jewish culture as this one, legitimating his view of

Augustine, *Trinity* 1.13). He is not worried about the man's Christology, and therefore one should not take Jesus' answer as evidence of the Gospel writers' or Jesus' Christology. Compare Mk 10.19 with 12.28-31; Mt. 19.18-19 with 22.36-40; Lk. 18.20 with 10.27-28.

73. Dunn, in my opinion, here misses the traditional doctrine of the incarnation which holds that it was not the man Jesus Christ who entered the Virgin's womb but the pre-incarnate Son of God who became incarnate there. The traditional view holds that before the incarnation, the Son of God was not a man even though the Son of God had personal distinction from the Father (see Irenaeus, *Against Heresies* 18.3.1 [from R.A. Norris, *The Christological Controversy* (SECT; Philadelphia: Fortress Press, 1980), p. 49]; and Justin Martyr, *First Apology* 63).

74. Dunn, *Christology*, p. 43.

75. Casey, *Prophet*, p. 114, defines incarnation, 'In this book, a relatively strict definition of the term has been used to refer to the process by which a fully divine being is born as a person'.

Jesus from the Adam story and from Isaiah 45.18-25, does not say that Jesus is God, we must infer that he did not believe that Jesus was God. Only the clarity of the Johannine prologue should convince us that such an author did believe in the deity of Jesus.[76]

Both writers hold the axiom: what is not explicit, is not the case. If one holds this axiom, there is a measured truth in Casey's and Dunn's evolutionary Christologies, since there are few undisputed, early texts which explicitly class Jesus as divine in terms of the divinity of the one God of monotheism. But this starting point seems to deny the possibility that early Christians held a belief which was so fundamental that New Testament writers never chose to explain it. In addition, neither Casey nor Dunn deals with the distinctiveness or enigmatic nature of early Christianity (1 Cor. 13.12; Gal. 5.11; Phil. 3.13; Heb. 13.13).[77] Yet elements within Christianity remained a mystery and veiled to the eyes of non-believing Jews.[78] Thus, I see no clear evidence of the limitations of that distinctiveness or the depths of the mysterious Christian enigma.

Other Hermeneutical Axioms

I now turn to a brief look at some other hermeneutical axioms in the early Church. A wide range of tradition suggests that first-century Christians believed they were living in the last days.[79] Other passages affirm only a remaining final consummation.[80] Christians also believed that much prophecy pointed to their own time[81] and saw their message as 'nothing but what the prophets and Moses said would take place' (Acts 26.22; see too 24.14 and 28.23). They believed that the Old Testament pointed to Christ's ignominious sufferings and his subsequent

---

76. Casey, *Prophet*, p. 114.

77. See too Augustine, *Trinity* 5.1.

78. Jn 3.10, 12; 1 Cor. 2.1, 7; 4.1; 2 Cor. 3.14-18; 4.4; Mt. 13.11; Mk 4.11; Lk. 8.10; Rom. 11.25; Eph. 3.3; 6.19; Col. 1.26; 2.2; 4.3; 1 Tim. 3.16.

79. See 1 Cor. 10.11; Heb. 9.26; 1 Jn 2.18; 1 Pet. 1.20; 4.7; 2 Pet. 3.3; and by implication 2 Tim. 3.1 and Jude 18.

80. See Acts 1.6; 3.21; 1 Cor. 5.5; 2 Cor. 1.14; 1 Thess. 5.2; 2 Thess. 2.2; 2 Pet. 3.10; and 2 Pet. 3.12.

81. Lk. 1.70; 24.27, 44; Acts 2.16; 3.18-24; 7.52; 10.43; 26.22; 1 Cor. 10.11; Heb. 9.9; 1 Pet. 1.10-12; Rev. 10.7. This early Christian view of scripture corresponds to *1 En*. 1.2 where the writer states he is not writing for his own generation but one to come.

exaltation (Lk. 24.44; Acts 3.18-24; 10.43; 1 Pet. 1.11).[82] Moreover, Christians believed that with Jesus the Old Testament found its fulfilment (Mt. 11.3; Lk. 16.16; perhaps 2 Cor. 1.20) and that a decisive break with the past has taken place (Gal. 4.4; Heb. 1.1-3; 9.6-7). Furthermore, some believed that the long awaited new exodus had begun.[83] Jesus as messiah is a participant in the final victory, and the nations will hope in his name (Mt. 12.20-21). New Testament writers affirm that the Old Testament prophets did not understand clearly the objects of their prophecies (1 Pet. 1.11 and perhaps Mt. 13.17 and Lk. 10.24). Thus, the Christian interpretation of Scripture was one not clear to the normal Jew or even to Jesus' disciples without instruction (Lk. 24.27, 44 and by implication Jn 12.41). Two writers present the view that the disciples' understanding of scripture was the result of exegetical work (Lk. 24.46-47; Jn 20.9). Some documents suggest that Jesus pointed the way for the New Testament Christocentric understanding of scripture (Lk. 24.27, 44; Jn 5.39, 46). All these perspectives may contribute to the early Church's application of Isa. 40.3 and Joel 2.32[3.5]a to Jesus.

Points of Contact Between Isa. 40.3 and
Joel 2.32[3.5]a and their Popularity

In Chapters 3–4, I showed that Isa. 40.3 and Joel 2.32[3.5]a proved extremely popular in early Christianity. The question remains whether there are points of contact between the two passages which might explain some of that popularity. First, one point to notice is both these passages reflect central ideas in Judaism. 'Calling on the name of the LORD' was an activity fundamental in Jewish history. Belief in God's intervention during the exodus was a Jew's proud heritage. Yet it was precisely these two fundamental ideas about God which New Testament writers adapted in their application of them to Christ. Such suggests that this practice was no accident but a radically new belief on the part of Christians. This practice in regard to Joel 2.32[3.5] demonstrates a real difference with pre-Christian and first-century Judaism because in Judaism it was those texts which were problematic which writers primarily reinterpreted as referring to a second figure. Joel 2.32[3.5] was

82. I suggest, along with the editors of NA[26], that two Old Testament sources for such belief are Isa. 52.7–53.12 and Psalm 22.

83. 1 Cor. 10.1-11; Mk 1.2; Mt. 3.3; Lk. 3.4-6; Jn 1.23; perhaps Heb. 4.3-11; Mk 14.1; Mt. 26.2-5 and Lk. 22.1; Jn 19.14; 1 Cor. 5.7.

only marginally in that category. Secondly, both passages come from larger contexts where New Testament writers apply other passages about God to Christ.[84] For instance, Rev. 14.1 may allude to Joel 2.32[3.5]b in clear application to the Father and Jesus. Joel 3.1-21[4.1-21] includes the idea of the day of the LORD which New Testament writers have applied to the coming of Christ. Mt. 24.29-30 and Mk 13.24-26 reflect the development of Joel 3.15-16[4.15-16], Isa. 13.9-10 and the day of the LORD, and the coming one in Matthew and Mark is the Son of Man. Rev. 6.12-17 gives the day of the LORD a binitarian interpretation of Joel 3.15[4.15] and context by mentioning the one seated on the throne and the wrath of the Lamb (Rev. 6.16). Jn 7.38 may reread Joel 3.18[4.18] in connection with Jesus where the source in Joel is the LORD's house. In regard to Isaiah 40, Rev. 1.5 identifies Jesus as the one who has loosed Christians from sin (see Isa. 40.2[LXX]); and Rev. 18.5-6). Isa. 40.8 contrasts Mt. 24.35, Mk 13.31, and Lk. 21.33 in one point: Jesus' words are eternal like God's words. Rom. 10.15 alludes to Isa. 52.7 which has a context similar to that of Isa. 40.9 in the coming of God to Judah. Interestingly, the context of Rom. 10.14-15 connects the message about Jesus as Lord with proclamation which Isa. 40.9 and 52.7 connect with the messenger's duty to proclaim God's coming. Isa. 40.9 speaks of the coming of God which puts to flight the fear of Zion; Jn 12.15 says the same of Jesus' coming to Jerusalem. Rev. 22.7 and 12 speak of the coming of the Alpha and Omega, Jesus (22.20), who will bring his reward with him; Isa. 40.10 ascribes this action to the LORD God. 1 Cor. 2.16 compares the mind of Christ to the mind of the Lord which Isa. 40.13 uses to distinguish the one LORD God from all his rivals. I believe that Paul makes a similar inclusion of Christ in Rom. 11.34-36 which also uses Isa. 40.13 (compare my above comments on 1 Cor. 8.4-6 and Rom. 11.36). Acts 19.27 may be Luke's ironic echo of Isa. 40.17 only now it is Christ's greatness before whom all nations are nothing. The wider contexts of Isa. 40.3 and Joel 2.32[3.5] thus were ones in which writers found a number of passages about the divine which they applied to Christ. Another point of contact between the New

84. See too Rom. 1.20; Eph. 1.19-20 and Isa. 40.26; Rom. 1.20 and Isa. 40.28. Tit. 3.6 also understands Joel 2.28[3.1] as referring to God pouring out his Spirit through Jesus. Joel 3.1-2[4.1-2] may be in the background of Mt. 25.31-46. The text furthermore may have provided much information on the day of the Lord in Christian understanding (see too A.M. Hunter, *Paul and his Predecessors* [London: SCM Press, rev. edn, 1961], p. 132).

Testament usage of Isa. 40.3 and Joel 2.32[3.5] is the connection with God's eschatological outpouring of the Spirit (see Mk 1.8; Mt. 3.11; Lk. 3.16; Joel 2.28[3.1]). Matthew, Mark and Luke closely connect the promise of Isa. 40.3 and baptism with the Spirit. The eschatological outpouring of the Spirit would occur in the new exodus; God, in a new Sinai, would write his laws on human hearts. This connection may betray an underlying hermeneutical axiom: if Jews associated Isa. 40.3 with the eschatological outpouring of the Spirit, and if Christians had experienced this outpouring, they would reason that Isa. 40.3 and Joel 2.28[3.1] had already taken place. Thus, both passages may have proved popular because of the connection with this new exodus event. Acts 1.5-6 makes a connection between Israel's future and the coming of the Spirit. Another possible connection between the two passages is that they could be read as about a salvation event centred around Jerusalem.[85]

A further point of contact is that they are both about κύριος. It is possible that New Testament writers applied 'God'-texts basically to the Father and 'Lord'-texts basically to Christ; however, since the New Testament writers apply some κύριος passages to God, it is unlikely that this connection is decisive in the popularity of these verses.[86] Another possible connection is that if one connects 'the angel in whom God's name dwells' and 'calling on the name of the Lord', one could connect the new exodus event and invocation of the name of God with a second figure. Jesus bearing the name of God (Phil. 2.10-11) would connect him as the object of invocation and this new exodus deliverer. Yet in my examination of the data, little objective evidence supports this connection.

The New Testament writers understood the salvation promised in Isa. 40.3 and Joel 2.32[3.5]a as having taken place after Jesus death. They believed a new Passover and exodus had taken place. One possible scenario is that they understood such events promised the manifestation of God's presence, and firmly convinced that Scripture was true and had been fulfilled in the Jesus event, they believed that God's particu-

---

85. Reading Isa. 40.1-10 as God's arrival to Jerusalem.

86. See Ps. 110.1 in Mt. 22.44; Mk 12.36; Lk. 20.42-43; Acts; 2.34-35; See too Rom. 8.34; 1 Cor. 15.25; Eph. 1.20; Col. 3.1; Heb. 1.3, 13; 8.1, 10, 12. Mk 11.9 (Ps. 117.26 [118.26]); 12.11 (Ps. 117.23 [118.23]); 12.29 (Deut. 6.4); 12.30 (Deut. 6.5); Heb. 7.21 (Ps. 110.4); 2 Cor. 6.17 (Isa. 52.11 and 2 Sam. 7.14); Rom. 12.19 (Deut. 32.35); Rom. 14.11 (Isa. 45.23); 1 Cor. 14.21 (Isa. 28.11); Rom. 4.8 ([Ps. 31.1-2 LXX]; Rom. 9.28; 9.29 (Isa. 1.9); 1 Cor. 3.20 (Ps. 93.11 LXX); 1 Thess. 4.6 (Sir. 5.3); 2 Tim. 2.19 a (Num. 16.5 ὁ θεός LXX, יהוה MT); Rom. 11.34 (Isa. 40.13); 2 Tim 2.19b (Isa. 26.13).

larized earthly presence was in the person Jesus. Yet at the same time, since Jesus had revealed God his heavenly Father, they believed he had introduced a complexity within the divine. They could claim God's presence indeed had come to Jerusalem, to Mount Zion and redeemed his people in the crucifixion and death of Jesus.

Also, both texts could be applied to a divine intermediary.[87] It may be that New Testament writers applied texts to Jesus which others applied to a divine intermediary such as the wisdom, word, or glory of God. This connection might explain Jesus and the day of the LORD expectation since later Jews understood that day as a revelation of the Shekinah. Also according to the New Testament, early leaders applied these texts to Jesus: John the Baptist associates Isa. 40.3 with Jesus (Jn 1.23-27);[88] Peter and Paul apply Joel 2.32 [3.5] to Jesus (Acts 2.21, 38; Rom. 10.13; 1 Cor. 1.2). Both passages also have some connection with 'all flesh'.[89] Lk. 3.6 explicitly quotes this section of Isa. 40.5, and Acts 2.17 relates the outpouring of God's Spirit 'on all flesh'.

Conclusion

In the previous chapter, I have suggested early evidence that Paul thought Jesus shared in the divinity of the one God of monotheism while distinct from God the Father. In this chapter, I posited that such a view of God explains the early Church's Salvation Historical perspective. Jesus is the climax of God's earthly revelation and the object of invocation because he is divine. I also suggested that the two passages have certain interesting contacts. The most important are the following: (1) one could read both as concerned with the Lord's eschatological deliverance around Jerusalem; (2) both could readily apply to divine intermediaries; (3) both occur in contexts where other passages about God are applied to Christ; and (4) the New Testament attributes the application of both texts to Christ as the act of a central figure in the Christian movement.

---

87. Wisdom is the object of invocation in Prov. 1.28; Wisdom is the deliverer of Israel in the exodus (Wisdom 10).

88. Compare too Mk 1.7 and parallels with Jn 1.27 and Acts 13.25.

89. See F.F. Bruce, *The Acts of the Apostles: The Greek Text with Introduction and Commentary*,(Grand Rapids: Eerdmans, 3rd edn, 1990), p. 121.

Chapter 7

CONCLUSIONS

I began this book with a survey of some of the recent theories regarding Old Testament passages about the divine which the New Testament applies to Jesus. I saw that these theories sought to answer two questions. What was the source and development of this practice, and what was its significance to Christians in the early decades of the Christian movement? To answer the latter question, I examined some of the pre-Christian parallels for applying a passage about God to a second figure. I found numerous examples of passages where a writer applies an earlier passage about God to a second figure. These figures included the angel, word, wisdom and glory of the LORD. The nature of these second figures is unclear: many scholars class them as divine yet the nature of that divinity is the subject of long standing dispute. Application of such passages to non-divine second figures is possible though does not appear common-place in pre-Christian Judaism. Application to the messiah or a messiah of such passages does not appear widespread. A number of parallels exist where the nature of the second figure is impossible to gauge with the evidence at hand. This is particularly the case with Melchizedek in 11Q Melchizedek. I suggested these parallels do not provide clear help in trying to assess the significance to early Christians of such application to Jesus.

My investigation, in many respects, is an examination of Maurice Casey's theory that pre-Christian parallels adequately explain the New Testament practice of applying such passages to Jesus. I have suggested, however, that while Casey's work has raised important issues, there are nevertheless problems with his argument. I pointed out his usage of 'divine', that is, a second god, which is not what most scholars mean when they affirm or deny that the New Testament presents Jesus as divine. Rather, Casey's presentation stands on a false dichotomy which limits the choices to seeing Jesus as a 'Gentile god' or as a creature. A third way, unexplored by Casey, is to see Jesus as divine in terms of a redefinition of monotheism. Besides the problem with terminology I have shown a problem with the argument about parallels since in the majority of cases parallel application occurs with a special class of second figures, the glory, angel, wisdom and word of the LORD. The debate over the first-century significance of these figures still rages with no end in sight; therefore, the parallels only bring interpreters to this difficulty, but they do not settle the significance.

I also examined the usage of Isa. 40.3 and Joel 2.32[3.5]a in pre-Christian and first century Judaism to see the kinds of ideas which these passages carried for most Jews. I posited that Isa. 40.3 suggested a new exodus in continuity with but surpassing the old in which God's glory would visibly rescue Israel. Some passages associated this new exodus with a second figure, though again the nature of that second figure was impossible to tell given the present state of the evidence. I found no clear pre-Christian evidence of the application of this verse exclusively to the or a Messiah. I pointed to some evidence in the Gospels which class Jesus as the presence of God. This association makes possible—at least for Matthew, Luke and John—the thesis that these writers understood the predicted coming glory of God as present in Jesus and that the new exodus promised in Isa. 40.3 took place with Jesus' death on the cross when God delivered his people from their enemies (the wrath of God and the power of Satan).

When I looked at Joel 2.32[3.5], I saw that 'calling on the name of the LORD' was an activity which characterized the people of God from the beginning of their relationship with God. I saw that this activity was frequently part of the cultic worship of God. Moreover, 'calling on the name of the LORD' was an activity which separated the people of God from unbelieving pagans. I then investigated the possibility of the application of this phrase to a second figure. Here the only real parallel I found was the possibility that some Semitic people may have understood 'the name' as somehow partially distinct from God. I found little New Testament evidence, however, that the New Testament writers understood Jesus as 'the name' of God, so this possibility proved somewhat of a dead-end in explaining how the New Testament applied this phrase to Jesus and what its significance was. I also surveyed the New Testament examples of the application of this phrase to Jesus. Interestingly, Luke attributes this practice to the first Apostles after the Pentecost event. According to Luke, the justification of the practice came form exegetical work seen against Jesus' exaltation. Luke described this practice as a necessity for salvation, that is, for inclusion in the new people of God. He also shared the view I saw in Isa. 40.3 that the salvation event described in Joel 2.32[3.5] had taken place. Luke also suggested that 'calling on the name of the Lord Jesus' was an integral part in the conversion experience of Paul. I also queried the question over the possible historicity of the event described in Acts 2 and came up with the verdict *non liquet*. I saw that Paul agrees with the sentiment expressed in Luke that 'calling on the name of the Lord Jesus' was a practice common to both Jews and converted Greeks. I saw that Paul makes this assumption in the fifties.

I then turned to outside evidence which might more clearly suggest the view of Christ which Christians had in the 50s. I looked primarily at 1 Cor. 8.4-6 which several recent commentators have put forward as evidence of a Christological redefinition of monotheism. I examined the passage and agreed that it implies that Paul had classed Jesus and the Father as divine while affirming the distinctiveness of the two as well as affirming monotheism. I then looked for any further evidence in the early Christian literature which might support this view. I also suggested that 1 Cor. 8.4-6 and the view therein contained swings the probability to the view that for Paul at least it was his redefinition of God which allowed for the application of passages about God to Jesus.

I asked if this hypothesis would explain any of the other New Testament data. I saw that the New Testament writers operated with a view that looked on the New Testament times as forming the high point of Old Testament times. I then asked what this view would mean for the idea of Jesus as the high point of revelation and as the object of invocation. I suggested that if the New Testament writers worked with a developed view of God they could indeed claim Jesus as the high point of revelation and as the object of invocation. If such were not the case, I found it difficult to understand their estimate of Christ as the high point of revelation and as the object of invocation.

Appendix

CITATIONS AND ALLUSIONS ABOUT THE DIVINE APPLIED TO CHRIST

Mt. 8.26 (Ps. 89.9); Mt. 13.14-15 (Isa. 6.9-10); Mt. 13.44 (Zeph. 1.3); Mt. 16.27 (Ps. 62.12); Mt. 18.20 (later traditions about Shekinah); Mt. 19.28 (Dan. 7.10); Mt. 21.16 (Ps. 8.2[3]); Mt. 21.44 (Isa. 8.14-15; Zech. 2.10; 13.7 and Dan. 7.13-14); Mt. 23.37 (Ps. 91.4); Mt. 24.29 (Isa. 13.10); Mt. 24.35 (Isa. 40.8); Mt. 25.31-46 (Zech. 14.5; Deut. 32.39-43; and Dan. 7.22); Mt. 25.32 (Joel 3.1-12 [4.1-12]; and Ezek. 34.17); Mt. 27.9 (Zech. 11.3); Mk 1.17 (Jer. 16.16); Mk 8.38 (Zech. 14.5); Mk 13.31 (Isa. 40.8); Lk. 10.19 (Ps. 91.13); Lk. 13.34-35 (Ps. 91.4); Lk. 19.10 (Ezek. 34.16, 22); Lk. 20.17 (Ps. 118.22); Lk. 20.18-19 (Isa. 8.14-15; Zech. 12.10; 13.7; Dan. 2.34-35, 44-45; 7.13-14); Lk. 21.33 (Isa. 40.3); Jn 10.28 (Wis. 3.1; cf. Deut. 32.39); Jn 12.38 (Isa. 53.1); Jn 12.41 (Isa. 6.1); Acts 2.21 (Joel 2.32[3.5]); Acts 18.10 (compare Josh. 1.9; Isa. 41.10; 43.5; Jer. 1.8); Rom. 8.26 (Ps. 44.22); Rom. 9.31-32 (Ps. 25.3); Rom. 9.33 (Isa. 8.14-15); Rom. 10.13 (Joel 2.28 [3.5]); Rom. 10.16 (Isa. 53.1); 1 Cor. 1.8 (transfer of the Old Testament day-of-the-LORD idea to day of the Lord Jesus); 1 Cor. 1.31 (Jer. 9.22-23); 1 Cor. 2.16 (Isa. 40.13); 1 Cor. 10.4 (Exod. 17.6; cf. Num. 20.7-11; and Ps. 78.15-16); 1 Cor. 10.9 (Ps. 78.18; and Num. 21.5-6); 1 Cor. 10.21 (Mal. 1.7, 12); 1 Cor. 10.22 (Deut. 32.21); 1 Cor. 10.26 (Ps. 24.1); 2 Cor. 3.16 (Exod. 34.34); 2 Cor. 5.10 (Eccl. 12.15); 2 Cor. 8.21 (Prov. 3.4 LXX); 2 Cor. 10.17 (Jer. 9.22-23); Eph. 4.8 (Ps. 68.19); Eph. 6.4 (Prov. 3.11); Phil. 2.9-11 (Isa. 45.23); 1 Thess. 3.13 (Zech. 14.5); 1 Thess. 4.6 (Ps. 94.2; and Sir. 5.3); 1 Thess. 5.2 (transfer of the day of the LORD to day of the Lord Jesus); 2 Thess. 1.7 (Zech. 14.5); 2 Thess. 1.8 (Isa. 66.15); 2 Thess. 1.9 (Isa. 2.10, 19, 21); 2 Thess. 1.10 (transfer of the day of the LORD to the day of the Lord Jesus); 2 Thess. 1.12 (Isa. 66.5; Mal. 1.11); 2 Thess. 2.2 (transfer of the day of the LORD to day of the Lord Jesus); 2 Thess. 2.8 (Job 4.9; Ps. 32.6 LXX); 2 Tim. 2.19 (Sir. 17.26 conflated with a common Old Testament phrase); Heb. 1.10-12 (Ps. 102.25-27); Jas 2.7 (a common Old Testament phrase); 1 Pet. 1.11 (Spirit passages); 1 Pet. 2.3 (Ps. 34.8); 1 Pet. 3.14-15 (Isa. 8.12-13); 2 Pet. 3.8 (Ps. 90.4); Jude 14-15 (Zech. 14.5; cf. *1 En.* 1.9); Rev. 1.7 (Zech. 12.10); Rev. 1.13-14 (Dan. 7.9); Rev. 2.17 (Isa. 62.2); Rev. 2.23 (Jer. 11.20); Rev. 3.5 (Exod. 32.32, 33; and Ps. 69.28); Rev. 7.17 (Ps. 23.2); Rev. 14.4 (first fruit passages); Rev. 17.14 (Deut. 2.47; 10.17); Rev. 19.16 (Deut. 10.17; and Dan. 2.47); Rev. 22.1 (throne passages).

BIBLIOGRAPHY

Aland, K., and B. Aland, *The Text of the New Testament: An Introduction to the Critical Editions and to the Theory and Practice of Modern Textual Criticism* (trans. E.F. Rhodes; Grand Rapids: Eerdmans; Leiden: Brill, 2nd edn, 1989).

Albright, W.F., and C.S. Mann, *Matthew: Introduction, Translation, and Notes* (AB; Garden City, NY: Doubleday, 1971).

Alexander, J.A., *Commentary on the Prophecies of Isaiah* (2 vols.; ed. J. Eadie; Edinburgh: Andrew Eliot and James Thin, rev. edn, 1865).

Alexander, P., '3 (Hebrew Apocalypse of) Enoch', *OTP*, I, pp. 223-54.

Alexander, P.S., 'Shekhinah', *DBI*, pp. 631-33.

Allen, L.C., *The Books of Joel, Obadiah, Jonah and Micah* (NICOT; Grand Rapids: Eerdmans, 1976).

Allo, E.B., *Première épître aux Corinthiens* (EB; Paris: Gabalda, 1934).

Anderson, A.A., *The Book of the Psalms* (2 vols.; NCB; Greenwood, SC: Attic Press, 1972).

Anderson, B.W., 'Exodus Typology in Second Isaiah', in *Isaiah's Prophetic Heritage: Essays in Honor of James Muilenburg* (ed. B.W. Anderson and W.J. Harrelson; New York: Harper & Row, 1962), pp. 177-95.

Anderson, H., *The Gospel of Mark* (NCB; London: Oliphants, 1976).

Attridge, H.W., 'Historiography', in *Jewish Writings of the Second Temple Period: Apocrypha, Pseudepigrapha, Qumran Sectarian Writings, Philo, Josephus* (ed. M.E. Stone; CRINT, 2.2; Assen: Van Gorcum; Philadelphia: Fortress Press, 1984), pp. 157-84.

Barrett, C.K., *A Commentary on the First Epistle to the Corinthians* (BNTC; London: A. & C. Black, 2nd edn, 1971).

—*A Commentary on the Second Epistle to the Corinthians* (HNTC; New York: Harper & Row, 1973).

—*The New Testament Background: Selected Documents* (London: SPCK, 1961).

Barth, M., *Ephesians* (2 vols., AB; Garden City, NY: Doubleday, 1974).

Bauckham, R., 'The Worship of Jesus in Apocalyptic Christianity', *NTS* 27 (1981): 322-41.

—'The Sonship of the Historical Jesus in Christology', *SJT* 31 (1978), pp. 245-60.

Baudissin, W.W. Graf von, *Kyrios als Gottesname in Judentum und seine Stelle in der Religionsgeschichte* (4 vols.; Giessen: Töpelmann, 1926-29).

Baumgarten, J.M., 'The Heavenly Tribunal and the Personification of Sedeq in Jewish Apocalyptic', *ANRW*, II.19.1.

Beale, G.K., 'Revelation', in *It is Written: Scripture Citing Scripture: Essays in Honour of Barnabas Lindars, SSF* (ed. D.A. Carson and H.G.M. Williamson; Cambridge: Cambridge University Press, 1988), pp. 318-36.

Beasley-Murray, G.R., *Jesus and the Kingdom of God* (Exeter: Paternoster Press, 1986).

Beckwith, R., 'Intertestamental Judaism, Its Literature and Its Significance', *Themelios* 15 (1990), pp. 77-81.

Benoit, P., J.T. Milik, and R. de Vaux, *Les grottes de Marabba'ât* (Discoveries in the Judaean Desert, 2; Oxford: Clarendon Press, 1961).

Berger, K., 'Apostelbrief und apostolische Rede/Zum Formular frühchristlicher Briefe', *ZNW* 65 (1974), pp. 190-231.

Best, E., *A Commentary of the First and Second Epistles to the Thessalonians* (BNTC; London: A. & C. Black, 1972).

Bethune-Baker, J.F., *An Introduction to the Early History of Christian Doctrine to the Time of the Council of Chalcedon* (London: Methuen, 1903).

Beyer, H.W., 'ἐπισκοπή', *TDNT*, II, pp. 606-608.

Black, M., *An Aramaic Approach to the Gospels and Acts* (Oxford: Clarendon Press, 3rd edn, 1967).

Blackman, P., *Mishnayoth* (7 vols.; New York: Judaica Press, 2nd edn, 1964).

Bock, D.L., *Proclamation from Prophecy and Pattern: Lucan Old Testament Christology* (JSNTSup, 12; Sheffield: JSOT Press, 1987).

Boers, H., 'Where Christology is Real: A Survey of Recent Research on New Testament Christology', *Int* 26 (1972), pp. 300-27.

Boobyer, G.H., 'Jesus as "Theos" in the New Testament', *BJRL* 50 (1967–68), pp. 247-61.

Bonnard, P.-E., *Le second Isaïe: Son disciple et leurs éditeurs, Isaïe 40-66* (EB; Paris: Gabalda, 1972).

Borgen, P., 'Philo of Alexandria', *ABD*, V, pp. 333-42.

Bousset, W., *Kyrios Christos: A History of the Belief in Christ from the Beginnings of Christianity to Irenaeus* (trans. J.E. Steely; Nashville: Abingdon Press, 1970).

Bowker, J.W., 'Speeches in Acts: A Study in Proem and Yelammedenu Form', *NTS* 14 (1967–68), pp. 96-111.

Braude, W.G., *Pesikta Rabbati: Discourses for Feasts, Fasts, and Special Sabbaths* (Yale Judaica Series, 18; New Haven: Yale University Press, 1968).

Braude, W.G., and I.J. Kapstein, *Pesikta de Rab- Kahana: Rab Kahana's Compilation of Discourses for Sabbaths and Festal Days* (Philadelphia: Jewish Publication Society of America, 1975).

Brewer, D.I., *Techniques and Assumptions in Jewish Exegesis before 70 CE* (Texte und Studien zum Antiken Judentum, 30; Tübingen: Mohr [Siebeck], 1992).

Brongers, H.A., 'Die Wendung יְהוָה בְּשֵׁם im Alten Testament', *ZAW* 77 (1965), pp. 1-20.

Brooks, J.A., and C.L. Winberry, *Syntax of New Testament Greek* (New York: University Press of America, 1979).

Brown, R.E., *Jesus: God and Man: Modern Biblical Reflections* (New York: MacMillan; London: Collier MacMillan, 1967).

Bruce, F.F., *The Acts of the Apostles: The Greek Text with Introduction and Commentary* (Grand Rapids: Eerdmans, 3rd edn, 1990).

—*The Book of Acts* (NICNT; Grand Rapids: Eerdmans, rev. edn, 1988).

—'Jesus is Lord', in *Soli Deo Gloria: NTS in Honor of William Childs Robinson* (ed. J.M. Richards; Richmond: John Knox, 1968), pp. 23-36.

—*This is That: The New Testament Development of Some Old Testament Themes* (Exeter: Paternoster Press, 1968).

—*1 & 2 Thessalonians* (WBC; Waco: Word Books, 1982).

Bultmann, R., *Theology of the New Testament* (2 vols.; trans. K. Grobel; New York: Scribner's, 1951, 1955).

Burton, E., *Testimonies of the Ante-Nicene Fathers to the Doctrine of the Trinity and the Divinity of the Holy Ghost* (Oxford: Oxford University Press, 1831).

Burton, E. De Witt, *A Critical and Exegetical Commentary on the Epistle to the Galatians* (ICC; Edinburgh: T. & T. Clark, 1921).

Caird, G.B., 'Jesus and Israel: The Starting Point for New Testament Christology', in *Christological Perspectives, Essays in Honor of Harvey K. McArthur* (ed. R.F. Berkey and S.A. Edwards; New York: Pilgrims, 1982), pp. 58-68.

Calvin, J., *The First Epistle of Paul the Apostle to the Corinthians* (trans. J.W. Fraser; ed. D.W. Torrance and T.F. Torrance; Edinburgh: Oliver & Boyd, 1960).

—*The Gospel according to St John 1–10* (trans. T.H.L. Parker; ed. D.W. Torrance and T.F. Torrance; Edinburgh: Oliver & Boyd, 1959).

Capes, D.B., 'Paul's Use of Old Testament Yahweh-Texts and its Implications for his Christology' (PhD dissertation, Southwestern Baptist Theological Seminary, 1990.

—*Old Testament Yahweh Texts in Paul's Christology* (WUNT, 47; Tübingen: Mohr [Siebeck], 1992).

Carmignac, J., 'Le document de Qumrân sur Melkisédeq', *RevQ* 7 (1969–71), pp. 343-78.

Carson, D.A., and H.G.M. Williamson (eds.), *It is Written: Scripture Citing Scripture: Essays in Honour of Barnabas Lindars, SSF* (Cambridge: Cambridge University Press, 1988).

Casey, M., 'Chronology and the Development of Pauline Christology', in *Paul and Paulinism: Essays in Honour of C.K. Barrett* (ed. M.D. Hooker and S.G. Wilson; London: SPCK, 1982), pp. 124-34.

—*From Jewish Prophet to Gentile God: The Origins and Development of New Testament Christology* (Cambridge: James Clarke, 1991).

Cassuto, U., *A Commentary on the Book of Exodus* (trans. I. Abrahams; Jerusalem: Magnes Press, 1967).

Cathcart, K.J., and R.P. Gordon, *The Targum of the Minor Prophets, translated with a Critical Introduction, Apparatus and Notes* (ArB, 14; Edinburgh: T. & T. Clark, 1989).

Cerfaux, L., *Christ in the Theology of St Paul* (trans. G. Webb and A. Walker; New York: Herder & Herder, 1959).

—*Recueil Lucien Cerfaux: Etudes d'exégèse et d'histoire religieuse* (Gembloux: Duculot, 1954).

Chamberlain, J.V., 'The Functions of God as Messianic Titles in the Complete Qumran Isaiah Scroll', *VT* 5 (1955), pp. 366-72.

Chambers, T., *The Homilies of Saint John Chrysostom Archbishop of Constantinople on the Epistles of Paul to the Corinthians* (Nicene and Post-Nicene Fathers, 12; Grand Rapids: Eerdmans, 1956).

Charlesworth, J.H., 'The Concept of the Messiah in the Pseudepigrapha', *ANRW*, II.19.1, pp. 188-218.

—*Jesus Within Judaism: New Light from Exciting Archaeological Discoveries* (AB Reference Library; New York: Doubleday, 1988).

Chester, A., 'Citing the OT', in Carson and Williamson (eds.), *It is Written*, pp. 141-69.

Chilton, B.D., 'Commenting on the Old Testament', in Carson and Williamson (eds.), *It is Written*, pp. 122-40.

—*The Isaiah Targum: Introduction, Translation, Apparatus and Notes* (ArB, 11; Edinburgh: T. & T. Clark, 1987).

Chouinard, L., 'Gospel Christology: A Study of Methodology', *JSNT* 30 (1987), pp. 21-37

Cockerill, G.L., 'Melchizedek or "King of Righteousness"', *EvQ* 63 (1991), pp. 305-12.

Cohen, A., *The Minor Tractates of the Talmud: Massektoth Ketannoth* (2 vols.; London: Soncino, 1965).

Collins, J.J., 'Testaments', in *Jewish Writings of the Second Temple Period: Apocrypha, Pseudepigrapha, Qumran Sectarian Writings, Philo, Josephus* (ed. M.E. Stone; CRINT, 2.2; Assen: Van Gorcum; Philadelphia: Fortress Press, 1984), pp. 325-55.

Colson, C., *Who Speaks for God? Confronting the World with Real Christianity* (Westchester, IL: Crossway, 1985).

Colson, F.H., G.H. Whitaker and R. Marcus, *Philo* (12 vols.; LCL; Cambridge, MA: Harvard University Press, 1929–53).

Conrad, E.W., 'The "Fear Not" Oracles in Second Isaiah', *VT* 44 (1984), pp. 129-52.

Conzelmann, H., *Acts of the Apostles: A Commentary on the Acts of the Apostles* (trans. J. Limburg, A.T. Kraabel, and D. Juel; ed. E.J. Epp with C.R. Matthews; Hermeneia; Philadelphia: Fortress Press, 1987).

—*1 Corinthians: A Commentary on the First Epistle to the Corinthians* (trans. J.W. Leitch; ed. G.W. MacRae; Hermeneia; Philadelphia: Fortress Press, 1975).

—*An Outline of the Theology of the New Testament* (trans. J. Bowden; New York: Harper & Row, 1969).

Cowley, A.E., *Aramaic Papyri of the Fifth Century BC* (Oxford: Clarendon Press, 1923).

Craigie, P.C., *The Old Testament: Its Background, Growth, and Content* (Nashville: Abingdon Press, 1986).

Cranfield, C.E.B., *A Critical and Exegetical Commentary on the Epistle to the Romans* (2 vols.; ICC; Edinburgh: T. & T. Clark, 1975–79).

—*The Gospel according to Saint Mark: An Introduction and Commentary* (Cambridge: Cambridge University Press, 1959).

—'Some Comments on Professor J.D.G. Dunn's *Christology in the Making* with Special Reference to the Evidence of the Epistle to the Romans', in *The Glory of Christ in the New Testament: Studies in Christology in Memory of George Bradford Caird* (ed. L.D. Hurst and N.T. Wright; Oxford: Clarendon Press, 1987), pp. 268-80.

Cullmann, O., *Christ and Time: The Primitive Conception of Time and History* (rev. edn with an new introductory chapter; trans. F.V. Filson London: SCM Press, 1962).

—*The Christology of the New Testament* (trans. S.C. Guthrie and C.A.M. Hall; Philadelphia: Westminster Press, rev. edn, 1959).

—'The Connection of Primal Events and End Events with the New Testament Redemptive History', in *The Old Testament and Christian Faith* (ed. B.H. Anderson; New York: Harper, 1963), pp. 115-23.

—'The Reply of Professor Cullmann to Roman Catholic Critics' (trans. R.P. Meye), *SJT* 15 (1962), pp. 36-43.

Curtis, A.W.H., 'Theophany', *DBI*, pp. 694-95.

Danby, H., *The Mishnah: Translated from the Hebrew with Introduction and Brief Explanatory Notes* (London: Oxford University Press, 1933).

Daniélou, J., *The Theology of Jewish Christianity* (trans. J.A. Baker; Chicago: Regnery, 1964).

Danker, F.W., *Jesus and the New Age according to St Luke* (St Louis: Clayton, 1972).

Davies, W.D., and D.C. Allison, Jr, *A Critical and Exegetical Commentary on the Gospel according to Saint Matthew* (ICC; Edinburgh: T. & T. Clark, 1988).

De Lacey, D.R., 'Jesus as Mediator', *JSNT* 29 (1987), pp. 101-21.

—' "One Lord" in Pauline Christology', in *Christ the Lord: Studies Presented to Donald Guthrie* (ed. H.H. Rowdon; Leicester: Inter-Varsity Press, 1982), pp. 191-203.

Delcor, M., 'The Apocrypha and Pseudepigrapha of the Hellenistic Period', in *The Cambridge History of Judaism* (ed. W.D. Davies and L. Finkelstein; Cambridge: Cambridge University Press, 1989), II, pp. 4409-503.

Delitzsch, F., *Biblical Commentary on the Prophecies of Isaiah* (trans. J.S. Banks and J. Kennedy; Edinburgh: T. & T. Clark, 4th ed, n.d.).

Dimant, D., 'Qumran Sectarian Literature', in Stone (ed.), *Jewish Writings of the Second Temple Period*, pp. 483-550.

Dodd, C.H., *According to the Scriptures: The Substructure of New Testament Theology* (London: Nisbet, 1952; New York: Scribner, 1953).

Dohmen, C., 'Zur Gründung der Gemeinde von Qumran (1QS VIII-IX)', *RevQ* 41 (1982), pp. 81-96

Doty, W.G., *Letters in Primitive Christianity* (Philadelphia: Fortress Press, 1973).

Downing, F.G., 'Ontological Asymmetry in Philo and Christological Realism in Paul, Hebrews and John', *JTS* 41 (1990), pp. 423-40.

Driver, S.R., *The Book of Genesis with Introduction and Notes* (London: Methuen, 3rd edn, 1904).

Duff, P.B., 'The March of the Divine Warrior and the Advent of the Greco-Roman King: Mark's Account of Jesus' Entry into Jerusalem', *JBL* 111 (1992), pp. 55-71.

Duhaime, J., 'Dualistic Reworking in the Scrolls from Qumran', *CBQ* 49 (1987), pp. 32-56.

Dulière, W., 'Theos Dieu et Adonai-Kurios: Conséquences de l'addition d'un Jésus-Kurios à l'Adonai-Kurios dans la terminologie chrétienne', *ZRGG* 21 (1969), pp. 193-203.

Dunn, J.D.G., 'Christology', *ABD*, I, pp. 979-91.

—*Christology in the Making: A New Testament Inquiry into the Origins of the Doctrine of the Incarnation* (London: SCM Press, 2nd edn, 1989).

—'In Defence of a Methodology', *ExpTim* 95 (1984), pp. 295-99.

—*Romans* (2 vols.; WBC; Waco, TX: Word Books, 1988).

—'Was Christianity a Monotheistic Faith from the Beginning?', *SJT* 35 (1982), pp. 303-36.

Durham, J.I., *Exodus* (WBC; Waco, TX: Word Books, 1987).

Du Toit Laubscher, F., 'God's Angel of Truth and Melchizedek: A Note on 11QMelch 13b', *JSS* 3 (1972), pp. 49.

Eichrodt, W., *Theology of the Old Testament* (2 vols.; trans. J.A. Baker; London: SCM Press, 1961–67).

Elliger, K., *Deuterojesaja: Partone Jesaja 40, 1-45,7* (BKAT; Neukirchen–Vluyn: Neukirchener Verlag, 1978).

Ellis, E.E., 'Biblical Interpretation in the New Testament Church', in *Miqra: Text Translation and Interpretation of the Hebrew Bible in Ancient Judaism and Early Christianity* (ed. M.J. Mulder; CRINT, 2.1; Philadelphia: Fortress Press; Assen: Van Gorcum, 1989), pp. 691-725.

—*The Gospel of Luke* (NCB; London: Oliphants, rev. edn, 1974).

—*The Old Testament in Early Christianity: Canon and Interpretation in the Light of Modern Research* (WUNT, 54; Tübingen: Mohr [Siebeck], 1991).

Elwell, W., 'The Deity of Christ in the Writings of Paul', in *Current Issues in Biblical and Patristic Interpretation: Studies in Honor of Merrill C. Tenney Presented by his Former Students* (ed. G.F. Hawthorne; Grand Rapids: Eerdmans, 1975), pp. 297-308.

Epstein, I., *The Babylonian Talmud* (34 vols.; London: Soncino Press, 1935–52).

Evans, C.F., *Saint Luke* (Trinity Press International New Testament Commentaries; London: SCM Press; Philadelphia: Trinity Press International, 1990).

Even-Shoshan, A., *A New Concordance of the Bible: Thesaurus of the Language of the Bible* (Jerusalem: Kiryat Sepher, 1985).

Fee, G.D., *The First Epistle to the Corinthians* (NICNT; Grand Rapids: Eerdmans, 1987).

Ficker, R., 'מַלְאָךְ', *THAT*, I, pp. 900-907.

Fishbane, M.A., 'The "Exodus" Motif: The Paradigm of Historical Renewal', in *Text and Texture: Close Readings of Selected Biblical Texts* (New York: Schocken, 1979), pp. 121-40.

Fitzmyer, J.A., *The Dead Sea Scrolls: Major Publications and Tools for Study* (SBLRBS, 20; Atlanta: Scholars Press, rev. edn, 1990).

—'Further Light on Melchizedek from Qumran Cave 11', in *Essays on the Semitic Background of the New Testament* (SBLSBS, 5; Missoula, MT: Scholars Press, 1974), pp. 245-67.

—*The Gospel according to Luke* (2 vols.; AB; Garden City, NY: Doubleday, 1981–85).

—'κύριος, ου, ὁ; κυριακός', in *Exegetisches Wörterbuch zum Neuen Testament* (ed. H. Balz and G. Schneider; Stuttgart: Kohlhammer, 1981), II, pp. 811-19.

—'The Languages of Palestine in the First Century AD', in *A Wandering Aramean: Collected Aramaic Essays* (SBLMS, 25; Chico, CA: Scholars Press, 1979), pp. 29-56.

—'New Testament *Kyrios* and *Maranatha* and their Aramaic Background', in *To Advance the Gospel: NTS* (New York: Crossroad, 1981).

—*Pauline Theology: A Brief Sketch* (Englewood Cliffs, NJ: Prentice-Hall, 1967).

—'The Semitic Background of the New Testament κύριος-Title', in *A Wandering Aramean*, pp. 115-42.

Flusser, D., 'Jesus in the Context of History', in *The Crucible of Christianity: Judaism, Hellenism and the Historical Background to the Christian Faith* (ed. A. Toynbee; London: Thames & Hudson, 1969), pp. 225-34.

—'Psalms, Hymns and Prayers', in Stone (ed.), *Jewish Writings of the Second Temple Period*, pp. 551-77.

Fokkelman, J.P., 'Stylistic Analysis of Isaiah 40.1-11', *OTS* 21 (1981), pp. 68-90.

Fossum, J., 'Kyrios Jesus as the Angel of the Lord in Jude 5-7', *NTS* 33 (1987), pp. 226-43.

—*The Name of God and the Angel of the Lord: Samaritan and Jewish Concepts of Intermediation and the Origin of Gnosticism* (WUNT, 36; Tübingen: Mohr [Siebeck], 1985).

—'The New *religionsgeschichtliche Schule*: The Quest for Jewish Christology', in *SBL 1991 Seminar Papers* (ed. E.H. Lovering, Jr; Atlanta: Scholars Press, 1991), pp. 638-46.

Frame, J.E., *A Critical and Exegetical Commentary on the Epistles of St Paul to the Thessalonians* (ICC; Edinburgh: T. & T. Clark, 1912).

France, R.T., *The Gospel according to Matthew: An Introduction and Commentary* (Tyndale New Testament Commentary; Leicester: Inter-Varsity Press, 1985).

—*Jesus and the Old Testament: His Application of Old Testament Passages to himself and his Mission* (London: Tyndale, 1971).

—'The Worship of Jesus—A Neglected Factor in Christological Debate?', *Vox Evangelica* 12 (1981), pp. 19-33.

Freeman H., and M. Simon (eds.), *Midrash Rabbah* (10 vols.; London: Soncino, 1939).

Fuller, R.H., *The Foundations of the New Testament Christology* (LL; London: Lutterworth, 1965).

—'Lower and Higher Christology in the Fourth Gospel', in *The Conversation Continues: Studies in Paul and John in Honor of J. Louis Martyn* (ed. R.T. Fortna and B.R. Gaventa; Nashville: Abingdon Press, 1990), pp. 357-65.

—'The Theology of Jesus or Christology? An Evaluation of the Recent Discussion', *Semeia* 30 (1984), pp. 105-16.

Furnish, V.P., *II Corinthians: Translated with Introduction, Notes, and Commentary* (AB; Garden City, NY: Doubleday, 1984).

Garrett, S.R., 'Exodus from Bondage: Luke 9.31 and Acts 12.1-24', *CBQ* 52 (1990), pp. 656-80.

Gasque, W., *A History of the Criticism of the Acts of the Apostles* (BGBE, 17; Tübingen: Mohr [Siebeck], 1975).

Gese, H., 'Wisdom Literature in the Persian Period', in *The Cambridge History of Judaism* (ed. W.D. Davies and L. Finkelstein; Cambridge: Cambridge University Press, 1984), I, pp. 189-218.

Gesenius, W., *Gesenius' Hebrew Grammar* (ed. and enlarged E.F. Kautzsch; trans. and rev. A.E. Cowley; Oxford: Clarendon Press, 2nd edn, 1985).

Gilbert, M., 'Wisdom Literature', in Stone (ed.), *Jewish Writings of the Second Temple Period*, pp. 283-324.

Ginsberg, H.L., 'Aramaic Letters', *ANET*, pp. 491-92.

—'The Legend of King Keret', *ANET*, pp. 142-49.

Glasson, T.F., ' "Plurality of Divine Persons" and the Quotation in Hebrews 1.6ff.', *NTS* 12 (1965–66), pp. 270-73.

—*The Second Advent: The Origin of New Testament Doctrine* (London: Epworth, 3rd edn, 1963).

Godet, F.L., *A Commentary on the Gospel of St Luke* (2 vols.; trans. E.W. Shalders; Edinburgh: T. & T. Clark, 5th edn, 1870).

Goldingay, J., 'Salvation History', *DBI*, pp. 606-607.

Goodenough, E.R., *An Introduction to Philo Judaeus* (Oxford: Basil Blackwell, 2nd edn, 1962).

Goppelt, L., *Theology of the New Testament* (2 vols.; trans. J.E. Alsup; ed. J. Roloff; Grand Rapids: Eerdmans, 1982).

Gould, E.P., *A Critical and Exegetical Commentary on the Gospel according to Mark* (ICC; Edinburgh: T. & T. Clark, 1901).

Grant, R.M., *Gods and the One God* (LEC; Philadelphia: Westminster Press, 1986).

—*Jesus after the Gospels: The Christ of the Second Century* (The Hale Memorial Lectures of Seabury-Western Theological Seminary, 1989; Louisville: Westminster/ John Knox, 1990).

Gray, G.B., 'The Psalms of Solomon', *APOT*, II, pp. 625-52.

Greeven, H., 'εὔχομαι', *TDNT*, II, pp. 800-808.

—'προσκυνέω, προσκυνητής', *TDNT*, VI, pp. 758-66.

Grillmeier, A., *Christ in Christian Tradition: From the Apostolic Age to Chalcedon (451)* (trans. J.S. Bowden; London: Mowbrays, 1965).

Groningen, G. van, *Messianic Revelation in the Old Testament* (Grand Rapids: Baker, 1990).

Guelich, R.A., *Mark 1–8.26* (WBC; Dallas: Word Books, 1989).

Gundry, R.H., *Matthew: A Commentary on his Literary and Theological Art* (Grand Rapids: Eerdmans, 1982).

—*The Use of the Old Testament in St Matthew's Gospel* (NovTSup, 18; Leiden: Brill, 1967).

Gunkel, H., *Genesis: Übersetzt und erklärt* (GHAT; Göttingen: Vandenhoeck & Ruprecht, 1917).

Guthrie, D., *New Testament Introduction* (Downers Grove, IL: Inter-Varsity Press, 1970).

—*New Testament Theology* (Downers Grove, IL: Inter-Varsity Press, 1981).

Haenchen, E., *The Acts of the Apostles: A Commentary* (trans. B. Noble, G. Shinn and H. Anderson; rev. R.M. Wilson; Philadelphia: Westminster Press, 1971).

—*Der Weg Jesu: Eine Erklärung des Markus-Evangeliums und der kanonischen Parallelen* (Berlin: Töpelmann, 1966).

Hagner, D.A., 'Paul's Christology and Jewish Monotheism', in *Perspectives on Christology: Essays in Honor of Paul K. Jewett* (ed. M. Shuster and R. Muller; Grand Rapids: Zondervan, 1991), pp. 19-38.

Hahn, F., *The Titles of Jesus in Christology: Their History in Early Christianity* (trans. H. Knight and G. Ogg; London: Lutterworth, 1969).

Hall, S.G., *Doctrine and Practice in the Early Church* (London: SPCK, 1991).

Hanson, A.T., *The Prophetic Gospel: A Study of John and the Old Testament* (Edinburgh: T. & T. Clark, 1991).

Hanson, J., 'Demetrius the Chronographer', *OTP*, II, pp. 841-47.

Hanson, R.P.C., *The Search for the Christian Doctrine of God: The Arian Controversy 318–381 AD* (Edinburgh: T. & T. Clark, 1988).

Hardy, E.R., *Christology of the Later Fathers* (in collaboration with C.C. Richardson; LCL, 3; London: SCM Press, 1956).

Harrington, D.J., 'Pseudo-Philo', *OTP*, II, pp. 297-303.

Harris, M.J., *Colossians and Philemon* (EGG; Grand Rapids: Eerdmans, 1991).

—*Jesus as God: The New Testament Use of Theos in Reference to Jesus* (Grand Rapids: Baker, 1992).

—'Prepositions', *NIDNTT*, III, pp. 1171-1215.

Hart, T.A., 'R.P.C. Hanson, *The Search for the Christian Doctrine of God*: A Review Essay', *EvQ* 64 (1992), pp. 155-64.

Hartman, L., ' "He Spoke of the Temple of his Body" (Jn 2.13-22)', *SEÅ* 54 (1989), pp. 70-79.

Harvey, A.E., 'Christ as Agent', in *The Glory of Christ in the New Testament: Studies in Christology in Memory of George Bradford Caird* (ed. L.D. Hurst and N.T. Wright; Oxford: Clarendon Press, 1987), pp. 239-50.

—*Jesus and the Constraints of History* (Philadelphia: Westminster Press, 1982).

Hay, D.M., *Glory at the Right Hand: Psalm 110 in Early Christianity* (SBLMS, 18; Nashville: Abingdon Press, 1973).

Hayman, P., 'Monotheism—A Misused Word in Jewish Studies?', *JSS* 42 (1991), pp. 1-15.

Hays, R.B., *Echoes of Scripture in the Letters of Paul* (New Haven: Yale University Press, 1989).

Heitmüller, W., *'Im Namen Jesu', Eine sprach- und religionsgeschichtliche Untersuchung zum Neuen Testament, speziell zur altchristlichen Taufe* (FRLANT, 2; Göttingen: Vandenhoeck & Ruprecht, 1903).

Hengel, M., 'Christology and New Testament Chronology: A Problem in the History of Earliest Christianity', in *Between Jesus and Paul: Studies in the Earliest History of Christianity* (trans. J. Bowden; London: SCM Press; Philadelphia: Fortress Press, 1983), pp. 30-47.

—'Hymns and Christology', in Bowden (trans.), *Between Jesus and Paul*, pp. 78-96.

—*Judaism and Hellenism: Studies in their Encounter in Palestine during the Early Hellenistic Period* (2 vols.; trans. J. Bowden; London: SCM Press, 1974).

—*The Son of God: The Origin of Christology and the History of Jewish-Hellenistic Religion* (trans. J. Bowden; Philadelphia: Fortress Press, 1976).

Herbert, A.S., *The Book of the Prophet Isaiah: Chapters 40–66* (Cambridge: Cambridge University Press, 1975).

Hess, R.S., 'Yahweh and his Asherah? Epigraphic Evidence for Religious Pluralism in Old Testament Times', in *One God, One Lord in a World of Religious Pluralism* (ed. A.D. Clarke and B.W. Winter; Cambridge: Tyndale House, 1991), pp. 5-33.

Hiebert, T., 'Joel, Book of', *ABD*, III, pp. 873-80.

Hodge, C., *An Exposition of the First Epistle to the Corinthians* (London: Banner of Truth Trust, 5th edn, 1958).

Holmberg, B., *Paul and Power: The Structure of Authority in the Primitive Churches as Reflected in the Pauline Epistles* (Coniectanea Biblica New Testament Series, 11; Lund: Gleerup, 1978).

Holtz, T., *Der erste Brief an die Thessalonicher* (EKKNT, 13; Neukirchen–Vluyn: Neukirchener Verlag, 1986).

—'Theo-logie und Christologie bei Paulus', in *Glaube und Eschatologie: Festschrift für Werner Georg Kümmel zum 80. Geburtstag* (ed. E. Grässer and O. Merk; Tübingen: Mohr [Siebeck], 1985), pp. 105-21.

—*Untersuchungen über die alttestamentlichen Zitate bei Lukas* (TU, 104; Berlin: Akademie, 1968).

Hooker, M., 'Mark', in Carson and Williamson (eds.), *It is Written*, pp. 220-30.

Horsely, R.A., 'The Background of the Confessional Formula in 1 Kor 8.6', *ZNW* 69 (1978), pp. 130-35.

Horton, F.L., Jr, *The Melchizedek Tradition: A Critical Examination of the Sources to the Fifth Century AD and in the Epistle to the Hebrews* (SNTSMS, 30; Cambridge: Cambridge University Press, 1976).

Howard, G., 'The Tetragram and the New Testament', *JBL* 96 (1977), pp. 63-83.

Hultgren, A.J., *New Testament Christology: A Critical and Annotated Bibliography* (BIRS; New York: Greenwood, 1988).

Hunt, A.S., and C.C. Edgar, *Select Papyri* (3 vols.; LCL; London: Heinemann, 1932).

Hunter, A.M., *Paul and his Predecessors* (London: SCM Press, rev. edn, 1961).

Hurd, J.C., Jr, *The Origin of 1 Corinthians* (Macon, GA: Mercer University Press, 1983).

Hurtado, L.W., 'The Binitarian Shape of Early Christian Devotion and Ancient Jewish Monotheism', in *Society of Biblical Literature 1985 Seminar Papers* (ed. K.H. Richards; Atlanta: Scholars Press, 1985), pp. 377-91.

—'New Testament Christology: A Critique of Bousset's Influence', *TS* 1979 (40), pp. 306-17.

—*One God, One Lord: Early Christian Devotion and Ancient Jewish Monotheism* (Philadelphia: Fortress Press, 1988).

—'Revelation 4–5 in the Light of Jewish Apocalyptic Analogies', *JSNT* 25 (1985), pp. 104-24.

Hull, S.D., 'Exceptions to Apollonius' Canon in the New Testament: A Grammatical Study', *TrinJ* 7 (1986), pp. 3-16.

Hyatt, J.P., *Commentary on Exodus* (NCB; London: Oliphants, 1971).

Iersel, B.M.F. van, *'Der Sohn' in den synoptischen Jesusworten* (Leiden: Brill, 1961).

Jeremias, J., *Jesus' Promise to the Nations: The Franz Delitzsch Lectures for 1953* (trans. S.H. Hooke; SBT, 24; London: SCM Press, 1958).

Johnson, A.R., *The One and the Many in the Israelite Conception of God* (Cardiff: University of Wales, 2nd edn, 1961).

Jonge, M. de, *Christology in Context: The Earliest Christian Response to Jesus* (Philadelphia: Westminster Press, 1988).

—'John the Baptist and Elijah in the Fourth Gospel', in *The Conversation Continues: Studies in Paul & John in Honor of J. Louis Martyn* (ed. R.T. Fortna and B.R. Gaventa; Nashville: Abingdon, 1990), pp. 299-308.

Jonge, M. de, and A.S. van der Woude, '11Q Melchizedek and the New Testament', *NTS* 12 (1965–66), pp. 301-26.

Juel, D., *Messiah and Temple: The Trail of Jesus in the Gospel of Mark* (SBLDS, 31; Missoula, MT: Scholars Press, 1977).

—*Messianic Exegesis: Christological Interpretation of the Old Testament in Early Christianity* (Philadelphia: Fortress Press, 1988).

Kaiser, O., *Isaiah 13–39: A Commentary* (London: SCM Press, 1974).

Käsemann, E., 'Blind Alleys in the "Jesus of History" Controversy', in *New Testament Questions of Today* (London: SCM Press, 1969).

Keck, L.E., 'Toward the Renewal of New Testament Christology', *NTS* 32 (1986), pp. 362-77.

Kelly, J.N.D., *Early Christian Doctrines* (San Francisco: Harper & Row, rev. edn, 1960).

Kim, S., *The Origin of Paul's Gospel* (WUNT, 4; Tübingen: Mohr [Siebeck], 1981; Grand Rapids: Eerdmans, 1982).

Kingsbury, J.D., *The Christology of Mark's Gospel* (Philadelphia: Fortress Press, 1983).

—'The Composition and Christology of Matt 28.16-20', *JBL* 93 (1974), pp. 573-84.

Kleinknecht, H., 'εἰκών', *TDNT*, II, pp. 388-90.

Knight, G.A.F., *Servant Theology: A Commentary on the Book of Isaiah 40–55* (International Theological Commentary; Edinburgh: Handsel Press, rev. edn, 1984).

—*A Biblical Approach to the Doctrine of the Trinity* (Edinburgh: Oliver & Boyd, 1953).

Kobelski, P.J., *Melchizedek and Melchiresa* (CBQMS, 10; Washington, DC: Catholic Biblical Association of America, 1981).

Koch, D.-A., *Die Schrift als Zeuge des Evangeliums: Untersuchungen zur Verwendung und zum Verständnis der Schrift bei Paulus* (BHT, 69; Tübingen: Mohr [Siebeck], 1986).

Kramer, W., *Christ, Lord, Son of God* (trans. B. Hardy; SBT, 50; London: SCM Press, 1966).

Kreitzer, L.J., *Jesus and God in Paul's Eschatology* (JSNTSup, 19; Sheffield: JSOT Press, 1987).

Kümmel, W.G., *Introduction to the New Testament* (trans. H.C. Kee; Nashville: Abingdon Press, rev. edn, 1975).

—*The Theology of the New Testament according to its Major Witnesses, Jesus-Paul-John* (trans. J.E. Steely; Nashville: Abingdon Press, 1973).

Kuhn, K.G., 'μαραναθά', *TDNT*, IV, pp. 466-72.

Labuschagne, C.J., 'קרא', *THAT*, II, pp. 666-74.

Ladd, G.E., *A Theology of the New Testament* (Grand Rapids: Eerdmans, 1974).

Lagrange, M.J., *Evangile selon Saint Luc* (EB; Paris: Gabalda, 1921).

Lang, F., *Die Briefe an die Korinther* (NTD, 7; Göttingen: Vandenhoeck & Ruprecht, 1986).

Leslie, E.A., *Isaiah Chronologically Arranged, Translated and Interpreted* (New York: Abingdon Press, 1963).

Liddon, H.P., *The Divinity of our Lord and Saviour Jesus Christ: Eight Lectures Preached before the University of Oxford in the Year 1866* (Bampton Lectures; London: Rivingtons, 7th edn, 1875).

Lightfoot, J.B., *Notes on the Epistles of St Paul* (Grand Rapids: Zondervan, 1957).

—*Notes on the Epistles of St Paul from Unpublished Commentaries* (London: MacMillan, 1895).

Limburg, J., 'An Exposition of Isaiah 40.1-11', *Int* 29 (1975), pp. 406-408.

Lindars, B., *New Testament Apologetic: The Doctrinal Significance of the Old Testament Quotations* (London: SCM Press, 1961).

Loader, W.R.G., *The Christology of the Fourth Gospel* (New York: Peter Lang, 1989).

—*Sohn und Hoherpriester: Eine traditionsgeschichtliche Untersuchung zur Christologie des Hebräerbriefes* (Wissenschaftliche Monographien zum Alten und Neuen Testament, 53; Neukirchen–Vluyn: Neukirchener Verlag, 1981).

Longenecker, R.N., *The Christology of Early Jewish Christianity* (London: SCM Press, 1970).

Lüdemann, G., *Early Christianity according to the Traditions in Acts: A Commentary* (trans. J. Bowden; London: SCM Press, 1989).

Lunt, H.G., 'Ladder of Jacob', *OTP*, II, pp. 401-406.

Lust, J., 'Daniel 7,13 and the Septuagint', *ETL* (1978), pp. 62-69.

Luther, M., *Luther's Works* (55 vols.; ed. H.C. Oswald and H.L. Lehmann; St Louis: Concordia, 1955–86).

Luz, U., *Matthew 1–7: A Commentary* (trans. W.C. Linss; Edinburgh: T. & T. Clark, 1989).

MacDonald, W.G., 'Christology and "The Angel of the Lord"', in *Current Issues in Biblical and Patristic Interpretation: Studies in Honor of Merrill C. Tenney*

Presented by his Former Students (ed. G.F. Hawthorne; Grand Rapids: Eerdmans, 1975), pp. 324-35.

Mack, B.L., and R.E. Murphy, 'Wisdom Literature', in *Early Judaism and its Modern Interpreters* (ed. R.A. Kraft and G.W.E. Nickelsburg; BMI, 2; Philadelphia: Fortress Press, 1986), pp. 371-410.

MacKintosh, H.R., 'Christ and God', *ExpTim* 31 (1919–20), pp. 74-78.

Mánek, J., 'The New Exodus in the Books of Luke', *NovT* 2 (1958), pp. 8-23.

Marcus, J., 'Mark 14:61: "Are You the Messiah-Son-of-God?"', *NovT* 31 (1989), pp. 125-41.

Marshall, I.H., *The Acts of the Apostles: An Introduction and Commentary* (TNTC; Grand Rapids: Eerdmans, 1980).

—*The Gospel of Luke: A Commentary on the Greek Text* (NIGTC; Exeter: Paternoster, 1978).

—*Jesus the Saviour: Studies in New Testament Theology* (London: SPCK, 1990).

—*Luke: Historian and Theologian* (Grand Rapids: Zondervan, 1970).

—*The Origins of New Testament Christology* (ICT; Leicester: Inter-Varsity Press, 1976).

—'Palestinian and Hellenistic Christianity: Some Critical Comments', *NTS* 19 (1972–73), pp. 271-87.

—*1 and 2 Thessalonians* (New Century Commentary; Grand Rapids: Eerdmans; London: Marshall Morgan & Scott, 1983).

Martin, B.L., *Christ and the Law in Paul* (NovTSup, 62; Leiden: Brill, 1989).

Martin, R.P., *Carmen Christi: Philippians 2.5-11 in Recent Interpretation and in the Setting of Early Christian Worship* (Grand Rapids: Eerdmans, rev. edn, 1983).

—*2 Corinthians* (WBC; Waco, TX: Word Books, 1986).

—*The Family and the Fellowship, New Testament Images of the Church* (Grand Rapids: Eerdmans, 1979).

—*New Testament Foundations: A Guide for Christian Students* (2 vols.; Grand Rapids: Eerdmans, 1975–78).

Martin, T.W., 'Hellenists', *ABD*, III, pp. 135-36.

Marxsen, W., *Der erste Brief an die Thessalonicher* (Zürich: Theologischer Verlag, 1979).

Masson, C., *Les deux épitres de Saint Paul aux Thessaloniciens* (CNT, 11a; Paris: Delachaux & Niestlé, 1957).

Matera, F.J., 'The Prologue as the Interpretative Key to Mark's Gospel', *JSNT* 34 (1988), pp. 3-20.

Mauser, U., *Christ and the Wilderness* (London: SCM Press, 1963).

McComiskey, T.E., 'Angel of the Lord', *EDT*, pp. 47-48.

McDonald, H.D., 'Cyril of Alexandria', in *Eerdman's Handbook to the History of Christianity* (ed. T. Dowley; Grand Rapids: Eerdmans, 1977), p. 174.

McKenzie, J.L., *Second Isaiah* (AB; Garden City: Doubleday, 1968).

Merendino, R.P., *Der Erste und der Letze: Jes 40-48* (VTSup, 31; Leiden: Brill, 1981).

Metzger, B.M., *A Textual Commentary on the Greek New Testament* (New York: United Bible Societies, 1975).

Middleton, T.F., *The Doctrine of the Article* (ed. H.J. Rose; London: Luke Hansard & Sons, 1808).

Milik, J.T., 'Milkî-sedeq et Milkî-resa' dans les anciens écrits juifs et chrétiens', *JJS* 23 (1972), pp. 95-144

Miller, M.P., 'The Function of Isa. 61.1-2 in 11Q Melchizedek', *JBL* 88 (1969), pp. 467-69.

Moberly, R.W.L., *At the Mountain of God: Story and Theology in Exodus 32–34* (JSOTSup, 22; Sheffield: JSOT Press, 1983).

Moffatt, J., *The First Epistle of Paul to the Corinthians* (London: Hodder & Stoughton, 1938).

Moo, D.J., *The Old Testament in the Gospel Passion Narratives* (Sheffield: Almond Press, 1983).

Moore, G.F., *Judaism in the First Centuries of the Christian Era: The Age of the Tannaim* (3 vols.; Cambridge, MA: Harvard University Press, 1927–30).

Morray-Jones, C.R.A., 'Merkabah Mysticism and Talmudic Tradition' (PhD thesis, Cambridge University, 1988).

Morris, L., *The Epistle of Paul to the Thessalonians: An Introduction and Commentary* (Grand Rapids: Eerdmans, 1957).

—*The First Epistle of Paul to the Corinthians: An Introduction and Commentary* (TNTC; Grand Rapids: Eerdmans; Leicester: Inter-Varsity Press, 1958).

—*The Gospel according to St Luke: An Introduction and Commentary* (TNTC; London: Inter-Varsity Press, 1974).

Moule, C.F.D., 'The Christology of Acts', in *Studies in Luke–Acts: Essays Presented in Honor of Paul Schubert, Buckingham Professor of New Testament Criticism and Interpretation at Yale University* (ed. L.E. Keck and J.L. Martyn; Nashville: Abingdon Press, 1966), pp. 159-85.

—*An Idiom Book of New Testament Greek* (Cambridge: Cambridge University Press, 2nd edn, 1959).

—'The New Testament and the Doctrine of the Trinity', *ExpTim* 88 (1976–77), pp. 16-20.

—*The Origin of Christology* (Cambridge: Cambridge University Press, 1977).

Mounce, R.H., *Matthew: A Good News Commentary on his Literary and Theological Art* (Grand Rapids: Eerdmans, 1982).

Munck, J., *Paul and the Salvation of Mankind* (trans. F. Clarke; London: SCM Press, 1959).

Mußner, F., *Apostelgeschichte* (EcB; Würzburg: Echter-Verlag, 1984).

Nagata, T., 'Philippians 2.5-11: A Case Study in Contextual Shaping of Early Christian Christology' (PhD dissertation, Princeton University, 1981).

Neil, W., *Acts* (NCB; London: Marshall, Morgan & Scott, 1981).

Newman, C.C., *Paul's Glory Christology: Tradition and Rhetoric* (NovTSup, 69; Leiden: Brill, 1992).

Newsome, C.A., *Songs of the Sabbath Sacrifice: A Critical Edition* (HSM, 27; Atlanta: Scholars Press, 1985).

Nickelsburg, G.W.E., 'The Bible Rewritten and Expanded', in Stone (ed.), *Jewish Writings of the Second Temple Period*, pp. 89-156.

—'Stories of Biblical and Early Post-Bibilcal Times', in Stone (ed.), *Jewish Writings of the Second Temple Period*, pp. 33-87.

Nickelsburg, G.W.E., and M.E. Stone, *Faith and Piety in Early Judaism: Texts and Documents* (Philadelphia: Fortress Press, 1983).

Noll, S.F., 'Angelology in the Qumran Texts' (PhD thesis, University of Manchester, 1979).

Nolland, J., *Luke 1–9.20* (WBC; Dallas: Word Books, 1989).

Norden, E., *Agnostos Theos: Untersuchungen zur Formengeschichte Religiöser Rede* (Stuttgart: Teubner, 1956).

Norris, R.A., *The Christological Controversy* (SECT; Philadelphia: Fortress Press, 1980).

North, C.R., *The Second Isaiah: Introduction, Translation and Commentary to Chapters XL–LV* (Oxford: Clarendon Press, 1964).

O'Neill, J.C., 'Heilsgeschichte', *NDCT*, p. 248.

Orr, W.F., and J.A. Walther, *I Corinthians* (AB; Garden City, NY: Doubleday, 1976).

Osterley, W.O.E., and G.H. Box, *Religion and Worship of the Synagogue: Introduction to the Study of Judaism from the New Testament Period* (London: Isaac Pitman & Sons, 2nd edn, 1911).

Pardee, D., *Handbook of Ancient Hebrew Letters: A Study Edition* (SBLSBS, 15; Chico, CA: Scholars Press, 1982).

Parsons, M.C., 'The Ascension Narratives in Luke–Acts' (PhD dissertation, Southern Baptist Theological Seminary, 1985).

Patte, D., *The Gospel according to Matthew: A Structural Commentary on Matthew's Faith* (Philadelphia: Fortress Press, 1987).

Payne, P.B., 'Jesus' Implicit Claim to Deity in His Parables', *TrinJ* 2 (1981), pp. 3-23.

Pesch, R., *Das Markusevangelium* (2 vols.; HTKNT; Freiberg: Herder, 1984).

Peterson, E., *ΕΙΣ ΘΕΟΣ: Epigraphische, formgeschichtliche und religionsgeschichtliche Untersuchungen* (FRLANT, 24; Göttingen: Vandenhoeck & Ruprecht, 1926).

Phelps, D.L., 'Implications of Lucan-Peter's Pentecost Homily for Christian Preaching of the Old Testament' (PhD dissertation, Southwestern Baptist Theological Seminary, 1990).

Pietersma, A., 'Kyrios or Tetragram: A Renewed Quest for the Original Septuagint', in *De Septuaginta: Studies in Honour of John William Wevers on his 65th Birthday* (ed. A. Pietersma and C. Cox; Mississauga, Ont.: Benben, 1984), pp. 85-101.

Plummer, A., *A Critical and Exegetical Commentary on the Second Epistle of St Paul to the Corinthians* (ICC; Edinburgh: T. & T. Clark, 1915).

Pokorny, P., *The Genesis of Christology: Foundations for a Theology of the New Testament* (Edinburgh: T. & T. Clark, 1987).

Porter, S.E., 'Two Myths: Corporate Personality and Language/Mentality Determinism', *SJT* 43 (1990), pp. 289-307.

Prat, F., *The Theology of Saint Paul* (2 vols.; trans. J.L. Stoddard; London: Burns, Oates & Washbourne, 1957).

Priest, J., 'The Testament of Moses', *OTP*, I, pp. 919-26.

Puech, E., 'Notes sur le manuscrit de 11QMelkîsédeq', *RevQ* 12 (1987), pp. 483-513.

Rad, G. von, *Old Testament Theology* (2 vols.; trans. D.M.G. Stalker; London: SCM Press, 1975).

—'ἄγγελος: מַלְאָךְ in the OT', *TDNT*, I, pp. 76-80.

—*Genesis: A Commentary* (trans. J.H. Marks; London: SCM Press, 1961).

Rainbow, P.A., 'Jewish Monotheism as the Matrix for New Testament Christology: A Review Article', *NovT* 33 (1991), pp. 78-91.

—'Monotheism and Christology in I Corinthians 8.4-6' (DPhil thesis, Oxford University, 1987).

Ramsay, W.M., *St Paul the Traveller and Roman Citizen* (London: Hodder & Stoughton, 10th edn, 1908).

Rawlinson, A.E.J., *The New Testament Doctrine of the Christ: The Bampton Lectures for 1926* (London: Longmans, Green & Co., 1926).

Reiling, J., and J.L. Swellengrebel, *A Translator's Handbook on the Gospel of Luke* (Helps for Translators, 10; Leiden: Brill, 1971).

Rendtorff, R., 'The Book of Isaiah: A Complex Unity: Synchronic and Diachronic Reading', in *Society of Biblical Literature 1991 Seminar Papers* (ed. E.H. Lovering; Atlanta: Scholars Press, 1991), pp. 8-20.

Rese, M., *Alttestamentliche Motive in der Christologie des Lukas* (SNT, 1; Gütersloh: Gerd Mohn, 1969).

Ringgren, H., *Israelite Religion* (trans. D.E. Green; Philadelphia: Fortress Press, 1966).

—*Word and Wisdom: Studies in the Hypostatization of Divine Qualities and Functions in the Ancient Near East* (Lund: Ohlsson, 1947).

Roberts, A., and J. Donaldson, *The Ante-Nicene Fathers Translations of the Writings of the Fathers down to AD 325*, I (rev. A.C. Coxe; Grand Rapids: Eerdmans, n.d.).

Robertson, A., and A. Plummer, *A Critical and Exegetical Commentary of the First Epistle to the Corinthians* (ICC; Edinburgh: T. & T. Clark, 1911).

Robertson, R.G., 'Ezekiel the Tragedian', *OTP*, II, pp. 803-807.

Robinson G.L., and R.K. Harrison, 'Isaiah', *ISBE*, II, pp. 885-904.

Robinson, J.M., *The Nag Hammadi Library in English* (Leiden: Brill, 2nd edn, 1984).

—'The Witness of Paul: Christ, The Lord', in *Who Say Ye That I Am? Six Theses on the Deity of Christ, Written in Competition for the Robert A. Dunn Award* (ed. W.C. Robinson; Grand Rapids: Eerdmans, 1949), pp. 131-45.

Robinson, W.C., 'Jesus Christ is Jehovah', *EvQ* 5 (1933), pp. 144-55, 271-90.

Rowland, C., 'The Influence of the First Chapter of Ezekiel on Jewish and Early Christian Literature' (PhD thesis, Cambridge University, 1974).

—'John 1.51, Jewish Apocalyptic and Targumic Tradition', *NTS* 30 (1984), pp. 498-507.

—'A Man Clothed in Linen: Dan. 10.6ff. and Jewish Angelology', *JSNT* 24 (1985), pp. 99-110.

—'The Vision of the Risen Christ in Rev. i.13ff: The Debt of an Early Christology to an Aspect of Jewish Angelology', *JTS* 31 (1980), pp. 1-11.

—'The Visions of God in Apocalyptic Literature', *Journal for the Study of Judaism* 10 (1979), pp. 137-54.

Rubinkiewicz, R., 'Apocalypse of Abraham', *OTP*, I, pp. 681-88.

Ruddick, C.T., 'Behold, I Send my Messenger', *JBL* 88 (1969), pp. 381-417.

Runia, D.T., 'God and Man in Philo of Alexandria', *JTS* 39 (1988), pp. 48-75.

—*Philo of Alexandria and the Timaeus of Plato* (Philosophia Antiqua, 44; Leiden: Brill, 1986).

Sacchi, P., 'Esquisse du développement du messianisme juif à la lumière du texte qumranien 11Q Melch', *ZAW* 100 sup. (1988), pp. 202-14.

Sahlin, H., *Der Messias und das Gottesvolk: Studien zur protolukanischen Theologie* (Acta Seminarii Neotestamentici Uppsaliensis, 12; Uppsala: Almqvist, 1945).

Sanders, E.P., *Paul, the Law, and the Jewish People* (Philadelphia: Fortress Press, 1983).

—'Testament of Abraham', *OTP*, I, pp. 871-80.

Sandmel, S., *Philo of Alexandria: An Introduction* (Oxford: Oxford University Press, 1979).

Sandt, H. van de, 'The Fate of the Gentiles in Joel and Acts 2: An Intertextual Study', *ETL* 66 (1990), pp. 56-77.

Schelkle, K.H., *Theology of the New Testament* (4 vols.; trans. W.A. Jurgens; Collegeville, MN: Liturgical Press, 1971–78).

Schneider, G., *Die Apostelgeschichte* (2 vols.; HTKNT; Freiberg: Herder, 1980–82).

—'Gott und Christus als κύριος nach Apostelgeschichte', in *Lukas, Theologe der*

Heilsgeschichte: Aufsätze zum lukanischen Doppelwerk (BBB, 59; Bonn: Peter Hanstein, 1985).

Scholem, G.G., *Jewish Gnosticism, Merkabah Mysticism and Talmudic Tradition* (New York: Jewish Theological Seminary, 1965).

Schönweiss, H., and C. Brown, 'Prayer', *NIDNTT*, II, pp. 861-75.

Schulz, S., 'Maranatha und Kyrios Jesus', *ZNW* 53 (1962), pp. 125-44.

Schürmann, H., *Das Lukasevangelium* (HTKNT; Freiberg: Herder, 1969).

Schutter, W.L., *Hermeneutic and Composition in 1 Peter* (WUNT, 30; Tübingen: Mohr [Siebeck], 1989).

Schwab, M., *Le talmud de Jérusalem* (Paris: Besson & Chantemerle, 1960).

Schweizer, E., 'Discipleship and Belief in Jesus as Lord from Jesus to the Hellenistic Church' (trans. H.F. Peacock), *NTS* 2 (1956), pp. 87-99.

—*The Good News according to Luke* (trans. D.E. Green; Atlanta: John Knox, 1984).

—*The Good News according to Mark* (trans. D.H. Madvig; Richmond: John Knox, 1970).

—'What Q Could Have Learned from Reginald Fuller', *ATR* Supplement 11 (1990), pp. 55-67.

Schürer, E., *The History of the Jewish People in the Age of Jesus Christ (175 BC–AD 135)* (rev. and trans. G. Vermes, F. Millar, M. Goodman, and M. Black; 3 vols.; Edinburgh: T. & T. Clark, 1973–86).

Segal, A.F., *Rebecca's Children: Judaism and Christianity in the Roman World* (Cambridge, MA: Harvard University Press, 1986).

—*Two Powers in Heaven: Early Rabbinic Reports about Christianity and Gnosticism* (SJLA, 25; Leiden: Brill, 1977).

Seters, J. van, 'Isaiah 40.1-11', *Int* 35 (1981), pp. 401-404.

Sevenster, J., *Do You Know Greek? How Much Greek Could the First Jewish Christians Have Known?* (NovTSup, 19; Leiden: Brill, 1968).

Sherwin-White, A.N., *Roman Society and Roman Law in the New Testament* (Oxford: Clarendon Press, 1963).

Sievers, J., ' "Where Two or Three . . . ": The Rabbinic Concept of the Shekhinah and Matthew 18.20', in *The Jewish Roots of Christian Liturgy* (ed. E.J. Fisher; New York: Paulist Press, 1989), pp. 47-61.

Simon, U.E., *A Theology of Salvation: A Commentary on Isaiah 40–55* (London: SPCK, 1961).

Skehan, P., 'The Divine Name at Qumran, in the Masada Scroll, and in the Septuagint', *BIOSCS* 13 (1980), pp. 14-44.

Skinner, J., *The Book of the Prophet Isaiah Chapter XL–LXVI* (Cambridge: Cambridge University Press, 1954).

—*A Critical and Exegetical Commentary on Genesis* (ICC; Edinburgh: T. & T. Clark, 1910).

Smart, J.D., *History and Theology in Second Isaiah: A Commentary on Isaiah 35; 40–66* (Philadelphia: Westminster Press, 1965).

Smith, R.H., *Matthew* (ACNT; Minneapolis: Augsburg, 1989).

Snodgrass, K.R., 'Streams of Tradition Emerging from Isaiah 40.1-5 and their Adaptation in the New Testament', *JSNT* 8 (1980), pp. 24-45.

Soggin, J.A., *Introduction to the Old Testament: From its Origins to the Closing of the Alexandrian Canon* (trans. J. Bowden; Philadelphia: Westminster Press, rev. edn, 1980).

Sperber, A., *The Bible in Aramaic* (4 vols.; Leiden: Brill, 1959–73).

Spurrell, G.J., *Notes on the Text of the Book of Genesis* (Oxford: Clarendon Press, 1896).

Stanton, G., 'Matthew', in Carson and Williamson (eds.), *It is Written*, pp. 205-19.

Staton, C.P., '"And Yahweh Appeared..."': A Study of the Motifs of "Seeing God" and of "God's Appearing" in the Old Testament Narratives' (DPhil thesis, Oxford University, 1988).

Stauffer, E., *New Testament Theology* (trans. J. Marsh; London: SCM Press, 1955).

Steenburg, D., 'The Worship of Adam and Christ as the Image of God', *JSNT* 39 (1990), pp. 95-109.

Stendahl, K., *The School of St Matthew and its Use of the Old Testament, With an Introduction by the Author* (Philadelphia: Fortress Press, 1968).

Stevenson, J., *A New Eusebius: Documents Illustrative of the History of the Church to AD 337* (London: SPCK, 1968).

Stinespring, W.F., 'Testament of Jacob', *OTP*, I, p. 913.

Stone, M.E., 'Apocalyptic Literature', in *idem* (ed.), *Jewish Writings of the Second Temple Period*, pp. 383-441.

Strack, H.L., and P. Billerbeck, *Kommentar zum Neuen Testament aus Talmud und Midrasch* (6 vols.; Munich: Beck, 1961–65).

Strack, H.L., and G. Stemberger, *Introduction to the Talmud and Midrash* (trans. M. Bockmuehl; Edinburgh: T. & T. Clark, 1991).

Stuart, D.K., *Hosea–Micah* (WBC; Waco, TX: Word Books, 1990).

Suhl, A., *Die Funktion der alttestamentlichen Zitate und Anspielungen im Markusevangelium* (Gütersloh: Gerd Mohn, 1965).

Sznycer, M., 'Une inscription punique inédite de Carthage', *Semitica* 37 (1987), pp. 63-67.

Tabor, J.D., '"Returning to the Divinity": Josephus's Portrayal of the Disappearances of Enoch, Elijah, and Moses', *JBL* 108 (1989), pp. 225-38.

Tannehill, R.C., *The Narrative Unity of Luke–Acts: A Literary Interpretation* (2 vols.; Philadelphia: Fortress Press, 1986).

Thackeray, H.StJ., R. Marcus, A. Wikgren and L.H. Feldman, *Josephus* (9 vols.; LCL; Cambridge, MA: Harvard University Press, 1926–65).

Thielman, F., *From Plight to Solution: A Jewish Framework for Understanding Paul's View of the Law in Galatians and Romans* (NovTSup, 61; Leiden: Brill, 1989).

Tiede, D.L., *Luke* (ACNT; Minneapolis: Augsburg, 1988).

Tobin, T.H., 'Logos', *ABD*, pp. 348-56.

Turner, M.M.B., 'The Spirit of Christ and Christology', in *Christ the Lord: Studies Presented to Donald Guthrie* (ed. H.H. Rowdon; Leicester: Inter-Varsity Press, 1982), pp. 168-90.

Turner, N., *A Grammar of New Testament Greek*. III. *Syntax* (ed. J.H. Moulton; Edinburgh: T. & T. Clark, 1963).

Urbach, E.E., *The Sages: Their Concepts and Beliefs* (trans. I. Abrahams; Cambridge, MA: Harvard University Press, 1975).

VanderKam, J.C., 'The Theophany of Enoch 1,3b-7,9', *VT* 23 (1973), pp. 129-50.

Vermes, G., *The Dead Sea Scrolls in English* (London: Penguin, 3rd edn, 1987).

Vos, G., 'The Continuity of the Kyrios-Title in the New Testament', *PTR* 13 (1915), pp. 161-89.

Warfield, B.B., 'God our Father and the Lord Jesus Christ', *PTR* 15 (1917), pp. 1-20.

—*The Lord of Glory: A Study of the Designations of our Lord in the New Testament, with Especial Reference to his Deity* (London: Evangelical Press, 1907).

Watts, J.D.W., *Isaiah 34–66* (WBC; Waco, TX: Word Books, 1987).

Watts, R.E., 'Consolation or Confrontation? Isaiah 40–55 and the Delay of the New Exodus', *TynBul* 41 (1990), pp. 31-59.

—'The Influence of the Isaianic New Exodus on the Gospel of Mark' (PhD thesis, Cambridge University, 1990).

Webb, R.L., ' "In those days came John..." The Ministry of John the Baptist within its Social, Cultural and Historic Context' (PhD thesis, University of Sheffield, 1990).

Weinfeld, M., 'Kuntillet 'Ajrud Inscriptions and their Significance', *Studi Epigrafici e Linguistici* 1 (1984), pp. 121-30.

Weiss, B., 'Der Gebrauch des Artikels bei den Gottesnamen: Exegetische Studie', *TSK* 84 (1911), pp. 319-92.

Weiss, J., *Der erste Korintherbrief* (KEK, 5; Göttingen: Vandenhoeck & Ruprecht, 2nd edn, 1925).

Werner, M., *The Formation of Christian Dogma: An Historical Study of its Problem* (trans. and ed. S.G.F. Brandon; London: A. & C. Black, 1957).

Westermann, C., *Genesis 12–36* (trans. J.J. Scullion; Minneapolis: Augsburg, 1985).

—*Isaiah 40–66: A Commentary* (trans. D.M.G. Stalker; London: SCM Press, 1969).

White, J.L., *Light from Ancient Letters* (Philadelphia: Fortress Press, 1986).

Whiteley, D.E.H., *The Theology of St Paul* (Philadelphia: Fortress Press, 1964).

Whybray, R.N., *Isaiah 40–66* (NCB; London: Oliphants, 1975).

Wilcox, M., 'Maranatha', *ABD*, IV, p. 514.

Wiles, M.F., 'Some Reflections on the Origin of the Doctrine of the Trinity', *JTS* 8 (1957), pp. 92-106.

Williamson, H.G.M., 'Joel', *ISBE*, II, pp. 1076-80.

Williamson, R., *Jews in the Hellenistic World: Philo* (CCWJCW, 1.2; Cambridge: Cambridge University Press, 1989).

Wimsatt, W.K., Jr, and M.C. Beardsley, 'The Intentionality Fallacy', in *The Verbal Icon: Studies in the Meaning of Poetry* (Lexington: University of Kentucky Press, 1954).

Wintermute, O.S., 'Apocalypse of Zephaniah', *OTP*, I, pp. 497-507.

Witherington, B., III, *The Christology of Jesus* (Minneapolis: Fortress Press, 1990).

Wood, A.S., 'Awakening', in *Eerdman's Handbook to the History of Christianity* (ed. T. Dowley; Grand Rapids: Eerdmans, 1977), pp. 434-55.

Woude, A.S. van der, 'Melchisedek als himmlische Erlösergestalt in den neugefundenen eschatologischen Midraschim aus Qumran Höhle XI', *Oudtestamentische Studiën* 14 (1965), pp. 354-73.

Wright, N.T., *The Climax of the Covenant: Christ and the Law in Pauline Theology* (Edinburgh: T. & T. Clark, 1991).

Wright, R.B., 'Psalms of Solomon', *OTP*, II, pp. 640-50.

Young, E.J., *The Book of Isaiah: The English Text, with Introduction, Exposition, and Notes* (3 vols.; Grand Rapids: Eerdmans, 1972).

Young, F., 'Two Roots or a Tangled Mass', in *The Myth of God Incarnate* (ed. J. Hick; London: SCM Press, 1977), 87-121.

Zehnle, R.F., *Peter's Pentecost Discourse: Tradition and Lukan Reinterpretation in Peter's Speeches of Acts 2 and 3* (SBLMS, 15; Nashville: Abingdon Press, 1971).

INDEX OF REFERENCES

OLD TESTAMENT

NEW TESTAMENT

PSEUDEPIGRAPHA

QUMRAN

INDEX OF AUTHORS

JOURNAL FOR THE STUDY OF THE NEW TESTAMENT
SUPPLEMENT SERIES